TOWARDS ANOTHER MYTH:

A TALE OF HEIDEGGER AND TRADITIONALISM

Askr Svarte
(Evgeny Nechkasov)

Translated by Jafe Arnold

2024

PRAV Publishing
www.pravpublishing.com
prav@pravpublishing.com

Originally published in Russian by Totenburg
(Moscow, Russian Federation) under the title
K Drugomu Mifu
© E.A. Nechkasov, 2023
© Izdatel'stvo Totenburg, 2023

Translation copyright © PRAV Publishing, 2024

Copy-edited by Charlie Smith

All rights reserved. No part of this book may be reproduced or distributed in any form or by any means, electronic or mechanical, including photocopying, recording, or by any information storage and retrieval, without permission in writing from the publisher.

ISBN 978-1-952671-82-1 (Hardcover)
ISBN 978-1-952671-83-8 (Paperback)
ISBN 978-1-952671-84-5 (Ebook)

Für die Zukünftigen

TABLE OF CONTENTS

I. BRANCHING OUT — 7
A Fork in the Road — 9
Mythos and *Poiesis* — 12
The Goddess Speech — 31
Odin's Sacrifice — 54
Poets and Philosophers — 82
We, Nothing — 101
Tradition as Language — 115
The Metaphysics of the Mask — 141

II. WHERE NO WORD IS — 153
Prolegomena — 155
Das Wort — 157

III. THE ESCHATOLOGY OF LANGUAGE — 171
The End of Speech — The End of the World — 173
Sacrifice, Chatter, Caesura — 183
Mathematics — 193
Towards Another Myth — 204

IV. HEIDEGGER AND TRADITIONALISM — 219
Heidegger and Traditionalism — 221
A Preliminary Exposition — 223
Metaphysics and Being — 228
Dasein — 232

The Holy	237
Theology	250
The Fourfold	271
The Last God	279
The Future Ones	286
Another Beginning	295
The Horizons of the Juncture	303

SELECTED BIBLIOGRAPHY   **330**

I
BRANCHING OUT

1
BRANCHING OUT

A Fork in the Road

"In the midst of the World Night, shouldn't we cease our tormented tossing and turning, instead take up silence and a foothold in the void of the Nothing to which we always have access, and from this quiet speechlessness bordering the Nothing bear forth in silence the new Word of the Divine?"

Preliminary reflections on this voiced proposal[1] take us down pathways of thoughts whose branches stretch throughout the myths of the great traditions. Given that the supreme Deity of the Germanic peoples is Odin of the Aesir, who manifests himself as a Wanderer hidden behind a mask, there is no need to delay being on our way.

Why "bear forth in silence" instead of straightforwardly speaking out? What is the "Word of the Divine?" Is it the utterance of a Deity, or an unknown name that gives grounds to be? The relationship between silence and saying, between speechlessness and telling, between word and name, and between the latter, the human being, and Divinehood — all of this plunges us into the question of language and speech.

Moreover, speaking of the "World Night" clearly refers us to the necessity of understanding our contemporary — or contemporal — moment, our location in a predetermined phase which is characterized by the acute problem of alienation not only in the social sphere but more importantly in the sphere of our relation to the Sacred and to Being as the first and foremost ontological and existential categories.

This, in turn, affects the very possibilities of speaking out. Can we blindly repeat the old myths as if the past thousands of years of the history of alienation, decay, and oblivion never happened? To us, such an approach seems impossible; it is based on an inertial faith or calculation that veils doubt. Friedrich

---

1 See Askr Svarte, *Gods in the Abyss: Essays on Heidegger, the Germanic Logos, and the Germanic Myth*, trans. Iliya Koptilin and Daniil Granovskiy (London: Arktos, 2020).

Georg Jünger maintained that every myth is a meta-narrative and meta-history, i.e., a plot unfolding over the course of all human history. In such a case, we need to adjust for the time and the events of its course. This brings us to the question, indeed the problem, of the possibility of a fundamentally new, Other Myth, another meta-historical and, on the whole, ontological tale.

Closely adjacent to this is the problem of correctly understanding the instance of Nothing touched upon in the above passage with which our journey begins. Superficial associations invariably push us towards a quick solution by way of reducing the problem merely to materialism and cultural nihilism, but such a turn of events in the sphere of thinking should be avoided, and the question should be posed in a more radical way in direct connection with language, speech, and the being of man and the Divinities.

The possibility of turning to Nothing opens up in our era over the course of the decay and ossification of the Western tradition of metaphysical thought that has run its course. Here we inevitably find ourselves meeting up with Martin Heidegger's fundamental posing of the problem of the eschatology of Being. The question of an Other Beginning beyond Western metaphysics and its structures was at the heart of Heidegger's thinking. In the mythological picture of the world, the end is followed by a new beginning, the cyclical rebirth and return of the world, i.e., the reoccurrence of the very same that was. But Tradition also teaches that death and the end are an integral part of the trial, sacrifice, and ritual passage of initiation. The eschatological moment opens up before us a subtle, hardly tangible gap, a fork in the roads of fate, and poses the metaphysical problem of the new, or rather the Other, in the midst of the very same.

All of this, of course, is a pressing problem for European man first and foremost. It is our reflection of and on our own fate, which has been outlined in two formulations. The first is from

Julius Evola, and it says that if it has befallen Europe to be the first to descend into the abyss of decline, death, and darkness, then Europe will also be the first to emerge, purified, on the other side. The second formulation is from Martin Heidegger, and it speaks of the infinite possibilities of our history if only man dares to be authentic and takes the risk of fundamentally re-establishing the truth of Being.

We dare to question all of this and wander among the heights of these questions in anticipation of a silent response.

Mythos and Poiesis

Myth is primary ontological reality. Myth is the fundamental way of perceiving and expressing Being. It possesses all the necessary structures and procedures of thinking for describing all phenomena and for giving answers to all questions. Myth is the root structure of human being-in-the-world and thinking. We, in essence, are *Homo Mythicus*.

Myth was not fully uprooted by the Enlightenment, but it was to a considerable degree pushed into the periphery. In Postmodernity, myth has been partially rehabilitated, but it has been significantly devalued from the status of a grand narrative down to the level of a stereotype or a fluid identity of subcultures of choice.

The use of the term "reality" to explain the essence of myth imposes specific restrictions bound to the implicit distinction between "real and credible" and "unreal, false, fictitious." "Reality" comes from the Latin *res*, that is "thing," "property," "matter," and "deed." Taken literally, "reality" means thingness, objectiveness, in its visible presence as a property. This trajectory directly leads us down to materialism and then all the way down to naive positivism and empiricism, in which miracles are completely "cancelled" or simulated.

Evgeny Golovin said the following of myth:

> Myth cannot be studied or interpreted. One cannot "come to conclusions" of a scientific, psychological, or ethical character on the basis of myth. Myth simply makes its presence known — like how lightning warns an elder tree: I am coming, hide. The tree has the quality of evading the lightning. Myths tell us about heroes of divine origin, and the active space of myth is not our space.[2]

If the use of the word "reality" is intended to emphasize the concreteness or visible givenness of the truth of myth, then the case is actually more like this: there is nothing "unreal" in myth, and the above-mentioned division only appeared in creationism

---
2   Evgeny Golovin, *Priblizhenie k Snezhnoi Koroleve* (Moscow: Arktogeia, 2003).

and was fully inherited and cemented in Modernity. Therefore, defining myth as "real" is redundant and tautological. We ought to pick up a replacement for the word "reality" in order to avoid the smuggled, shadowy pole of the exclusion of the unreal from the sphere of reality. The Slavic word *yav'*, that is "manifest," and its derivatives associated with the middle world and manifest presence, are preliminarily suitable for this. The word *yav'* is "what is [manifestly] seen."

"Myth" comes from the Greek μῦθος, which literally means an oral story, narrative, and history. As has been said, myth wields explanatory power for the whole cosmos and answers all the questions posed within folk cultures, legends, and traditions. If Tradition, from *tradere*, means transmission, then myth is the way of being of Tradition, the oral transmission of the story of whence, why, and how everything exists, what laws and fate are assigned to everything, and what lots are to be drawn. These matters are told by the Norns or Moiras, the Deities or their messengers, the souls of ancestors, and seers, shamans, or sages. Myth is expressed in speech, and the Indo-European peoples prioritized the oral transmission of tradition. Through speech, myth is closely intertwined with the language of the people that is its bearer and speaker (although the notion of language is broader than speech as speaking). Thus, somewhat stepping ahead, we could illustrate Tradition with the metaphor of a tree, which would be similar to the language family trees of linguistics. But we would be even closer to the essence of the matter if we used the metaphor of a forest where each tree embodies what on the linguistic tree would correspond to a language family with different branches. We know that the peoples of one language family express one and the same tradition, but with their own lingual and local variations.

Two questions arise before us: Who is the one uttering and speaking, or rather who is the one who tells of all that there is, of beings as a whole (*Seiende-im-Ganzen* per Heidegger)? And what is the origin of language in the middle world of people?

The question of the origin of language, and therefore speech, is decided and resolved only in myth. No scientific hypotheses can answer this question; it is absolutely beyond their sphere of competencies. Science proposes a mere spread of weak, unconvincing, and at times downright vulgar guesses as to the origin and evolution of language. Language and speech are gifted to people by the Divinities, and this is quite likely the most important and key gift, the meaning and purpose of which runs much deeper than simple communication and ensuring that people can talk with one another. In the steppes, in the mountains, in the thick of forests, on the banks of rivers and across islands, in the dead of night around the fire, among other sounds, the song of the Divinities or spirits was heard by people. It was heard, "listened to," "caught on to," and "sung along with." For song — a hymn, a *galdr* — is the primary and highest form of human speech addressed to the inhabitants of the upper and lower worlds as well as the beings of the middle world. It is no coincidence that the sacred texts of traditions were written and have come down to us in various poetic forms, as have the legends of folklore (which is also called "oral lore").

Myth tells itself. This fully corresponds to the holistic perception of the world: the interconnectedness of everything, the inhabitedness of every corner of the world by the spirits of rivers, lakes, mountains, fields, ravines, pebbles alongside a road, and the infinite "and so on." The world is full of mythical beings, of the selves of animals or plants, the living and the dead, humans and Divinities. The person who tells myths is not an author but a participant in the uttering of truth, which passes through him from the Muses, spirits, ancestors, or Deities and their messengers. Other myths are transmitted to man by other tellers. Tradition, thus, is the polylogue of the whole beingful world.

But if myth tells itself, then what is the status of the Deities, especially the supreme ones who, according to myth, lay down the harmony, order, and law of the cosmos? Mystical and metaphysical monism maintains that the whole cosmos is the unfolding of the play of the mind or imaginational theater of the Absolute Divine. In this case, the Divine itself is the Teller and the Sayer of myth. But the descriptions, images, attributes, stories and histories associated with this Divinity, as well as the mystical path of becoming one with it and revealing the true nature of the cosmos, are told in myths. The criteria of linear logic, cause-and-effect relationships, and temporal sequentiality are inapplicable here, for they introduce measure and fixation into a realm that is above the conventions of the middle world. The truths of these higher spheres do not bear being unraveled and sorted into categories in the likes of "first there was this, then there was that," but should be grasped in an integral, symbolic unity that is broader than the rational. Everything else consists of interpretations generated by the adoption of one or another starting point for ensuing unraveling. In other words, many different forest paths can lead to a clearing, but in leading to it, they all merge into a single floor of flowers and grasses.

So, is it myth telling itself, the Divine telling itself about itself, as if uttering itself in play with itself? Both of these affirmations are right, and the monistic schools of non-duality have developed and affirmed distinctive versions of this relationship, versions which can be understood as formulations that richly express the ultimate unity that lies beyond the expressive means of discursive speech — expressions that have a grammatical structure and continuous sequence of utterances. Such, for example, is the phrase *tat tvam asi*, "thou art that," which has grammar and vocabulary, in contrast to the *maha mantra, AUM*, which is an independent syllable that tends towards the form of pure vocalization.

Searching for primacy in either subject or object plays no role here, because the traditional world of the sacred knows no such clear-cut and categorical distinction, and at times does not even recognize the present existence of either. Although such would be burdened by a definite share of conventionality, we could clarify that the subject is the principle of the Sky-Father, while the object is the principle of Mother-Earth.

Mythos — speech and language — is primary. Telling itself generates, describes, and sets up the very structure of the cosmos. Myth, placed in the center, tells us of which Divinity is telling the myth, and in the very same way, the myth's own tale and telling constitutes its listener, its form, and its content right down to the smallest details. Relatively speaking, myth creates out of itself in the center both the teller on the left, the listener on the right, as well as the speaking itself in one form or another (song, poetry, prose) and its content, or what the myth is about. Finally, myth creates the manifest world and its objects, which means that myth should not be taken to be speech suspended in the air in the middle of objective nature. When myth falls silent, both poles — the teller and the listener — are extinguished. Then the *mythos* can begin to unfold the next story, another history, as well as its heralds and listeners, or it can fall silent for a long time. If you hear a myth, this means only one thing: this myth, in this concrete instant, is telling not only what is said in its plot, but is telling you yourself, the one attentive to its telling, to its storytelling. This means that if all the beings of the world exist, then a myth is unfolding, a certain meta-history, as Friedrich Georg Jünger put it, is underway.

It is rightful and no coincidence that sacred texts (from the grandest compositions to folk tales and incantations like the Slavic *zagovory*) give priority to song and poetic form, to *mythopoiesis*. The rich ancient Greek word ποίησις can be translated as "creating," and in its philosophical dimension, it means bringing into presence something that was not present before, bringing-out-into-the-light-of-the-world, putting-forth-here. Well-known doctrines and traditions speak of the world being created by the Divinities' song, or of an important role being played by the appearance of speech and the naming of things (assigning them their essence and fates through their names) whereby chaos is brought to cosmic harmony. This is replicated in the middle world by the numerous incantations intended to influence reality, heal the sick, protect one's household or save one's life, call someone to accountability, etc., which are uttered both in everyday life and states of ecstatic enthusiasm (in the etymological sense of being "inspired" or "possessed" by Divinities). Mythopoiesis is at once, in the same instant, creation by the poetic word and the telling of myth. It is not that "the word is pronounced first" and then a certain thing or phenomenon appears as a consequence, but rather the very emergence of things is a form of speaking.

The very word for "thing" in the Slavic languages, *veshch'* in Russian, is related to the *veche*, the assembly of free, arms-bearing men who gather to resolve a community issue, to legislate (to speak forth the law), to convene to discuss (Russian *soveshchanie*), etc. On an even deeper level, the word means "speaking" or "that which is said," such as in the Old Czech *věce* (*veche*) and the modern Czech *věc* ("thing"). In the ancient understanding, a "thing" coincides with an affair, a matter, a question for which dignified people gather to discuss and on which they must come to a decision. A "thing" was no mere material object like the Cartesian *objectum*. Likewise, the German *Ding* and the English "thing" belong in the same semantic field of "thing" and "affair" along with the Icelandic *þing*, which is analogous to the Slavic *veche* and goes back to the Proto-Germanic *þingą.

The Russian language also knows the forms *veshchat'* ("to say, to tell"), *predveshchat'* ("to foretell"), the epithet *veschchii*, meaning one who "foresees," "foretells," i.e., one who is wisely perspicacious, as well as *uveshchevat'* which like *ugovarivat'* means "to persuade," "to urge," wherein the root for "speaking," "*govor-*" refers to the semantic layer of oral speech, the voice (*golos* — vocalization), and language (*iazyk*, which also means "tongue"). Thus, in the Russian field, mythopoiesis is linked to these roots and is etymologically and semantically connected with "thing" (*veshch'*) in the sense of an affair and an occasion for gathering arms-bearing men to tend to affairs, to certain matters (cf. the Greek ἀρχή, which means at once "ground," "beginning," "principle," "authority," and "reign"). All of these are expressly spoken out, uttered, pronounced, foretold or discussed, and wield power like incantations (*zagovory*).

At an earlier stage, the word ποίησις was synonymous and used on an equal basis with τέχνη ("craft," "skill," "cunning"), but in the sense of a specific masterful work. This is similar to the situation with the altogether weak distinction between the words μῦθος and λόγος, both of which mean speech. Τέχνη is traditional craft and sublime art, which is closely connected with a whole mytho-ritual array of practices, such as appeasing the spirits of a workshop and the patrons of the craft, the ritual extraction of raw material for crafting, sacrificing to the Deities, and the ubiquity of poetic incantations (for defense, for magical powers, for spells, for praising, for frightening off). Sacred art fascinates us, inspires us, enraptures and whisks us out of everyday life, for through it we see the Divine illumination and insight gifted by the Muses to the master or at work in holding the power of chthonic matter in divinely-inspired forms of harmony (this is relevant, for instance, to the Germanic tradition, where the best craftsmen were the underground dwarfs). The same can be seen in roof rafting or in carving out a log or beam for building a hut. Τέχνη is directly connected to the Greek words τέκτων, "carpenter" (for Aristotle, ὕλη, "wood," is the category of matter as such), τίκτω, "to bring forth, to generate," to the Sanskrit *takṣati* ("to give form," "to yield an image," "to cut off or cut out"), and the Proto-Germanic cognate **paḥsuz*, which is also associated with generating and, quite possibly, spinning and weaving (Russian: *tkat'* — "to weave"; *tkan'* — "fabric").

If *poiesis* is creating in the word, in a specific vocalization and in giving a name to a thing, then authentic τέχνη is creating with the hands, which is a rougher, material form of embodying the same *mythos*. Μῦθοποίησις is telling-bringing-into-the-world (telling a myth defines the teller and the told), while μῦθοτέχνη is telling-embodying-in-things, the vesting of the whole array of incantational, mythical, and lingual forms into a specific piece of matter, whether wood, stone, metal, or fabric, by the master craftsman. In relation to material objects, *mythos* acts as the maieutic, that is the midwifery art of assisting during childbirth, which is yet another thing associated with ritual chants and songs. In philosophy, maieutics is raised to the level of a practice and method for revealing truth, such as in the Socratic style of questioning. But the roots of the Greek word μαιευτική have much to say and touch upon wide semantic fields. The root μαῖα means midwife, and was a respectful way to address a woman, a mother. In Greek mythology, Maia was one of the Pleiades who gave birth to Hermes by Zeus.

There are no grounds to speak of any etymological kinship between the Greek μαῖα and the Sanskrit *māyā*, but their homonymy and semantic overlaps speculatively lend to enriching our study. In Hinduism, *Maya* means not only the illusion of the world, but also the creative, generative force. The world is manifest to the eye thanks to Maya, and Maya is the veil (once again the motif of weaving and fabric) of the highest self of Brahman, his creative force and Shakti. The Sanskrit roots of Maya speak to the meaning of "linking, binding, and deceiving," and these motifs are highly developed in non-dual metaphysics. Here we can recall Jan de Vries' interpretation of the Germanic root *ginn* as "enchanting," i.e., "magically misleading," which appears in the word *Ginnungagap* (the Germanic-Scandinavian Abyss out of which the cosmogony begins).

The Greek μαῖα is not only a midwife or a female assistant[3], but a mother. The whole category of "matter" comes from understanding the mother as a nurse, as the one who nurses and nurtures life. In Plato, the maternal nursery that yields the place and material for the ideas and forms is called χώρα, which literally means "wide" and also referred to the special free lands surrounding the Greek *polis*. Plato's idealist metaphysics subsequently contrasted this with the ideal world that is not embodied in objects.

Thus, we can see and understand how *mythos* is revealed in oral poetry and folk tales as well as in the material world of craft and art, where the emphasis is shifted onto the feminine and maternal element. But authentic, mythological τέχνη should not be equated with the "technology" (or "technics") of the later eras

---
[3] It is noteworthy that in archaic societies the role of midwife could also be assumed by a male "witch doctor" or shaman.

of the Renaissance and the Enlightenment. Modern technology has no relation whatsoever to the [μῦθο]τέχνη of antiquity. The claim that the historical roots of technological progress go back to antiquity and archaic society is nothing more than a manipulative trick employed by a false *historial* in an attempt to cast the shadow of this paradigm backwards onto the past while ignoring the qualitative difference in natures. Modern technology and its triumph are upheld by the machinery of mass, uniform production, the triumph of the quantitative economic approach (whose fullest expression is capitalism), and the natural science institute of the university of "science." All of this is based on positing the calculability of the whole beingful world, of all beings. Martin Heidegger called this phenomenon the *Gestell*, the "Enframing," and described it as a particular relation to the truth of Being, from which modern technology and its demonic alienation of man from his own nature and Being is only consequently manifested in such technological forms. Within the framework of the Gestell, truth must correspond to predetermined (but not mythological), rigidly anti-sacred, scientific methods which are tightly interwoven into the closed system of "Capital — Institute — Production." Within the inner workings of the Gestell, the production of things is excessive (ὕβρις — hubris), dull, and parodies genuine handicraft. Things created in this stream are devoid of mythopoetics. They are not created in the proper ritual silence that is the condition of the mystery of creation in silence; instead, they are produced in a mere void of any talking about what is going on in such production. Things are made without the slightest thought about the Divinities, without inspiration by the Muses, without sacrifices to the spirits, without sending off the accursed share to the beyond. The only music that can exist in such a framework is the meaningless stream of vulgarities broadcasted by the radio in the back of the factory. This is how matter spawns and reassembles itself amidst the sterile deprivation of the Divine.[4]

---

[4] The question of technology and the negative formation of the Gestell is examined in more detail in Askr Svarte, *Tradition and Future Shock: Visions of a Future that Isn't Ours* (PRAV Publishing, 2023).

If *mythopoiesis* is creation by the word, substantive craft, and the singing of things into production (maieutics), then mythopoiesis also has to do with what is regarded as natural growth, procreation, and the manifolding of beings and life, i.e., φύσις. The Greek word φύσις (*physis*) gave the root for what with the Enlightenment came to be known as "physics" and, more broadly, physicalism as an umbrella term for all the natural sciences of objective nature (*natura*). We have already encountered a number of meanings of the word φύσις: to give form, to give birth, to bear, to bring forth. This picture can be complemented with other facets: φύσις is growth and manifestation, like a plant breaking up through the soil, upon which we see its shaft and shoots, or like a source of water pouring out through a crack in a rock. Going even deeper, the root φύω is related to the Proto-Indo-European *b^huH, which is cognate with the Old English *bēon*, "to be," "to become," as well as all the Germanic verbs for being/existing.

Thus, we discover a certain duality within the manifest world that first unfolds out of *mythos*. There are beings that are unconcealed through sacred mythopoiesis and mythotekhne, and there are beings that grow of and out of themselves, that is the whole beingful world, *physis*. On the whole, this fully corresponds to the hierarchical movement of the emanations of the One down to its lower boundary of the many, that is the movement of πρόοδος, the gradual division into dyad, triad, and many.

We can, however, quite easily find our way out of this dualism in the different emanations of the beingful world. We can do so without discarding or cancelling φύσις as something non-extant; instead, we can expand our understanding to include and encompass it within the holism of non-dual *mythos*. We merely have to recall that the properties of the surrounding nature, landscape, climate, as well as flora and fauna, are put in place by the Divinities and spirits that create the worlds. A number of myths, legends, sagas, epics, and folklore tales tell us why there are specific plants and cereals on this earth (e.g., they are gifts from Demeter, or, for instance, mushrooms and plants are a separate species of living beings with their own history), where the animals here came from and how they came here (e.g., the Fijian myth of the birth of pigs as gifts from a spirit that answered a petition for defense), how mountains are sleeping giants or the refuges of hidden heroes and kings, just as boulders are trolls and rivers are living beings, etc. We can recall the Scandinavian myth of how the whole cosmos is the body of the giant Ymir, whose brains became the clouds, his eyelashes the forests, and his blood the waters. Thus, φύσις is not autonomous like the Cartesian objective nature of Modernity, which is given to man at his disposal as a resource at hand, but is mythologically predetermined, incanted, foretold, and "thinged," sketched out and projected like a story about what something is, why it grows here, what it is for, or how it was gifted in response to an act or request on the part of humans. This directly leads us to the thesis that there is a fundamental ontological plurality of natures: there is no single φύσις for all in the likes of that which the European sciences of Modernity allege to describe the most accurately. There are many φύσεις, many natures, as many as there are authentic, living mythologies and their peoples who live in, speak, and transmit them. There is not an infinite number of them, but an organic plurality. Furthermore, the authentic mythopoetic being of a people and its Divinities is possible only in a fine balance between myth-culture and myth-φύσις ("mythic nature"), such as in rural life without technological process and urbanization, where the φύσις of the world of plants and animals is still accessible to one's sight and for mystical communication just beyond the fence, and where the Divinities and spirits of ancestors still walk among clearings and yards. In principle, the urban environment is not φύσις, but rather a physicalist spawn of the Enframing. It grows neither by itself nor under the influence of mythological maieutics, but merely reproduces out of its own inner poverty a uniform landscape of alienation that is divorced from life.

Why is everything in our era reduced to *natura* and physicalism? Here we should turn to Indian metaphysics. Our era is marked by the total dominance of the *tamas guna*, that is the quality of ignorance, darkness, crude matter, death, and inertia. The well-known doctrine of cycles states that with each successive era the quantity of goodness and light diminishes while the density of time and the hardening of beings within the world increase. This is *tamas*, "darkness" in Sanskrit, *tenebra* in Latin, and *t'ma* in Russian. The primacy of the *tamas* principle in our era means the domination of the sheerly material existence of the world and crude material descriptions of it. Physics, of course, is real, but it is not the entirety of truth — physics is merely the bottom sediment of the viscous silt into which the entire cosmos has been submerged. It is neither the end, peak, nor center of truth, but rather the bastard "truth" of ignorance, the "truth" of the condition of not knowing the other gunas and qualities of the cosmos, of our being deprived of their manifestations and presence. The diminution of the light of Divine freedom and "ease" has reached such depths that the majority of people now believe that there never was any such light before, and that any talk about such pertains merely to mankind's old superstitions and delusions. They believe in the physicalist picture of the world not because it is actually the truth, but by dint of their own ignorance of any other and out of the sheer lack of any heroic or mystical audacity and freedom to think about another. Such a state of affairs is real because the myth that tells of the sacred "lightheartedness" that easily overcomes any gravity is no longer sounded and heard in the midst of the crude noise of our days. Meanwhile, an altogether other eschatological tale is unfolding.

Another word that is of no small importance and should not be sidestepped is λόγος. The word λόγος has an enormous quantity of meanings, yet this is a common quality of sacred languages and archaic speech, where every word is multifaceted, rich in semantics, and is not so much a set of concrete significations and names as it is a principle or element in the structure of the cosmos, one that is expressed in the language of the creative tale. The word λόγος comes from the verb λέγω — "to speak," "to name," "to tell," which, once again, in archaic times rendered it practically a synonym for *mythos*. Furthermore, from λόγος comes the notion that words are concepts and teachings, as in the various "-logies" of sciences. But the original meaning of the word λόγος, traceable back to the Proto-Indo-European root *leǵ, means cutting into an array and gathering together. Martin Heidegger explains the meaning of the verb *legein* with the image of a harvest: the ears of grain are cut, arrayed, and gathered together in a fold of like to like and then tied together into a bundle and sheaf. There is an inherent separation of one thing from another at work here, just as berries and wormwood are not bundled together with ears of wheat. In turn, λόγος is gathering in word, in thought, in reflective thinking, as well as in artistic creation. The craftwork of a master is also a manifestation of λόγος.

The term "mythology" now no longer looks so tautological, even though both Greek roots are synonymous in denoting speech and word. Mythology is the gathering into one sheaf of all the myths of specific Divinities and traditions as a whole. Mythology is no mere polylogue of tales about everything, as if overflowing into glossolalia, but the distinctive narratives proper to cults and peoples. In mytho*logy*, the gathering principle of *logos* is more strongly at play, coming close to the*ology* and philosophy, which are themselves often difficult to distinguish from each other. Further empowering the *logos* at work here leads to it being torn away from the roots of *mythos* and developed into *ratio*. *Logos* also refers to the passage from speech to writing, from oral telling to text, which means more fixed versions of a myth and to a certain ossification of *koine*.

Another most important dimension of λόγος is truth — or rather the question of truthfulness. If λόγος is λέγειν, the gathering-together-of-the-like, then the very distinction between like and other — e.g., an ear of cereal vs. a branch of wormwood — must be deliberately predetermined. Thus, the truth of *logos* is the correspondence between what is gathered together and what ought to be gathered together. The very principle of distinguishing one thing from another is the gnoseological dimension of Heraclitus' πόλεμος.

Herein lies the correspondence theory of truth which, known to us since Plato and Aristotle, has in different variations constituted the essence of Western metaphysics and its approach to truth. Instead of delving into the history of how metaphysics became meta-physics (τὰ μετὰ τὰ φυσικά) over the course of the arrangement of Aristotle's books, let us once again turn to the words themselves, for they do not contradict the essence. Μεταφυσικά is that which is above physics, i.e., the sphere of ideas, the realm of ontological principles and laws. The manifest world must correspond (*correspondentia*) to the forms residing in the upper, heavenly world, the embodiment of which in matter introduces distortions, aberrations, and the diversity of all beings. For Plato, this is the heavenly world of intelligible ideas, the Greek word ἰδέα literally meaning that which is visible, a directly seeable being. In Aristotle, this *eidos* is the form of a thing, while ἐντελέχια (entelechy) is the completeness of a thing in its purpose (that for which it exists) and in its place; all things move towards realizing the life force inherent in them or in the intent of their creator. The truth of things and phenomena is determined through their correspondence to their higher predetermination. We see the same metaphysical structure in the scientific picture of the world, but unfolded towards matter and its laws. What is true is what corresponds to the accepted scientific methodology, the physical-mathematical corpus and descriptive language of which are held to be the most accurate. That which is true is that which corresponds to pure nature and the material approach (the principle of *adaequatio*). Thus, what Plato considered to be the bastard *logos* is elevated to replace the Apollonian harmony of the world of ideas. Both Nietzsche and Heidegger arrayed strategies for overcoming the whole of Western metaphysics stretching from Plato to modern science, and they pointed out that it has been completely exhausted and reached its end. In Traditionalist doctrine, this corresponds to the oblivion and death of Tradition in the descending eschatological cycle.

One specific feature of Western metaphysics — one which, in our opinion, could not have come about without the colossal and decisive influence of the ontology of creationist monotheism from which all the key provisions of Modernity proceeded — is the idea of searching for one final truth for all, a certain supra-idea or supra-being, a highest possible form, of which the entire cosmos is an imprint. Heidegger saw precisely this as the erroneous resolution — or decision — of the question of Beyng[5] among the ancient Greeks that was inherited by the West. The truth of Beyng was substituted by a being, by something that "is," such as Plato's ἰδέα of the Good, which *a priori* inlays a distortion and inconsistency between phenomenal here-being and what is "above."

From this point we can expand the question of the status of truth: is there one truth or many? Is there an absolutely universal set of procedures and judgments that confirm and affirm truth? This would be a metaphysical approach, from which we must move to Heidegger's proposal to understand truth as unconcealment, as *aletheia*. The Greek word ἀλήθεια consists of the private negation ἀ- and the root λήθε, which means oblivion, concealment, obscuration. In the Greek myths, Lethe (Λήθη) is the river of forgetfulness in the subterranean kingdom of Hades, the latter of which, Ἀΐδης, from the same root as ἰδέα, literally means a lack of visibility. In Plato's *Republic*, Lethe is not called a river, but a plain — the Plain of Oblivion — which refers us to *topos* and space, whereby we come close to *khora*.

Heidegger describes *aletheia*-truth with his overarching metaphor of a forest. Imagine that we are walking along a trail

---

[5] This manner of writing "Being" refers to the difference between *Sein* and *Seyn* in the later Heidegger, wherein *Seyn* is apophatic. We will explore this in depth below. See Askr Svarte, *Gods in the Abyss*; Alexander Dugin, *Martin Heidegger. Poslednii Bog* (Moscow: Academic Project, 2014); idem, *Martin Heidegger: The Philosophy of Another Beginning*, trans. Nina Kouprianova (Arlington: Radix / Washington Summit Publishers, 2014).

in the Black Forest, and the tops of the dense, dark forest close in over our heads. But now ahead of us is a small, illuminated clearing. The light penetrates through a hole-like gap in the thicket of the forest tops. This gap is *aletheia*. Understanding truth as *aletheia* means understanding truth to be the unconcealment that gives a being (any and all things) the space to manifest itself as present and whole; the very same light shining through the clearing provides space for the forest around it to figure as an accentuated border, a rim, a framing of the clearing (like the being that frames the Greek openness of χάος as well as the Scandinavian gap). In *aletheia*, there is no criterion of truthfulness-as-correspondence, there is only the clearing that reverently offers itself to things for them to be brought into being. Thus, *aletheia*-truth comes close to *poiesis* and speech — after all, we can easily utter contradictory statements, speak the truth as well as lie, but both belong to the essence of speaking. This luminous clearing itself is in essence not some-thing, it is "no-thing," and it does not affect a being, which is to say that it is not *khora*-matter. *Aletheia* does not certify what is true and what is not, for its truth rests in the un-concealment, the un-hiddenness, of beings and the beingful world.

At this point, we can raise the question of the metaphysical structure of language itself, i.e., how, despite the freedom of arbitrary utterances, it is still necessary for a phrase to correspond to grammar in order for it to be intelligible independently of the truthfulness or falsity of its content. There are some grounds to the opinion that the structure of Western metaphysics reflects and embodies on a new level the grammatical structure of the ancient Greek language. But if we look beyond the European and Indo-European grammatical canon, then we see that there are many different grammars and ways of categorizing the basic experience at play in thought, language, and speech.[6] The primal element at play in language turns out to be broader than any specific grammar, and there can be numerous grammars within

---

6 See Sergei Borodai, *Iazyk i poznanie. Vvedenie v postreliativizm* (Moscow: Sadra, 2020).

a language, not to mention semantics, vocabulary, styles of thinking, an abundance of regional dialects, phonetic variations, and isogloss boundaries. Both metaphors are true for language (as well as thinking): the clearing that encompasses various beings (linguistic, grammatical, and other variations) and the soil from which various tradition-language-trees grow.

If we immerse ourselves in one of the modern European languages, then it bears granting priority to the poetic forms which allow for flexible play with word order, verb arrangement, phonetics, stresses (archaic languages generally have arbitrary word stresses), and the interweaving of vocalizations, colloquial sayings, refrains, and an immense quantity of metaphors, paraphrases, riddles, kennings, idioms, etc., all of which create in the stanzas of songs a multiplicity of tones and halftones of meaning that might reach the point of contradiction. *Mythos* turns out to be existentially richer than *logos* in manifesting the Dionysian nature of language, whereby strict statements, ecstatic exclamations, and glossolalia are the extremes of one and the same speech — just as a person with two hands can grasp the opposite ends of a staff or the different scales of a pine cone.

We do not have to face the problem of choosing between one of these two theories of truth and deciding which approach is more truthful: metaphysics or unconcealment. This duality finds resolution in a different way: as the telling of beings and the beingful world, a myth is the truth within its tradition, within the bosom of the people that transmits it. Here we should return to the metaphor of the tree. The tree's different branches originate from a single trunk — this is the variability of the interpretations and cults of different Divinities, or the truths of different estates within one and the same tradition. It is all the same tree, preserving its rootedness and collectedness within one body. The multiplicity of such trees forms the forest of traditions. The plurality of mythologies means a plurality of truths and a plurality of *logoi*. When we gaze deep into a tradition, we see that its truth, even metaphysical, is absolute within its world. Within its sphere of being, truth is conditioned by its myth, by its Divinities, by its cosmic laws, by its morality and customs. But it is enough for us to "surface" again and we will see the forest beyond the trees, and beyond the forest the clearing of unconcealment that gives many truths their space and light. This is how we come to know plurality and relativism as understandably limited by the sacred measure of Divine laws within different mythologies' frameworks, while avoiding total nihilism and the denial of grand truths (grand narratives) in favor of the Postmodern era's endless flow of "individual truths."

It is no coincidence that the word for truth is formed by the negation of concealment, as none other than ἀ-λήθεια. Through it constantly resounds the bringing forth of beings into unconcealment, the interplay of revealing-and-concealing. Heidegger points out that this concealing aspect was accomplished through ἰδέα and φύσις.[7] A being, manifesting itself primarily through growing and coming into the clearing of Beyng, fixes attention on itself as an extant thing that possesses a form and is literally visible. This appearance at once affirms metaphysical truth through the intelligibility of *logos* as thought (νόημα, νοεῖν) while pushing truth as unconcealment, as the unconcealing that gives space for manifesting and for being gathered-into-being-told, into the backdrop of oblivion. However, even while remaining within any metaphysical truth, in the *logos*-gathering, we can ecstatically break through to the illuminated insight that if truth exists as truth, then it has already passed into the illuminated clearing of unconcealment. This does not double metaphysics, nor does it create a meta-metaphysics (as if one more level on top), but rather is always immanently present like water in water.

Physis is the growing flow of beings in the *aletheia*-clearing of Beyng, a flow that is facilitated by midwife-like mythologies. Thusly are the trees of traditions, peoples, and civilizations

---

[7] See Martin Heidegger, *Contributions to Philosophy (Of the Event)*, trans. Richard Rojcewicz and Daniela Vallega-Neu (Indianapolis: Indiana University Press, 2012).

formed. The Divinities act as the *logoi* singing the *mythoi* of themselves, embodied in an ordered cosmos, in the caring and gathering of peoples who live in this nature and who sing songs and hymns to the Divinities in response. Thus, we understand the formulation "myth is our homeland" to mean not only our heavenly roots, but also the particular nature in whose bosom man and peoples live. This is *mythopoiesis*.

But are there many Deities or is the Divine one? Here we should point to Martin Heidegger's elegant and koan-like decision: the decision as to whether they are many or one belongs to the Divinities themselves as they gather at the Thing around the hearth of Being to resolve this question.

Paradoxically, this formulation does not utterly refute the polytheism that we defend, nor does it yield the opposite judgement. Instead, it brings us closer to the topic of theistic monism, Neoplatonic henology, and Advaita.

The Goddess Speech

The Sanskrit word *śabda* means oral speech, utterance, speaking out. According to Indian grammarians, who have erected some of the deepest systems of knowledge of the entire manifest world through the grammar, phonetics, and poetics of Sanskrit, speech manifests itself through, and is inextricable from, *sphoṭa*. The term *sphoṭa* is found in some of the most ancient grammatical accounts of Sanskrit, but its meaning was later expanded and elevated by Patanjali (2nd-1st centuries BCE) and Bhartrhari (c. 5th century CE). *Sphoṭa* means not only the content or meaning of uttered speech, but etymologically means to push out, to push forth, to give impetus. We can see in this a semantic and metaphysical proximity to the Greek *poiesis* as a form of the manifestation of *mythos*.

Sphoṭa is the quality of speech that is directed towards sound; it begins with the air that arises out of the chest and goes into the uttered word. The *Shatapatha Brahmana* (c. 1st millennium BCE) states that breath is at the heart of everything. The Greek word ψυχή (*psykhe*) as well as the Russian *dusha* (soul) and *dukh* (spirit) also etymologically take us back to breathing, inhaling, and blowing, i.e., to the movement of air within the chest, which is identified with the element of life as such. In the same text, breathing is identified with fire and Indra. Fire refers to the heart, to the heart's heat mixed with breath in the chest, which is reflected in the light of the mind, the heat of emotions, and the heat in one's loins. Fire is further differentiated to be identified with speech, vision, thought, and hearing. Everything belongs to the primal element of fire, for fire is everything, and fire itself is breath. Here we can recall the words of Heraclitus the Obscure:

Κόσμον τόνδε, τὸν αὐτὸν ἁπάντων, οὔτε τις θεῶν οὔτε ἀνθρώπων ἐποίησεν, ἀλλ' ἦν ἀεὶ καὶ ἔστιν καὶ ἔσται πῦρ ἀείζωον, ἁπτόμενον μέτρα καὶ ἀποσβεννύμενον μέτρα.	This cosmos, the same for all, was made neither by gods nor by humans, but was, is, and will be ever-living fire that is lit in measures and extinguished in measures.

The metaphysical identity of language, speech, and fire has long been known and is enshrined in language through various metaphors and poetics, such as tongues of flame and heated or fiery (sharp) words and speeches. The prophet Alexander Pushkin called for "burning the hearts of men with the verb-word."

The *Shatapatha Brahmana* asserts that everything has arisen out of non-being. This thought is so utterly inexpressible that it is described in the sheerly negative categories of "neither non-existent nor existent." The border region between non-being and being includes thought, which is higher than speech, but the greatness of speech hardly yields to being considered inferior. The higher position of thought is explainable in terms of how thought is able to exist while being held in the mind and not being uttered. Thought, therefore, is close to primordial non-being in that it cannot be seen. But when thought, through *sphoṭa*, passes into oral speaking, into speech and sound, it becomes coarse and like an "idea," that is something audible, "visible," manifest. Here it bears clarifying that, from our point of view, both thought and speech are the unfolding or manifesting of language. Language is closest of all to non-being, because it is latently present in and affects verbal speech, while remaining concealed-in-unconcealment, as well as thinking, just as internal monologue is still "sounded" in one's native language and uses its categories. When it comes to the question of the unambiguous primacy of either language or thinking, one cannot simply decide to abandon this division as a false formulation of the question, for being, language, and thinking form a complex, indivisible structure of densely mutual influences. It was therefore quite right of the Sanskrit grammarians to build their hierarchy on the principle of compression or compaction, moving from (one) non-being towards the multiplicity of manifest things and situating the fire of thought and speech on the highest levels. Likewise, seeking to pass judgment on the truthfulness of one hierarchy and the falsehood of others would be an erroneous, rationalist approach to the element of myth.

In the hierarchy of manifestation, speech, seeking for itself a form, generates breath, gives rise to vision, and vision creates hearing for taking in and confirming the act of speech. The act unfolds in the closest proximity to the material world, since it directly operates with things, objects, and performs actions. This also has to do with the ready-to-hand nature of beings that are always at the fingertips of the actor. Speech is above hearing, because speech gives an order to do something, while hearing is what receives this behest and prompts a person to act, such as to kindle the specific flame for the sacrificial fire. It is to this flame, which is the material reflection of the fire-breath-Indra, that thought and speech are offered as the first sacrifices, for they are "like a team of horses carrying offerings to the gods." Thus is completed the circle of the manifestation and ordering of that which is integrally proper to the beingful world, to the manifest, to that which has come into the clearing of non-being.

The hierarchy of the manifestation of fires is completed with the identification of man and the cosmos in the following lines:

> 6. He said, - Verily, that Agni [fire] is the breath; for when man sleeps, speech passes into the breath, and so do the eye, the mind, and the ear; and when he awakes, they again issue from the breath. Thus much as to the body [atman].
>
> 7. Now as to the [deities]. That speech verily is Agni [fire] himself; and that eye is yonder sun; and that mind [thought] is that moon; and that ear is the quarters; and that breath is the wind that blows here [in this world].
>
> 8. Now, when that fire goes out, it is wafted up in the wind (air), whence people say of it, 'It has expired [blown out or up]', for it is wafted up in the wind. And when the sun sets it enters the wind, and so does the moon; and the quarters are established in the wind, and from out of the wind they issue again. And when he who knows this passes away from this world, he passes into the fire by his speech, into the sun by his eye, into the moon by his mind [thought], into the quarters by his ear, and into the wind by his breath; and

being composed thereof, he becomes whichever of these deities he chooses...[8]

Continuing the analogy between the cosmic "body" of the Divine and the human body of the middle world, the emphasis on the mouth should not escape our attention. The *Shatapatha Brahmana* speaks of how Brahman was first created out of the body of Purusha. Brahman was created out of his mouth, that is the "mouth of fire." The mouth of Brahma also generates the estate of Brahmins — the priests and philosophers — within the single body of Indian society.

On the bodily level, the mouth figures as the physiological embodiment of the primordial Chaos or Abyss. Let us recall the etymology of the Greek χαίνω and the Germanic *gap*, as well as one of the *heiti* of Odin, *Gapþrosnir*, that is "the one whose mouth is wide open [in astonishment]." Etymologically complementary to the Greek and German array is the Russian word *zev*, which means gap, hole, open earth, the female womb, and mouth — meanings which were displaced by the later identification of *zev* with bored yawning (*zevanie*).

The mouth is the gateway[9] through which Brahma creates the world with the sacred syllable Ōṃ. Sound and vibration are fundamental. Creation happens through the pronounced sound (fire) that bursts into presence (*sphoṭa*). This corresponds to the vibration of the body in the area of the chest and larynx when singing vowels, chanting hymns and invocations, or speaking in general. In the *mahamantra*, the vowels *a* and *u* are responsible for the creation and the upholding of the external world. The situation with the consonant *m* is more interesting, as the latter is a nasalization of the declining vibration of the vowel *u* heading through the palate and paranasal sinuses to the top of the head.

---

8   *The Satapatha-Brahmana (Part IV)*, trans. Julius Eggeling, *Sacred Books of the East* 43 (Oxford: Clarendon Press, 1897), X.3.3.6-8 [Translation modified to correspond to the author's Russian].

9   Let us mention that the Latin Deity of Beginnings and the masculine personification of Chaos, Janus Bifrons, was also the Deity of Gateways and passages, doorways, and portals of all kinds, over which his image was hung. The Winter Solstice also took place under his aegis.

In other words, the descent of *u* into *m* is directed from the external world into the mind and achieves the most precise vibration at the highest point of the body. The vibration of the syllable comes to completion with the calming of any movement and images in the depths of the mind, or more precisely beyond the boundaries of the *atman*. This is suggested by the accent dot under the consonant *ṃ*, which is the *bija*, that is the seed from which fire, thought, mantra, and speech are regenerated.

Here we are encountering the monism of speech in the sacred proto-syllable and first word, *Ōṃ*. Brahman, who creates the world with the spoken word, is called *Shabdabrahman*, that is Word-Brahman. *Śabda* is word, sound, verbal speech. Accordingly, we now find ourselves in the bosom of *śabda-advaita* as based on classical Vedism.

Also of interest is how the vibration of the vowel u can come to a head not only by way of nasalization into the consonant *ṃ*, but also by keeping it as a vowel that passes into pure vibration. In this case, it does not ascend to the mind in the head, but is localized in the chest and heart and envelops the larynx. Here lies the very same "breath" and "fire" of which the Brahmana texts and the Upanishads speak. We know that in sacred anthropology the point of selfhood is the heart. This especially shines through such epithets attached to the heart as "blazing," "flaming," and "hot." The light of the heart is reflected in the mind and bursts through the mouth like fiery wind. Its heat is reflected in the lower part of the body, where it generates passions and corporeality. The sternum itself is the receptacle of Indra, in which there is not yet any division between breath, fire, thought, and speech.

Breath is *atman*, the soul is *jiva*. But we find both breath and fire not only among people, but among the Divinities and in the One. Everything is intertwined, and the peaks are reflected in the valleys. If the human being of the middle world is "the one who utters sacred syllables to the Deities," then *Shabdabrahman* is the absolute utterer. Brahman creates the myriads of worlds with the word.

The reverse of what unfolds in the speech of creation is described as the folding back of the various manifestations of fire (hearing, vision, speech) into breathing while dreaming, and then into a deep, dreamless slumber, which is considered to be a step closer to Brahma. Inhalation is the silencing of speech, the opposite movement to *sphoṭa*. In this metaphysics, this already means that there is death, of which slumber is one of the most common metaphors. The folding back and closing of seeing into breathing and sleep means the extinguishing of the entirety of the visible, phenomenal manifestness that is the cosmos. When Brahma falls silent, the same thing happens as when he closes his eyes: the worlds of Maya and objects disappear.

Herein lies the difficult point of the problem of truth. Scholars maintain that there is a firm connection between ancient peoples' notion of truth and metaphors of the visible and luminous. True is what is seen by the eyes and sight (ἰδέα) — this is the semantic, gnoseological, and even moral canon. On the one hand, it is indeed the case that sacred texts indicate this. The *Shatapatha Brahmana* says that "the true is sight." What is the seeable? The things and phenomena of the manifest world, including the theophanies of Deities, the feats of heroes, the tragedies of kings, or the forgotten life of stones alongside a road. This is the reality of the middle world, the world of people, as an intersection of many roads. Over the course of the metaphysical degradation of eras, the semantic metaphor of "visibility—light—truth" directly leads us to this interconnection being reinforced by *ratio* and *logos* put into opposition to *mythos*. Truth as that which is visible becomes crude and leads us to vulgar materialism, empiricism, and positivism. "If I don't see Divinities, then that means their being is not true, and claiming their being is a lie," so to speak. This defect affecting ontology and gnoseology was inlaid in metaphysics in already the most ancient times, starting with the very principle of manifestation and passage into presence. Unconcealment is at once the concealment of what is unconcealed in the "what," "where," and "how" of unconcealing. In the harmonious Golden Age, truth as visibility was not a problem, but with the fall of tradition this imbalance logically led to an ossification of the notion of truth and its gradual inversion. Truth, as the unconcealment of non-being, was consigned to oblivion in the very first notes of the cosmogony.

This horizon of "truth" only intensifies in the final era, when the *guna tamas* — inertness, ignorance, ductility, the principle of earth and matter — takes the lead in the cosmos. The most ancient teaching of Maya even says that the manifest world (and all worlds) is essentially an illusion that should be dispelled, for the only true nature (authentic existence) is Brahman. Thus, we arrive at a contradiction: what is visible is in fact not the true, but rather is a lie, a deception that generates *avidya* (ignorance) in relation to the supreme being of Brahman.

This dialectic is rather subtle, and the problem has several resolutions within the various darshanas of Hinduism. The most consistent solution is offered by the sages of Kashmir Shaivist Advaita, who argue that Maya is indeed true and "real" for those who find themselves within it, and everything that is manifest in the worlds is genuine within Maya. The illusion is concealed in the subtle ignorance of the other, in the conviction that the only thing that is real is this reality and its laws. To explain this, the sages use the metaphor of a theater in which all the roles, scenes, stage, actors, and speculators are "played" by the one Absolute (Brahman or Shiva). When the actor puts on his mask, his face is truly hidden, but, at the same time, a role and drama truly are playing out on stage. Therefore, the visible is true for the plot of the play, for the actor, and for the gullible spectator, because it unfolds within the imagination of the Absolute Divine. Only Shiva is authentic, and therefore everything he imagines is also authentic. This approach affirms the paradoxical veracity of two principles at once, the Divine Absolute and Maya, the latter of which is elsewhere and otherwise easily discarded as merely an illusion of the world. But if Shiva alone is authentic, then so is everything that he imagines, dreams, and whatever appears to him in intoxicated visions. Gaudapada's *Mandukya*

Karika says: "The self-shining Atman, by the power of his own *maya*, imagines himself in himself. He alone creates and knows objects. This is the conclusion of the Vedanta."[10]

Thought poses a problem for the visual metaphor of truth. The *Shatapatha Brahmana* describes thought in an apophatic vein:

> 1. Verily, in the beginning this (universe) was, as it were, neither non-existent nor existent; in the beginning this (universe), indeed, as it were, existed and did not exist: there was then only that Mind [thought].
>
> 2. Wherefore it has been said by the *Rishi*, 'There was then neither the non-existent nor the existent;' for Mind [thought] was, as it were, neither existent nor non-existent.[11]

Thought is invisible to literal gaze, it is incorporeal and accessible to us only in thinking, in "inner contemplation." Nevertheless, it both "is not" and "isn't not," as it precedes all the senses in the hierarchy of manifestation.

The very manifestation of the manifest world (Maya) is the desire of (Brahman's) thought to manifest itself, for which it indulges in heat, desire, and will, all united in the principle of *tapas*, ascetic practice, purposefulness, and cosmogony. The essence of ascesis lies in belittling and limiting oneself. Thousands of atmans and sacrificial fires have been created by thought, and thousands of sacrifices have been offered, but they themselves were thoughts and were within thought. Thought is expressed in language, and at this point we pass from the metaphor of sight to the metaphor of speech. If sight affirms the truth of what it sees, then this is no more than a "vise" on what has already become manifest at the behest of and through speech. Both sight and speech are the principles of the concealment-in-unconcealment of whatever one sees and says. The passage from thought to speech and sight, and to hearing and acting, is a descent down the river of manifestation towards cruder forms. Let us ascend to the source.

---

10 [Translated from the author's Russian].

11 *Satapatha Brahmana* X.5.3.1-2.

The *Brahmana* calls thought the borderline between "is" and "is not" because it is not visible. We do not literally see thoughts with our eyes. We contemplate thoughts with our inner gaze. Thoughts are not material (they are not objects), but they still remain under the shadow of the predicate "is" (there "are" thoughts which we think, which "are" thought). Thus, behind the facade of the exterior affirmation of truth as that which is visible, there lie still subtler matters of truthfulness as that which "is," even if they are not always visible. This "is" exists in the inextricable connection of language, thought, and being(s). The higher status of sight that affirms truth turns out to be formal, while manifestation and being-in-the-world are much closer to speech and thought, the tightest link between which is language. The relationship of language to thinking and speech can be described with the metaphor of "water mixed in with water"; after all, we speak in language, we think and conduct internal monologue in language, we give orders (which give rise to actions) in language. Language connects humans into tribes and peoples, language is a gift given by the Divinities, and, finally, people sing hymns, offer praises, and present petitions to the Divinities in language. The *Chandogya Upanishad* says: "Just as, my dear, by one piece of clay everything made of clay may be known — the modification is merely a verbal distinction, a name; the reality is just 'clay.'" Earlier in the same text, we are told: "As all leaves are held together by a spike, so all speech is held together by *Om*. Verily, *Om* is the world-all. Verily, *Om* is this world-all."[12]

Speech is praeternal and primordial in relation to all objects and phenomena, to the whole of reality that only subsequently becomes visible to sight. In the Vedic period, speech appears as the Goddess Vac or Vak, whom *Rigveda* hymn X.125 endows with the highest epithets of "begetting Rudra, Indra, and Agni," "bearing soma," "granting food to he who looks, breathes, and hears what is said," "the gatherer of treasures," etc. In this hymn,

---

12 *Chandogya Upanishad* 6.1.4, 2.23.3 in *The Thirteen Principal Upanishads*, trans. Robert Hume (Oxford: Oxford University Press, 1921).

we distinctly see the attribution of feminine semantics to speech, Vac, who is like a nurse, mother, and harvester. "Granting food" to those who see, breathe, and hear means giving birth to visible objects, to breath and wind, as well as to sounds. The poetic device of the hymn indicates the totality of her creative power as concentrated in the syllable Ōṃ.

The *maha mantra* is at once a syllable and a word. In Indian metaphysics, *Om/Aum* is the root all-word to which numerous theories, darashanas, practices, and interpretations have been devoted. Aum is Brahman and is the seed of all speech and language. All subsequent phonemes, roots, words, objects, and the whole of reality are essentially only the unfolding of this primordial word's power within discursive speech and the phenomenal world. The entirety of the multiplicity of metaphysical triads corresponds to it.

The sound "*a*" corresponds to the principle of creation, and in the Trimurti of Divinities it is *Shabdabrahman*.

The sound "*u*" corresponds to Vishnu and the principle of maintaining the existence of the multiplicity of manifest worlds.

The sound "*m*" (as a nasalization of "*u*") corresponds to Shiva and the principle of destruction in the cosmogonic cycle.

The passage from the lighter and primary vowels to the consonant is interpreted as marking the strengthening and triumph of the *guna tamas* at the lower levels of emanations at the end of the life-cycle of the cosmos as well as in language and speech.

This syllable is the past, present, and future. Line 1.23 of the *Mandukya-Karika* says that the sound "*a*" leads to the Universal, "*u*" to the Luminous, and "*m*" to the Conscious, and above them all is the One, for which there is no measure and no motion. Despite the fact that *Aum* is divisible into phonemes bearing different interpretations and divine personifications, it is always to be thought in indivisible unity: the separate phonemes stand out from, but are not set apart from, the resounding oneness of *Shabdabrahman*.[13]

Sounding, expressed speech — the Goddess Vac — is *shakti*, the power of the manifestation of the Absolute and the fabric of matter. But speech occupies an intermediate position. When it sounds, thereby unifying breath and fire, it moves away from the center and creates worlds, but it is not sounded out on the level of thought, which means that our understanding of the nature of speech needs to be subtler and more refined. There is "thought-speech," but it is invisible, and within consciousness it continues to generate purer worlds, objects, and phenomena which are not burdened by matter. This is the world of the imagination, the theater within the consciousness of atman-Brahman. Finally, speech-thought can be extremely borderline in its orientation towards what is neither a sound nor a thought or utterance, but rather the *bija* under the phoneme m, which indicates an ineffable and inexpressible oneness, the seed from which the future syllable $Ōm$ fore-sounds and into which it will later fade away.

We might notice a certain contradiction in how the sound "*m*" simultaneously means both *tamas* and the path to the Conscious. How is this possible? At this point, we must digress and take a side path to pose the question: Who is the Uttering and Conscious one?

All the worlds and the manifest world are created by *Shabdabrahman*, that is by Brahma who creates the world by chanting the word, through unfolding the *maha mantra Aum* into the infinite diversity of beings. He is the first in the

---

13 Comparing both Hinduism and Neoplatonism's descriptions of the highest metaphysical and ontological levels (the supreme triads and the One) to the "unique" Christian teaching of the indivisible yet unmerged Trinity, we can state that the latter is deeply, metaphysically and historically secondary. Moreover, it is noteworthy that the Vedic grammarians regarded the Vedas and the Sanskrit script itself to be one of many literal embodiments of Brahman, which is to say that the Divine could be empirically beheld with one's own eyes in the lines of the holy texts, which were seen as an incarnation of the Absolute. This approach is superior to, for instance, Abrahamism's doctrine of the divine inspiration (mere inspiration) of its holy books.

classical Hindu Trimurti of Divinities. But the roles in the triad of *devas* are subject to the metaphysical law of cosmic decline, i.e., the change in eras from the Satya-Yuga to the dark era of ignorance and the destruction of the world that is the Kali-Yuga. The middle period is dominated by Vishnu, the Divinity of upholding order and the cosmos, the one who keeps the worlds created by Brahma in presence and in accordance with *rita* and *dharma*. The whole beingful world arises, flourishes, and wanes, and all the worlds are doomed to death, after which ensues rebirth in new cycles. Tradition does not know absolute death and is not afraid of it, for it knows the law of return and rebirth. The Divinity of death and destruction in the Trimurti, and also the Deity of supreme wisdom, is ascetic, ardent, mad Shiva.

The figure of Shiva can be traced back to deep antiquity, where he was known as Pashupati, the Shepherd of Flocks, and his name is already mentioned in the Vedas and means "Good" or "Blessing." Many centuries of theological and philosophical polemics among the non-dual teachings of Kashmir Shaivism led to the crystallization of the final theology of Shiva as *Mahadeva*, who has absorbed the main traits of the fearsome Rudra[14] as well as inherited the basic provisions of the Vedas and the Upanishads, all with the necessary adjustments for the degradation of the metaphysical conditions of the universe. In other words, Kashmiri Shaivism fully preserves the standpoints and aspirations of the classical epoch, but it adapted them specifically to the inevitably ensuing era of decline on the threshold of the destruction of all the worlds. Non-dual Shaivism is theistic monism, the highest peak of traditional theology and metaphysics, and it is extremely appropriate to the state of the cosmos on its deathbed. The grace revealed on the

---

14 Another of Rudra's names is Pashupati, and his traits are also especially reflected in Bhairava ("The Fearfully Roaring One"). Indra's traits can also be found in the figure of Shiva. These connections have been pointed out by Collin Cleary, a scholar of Indology and one of the leading American theologians of Odinism, in his article "What God Did Odin Worship?" See Collin Cleary, *Summoning the Gods: Essays on Paganism in a God-Forsaken World* (San Francisco: Counter-Currents Publishing, 2011).

path and in the rituals of the Vedas has been lost, and the union of this path and its adept has become fruitless, hence the fruit of enlightenment must be cultivated out of the same seed, but on different soil, in different metaphysical conditions, in other forms and even different aesthetics. Shiva thus becomes the integral monistic figure and the cornerstone of the entirety of high Hindu metaphysics as well as folk cults, among which today he remains one of the most revered Deities. Shiva inherited and reveals all the facets of the Divine figure who creates the worlds with the word. Shiva is *Shabdashiva*, the one riding on the Cow of Speech. He is the all-good destroyer of ignorance and the granter of liberation in the midst of the rotting corpse of this world.

The most important role for understanding the supreme nature of Brahman is played by the theological distinction between *saguna* and *nirguna*. Brahma Saguna is the Absolute manifested in qualities ("clad in gunas") and things. In this theology, Brahma is described through the attribution of various qualities, names, and epithets, and is conceived as the Deity embodied in the plurality of the phenomena and things of the cosmos. In the *saguna* mode, the Divinity can be described, given a form, an image, or even a multiplicity of manifestations ("he is that," "that is he"), hence the many names for the Divinities in all traditions. The multiplicity of names points to the infinite power and potency of manifestations in the most different aspects. The very doctrine of manifestationism, which speaks of the world-as-the-manifest-Divine, is also an embodiment of Brahma in the *saguna* aspect, i.e., the world is like the body of the Divine. Dominant here is the principle of movement from the center to the periphery, the unfolding of manifestation from the center of the One to the many, like the first drops that protrude from the pores of rock, already carrying within them a vast river delta flowing into the ocean. The theology of Brahma Saguna is cataphatic theology, the path of knowing through forms and atmans. Accordingly, oral speech and the spoken, sounded words of Speech are the cataphatic kingdom of *Shabdabrahman*. Moreover, the very determination of things through the verb "is" pertains to the *saguna* aspect even if what there is, is not material, but a form imagined or contemplated by the mind. Here we once again encounter the nurturing aspect of Speech, like a mother, like Mahadevi, like the *shakti* that gives to things their space-time-form of manifestation in discursive, creative speech. The dualist schools consider Brahma Saguna to be the supreme form of the Absolute, and they worship him as a manifest and personal Deity.

Brahma Nirguna, also called Para-Brahman, is the apophatic heart and the supreme, ineffable Brahman. Prominent Advaitists have correctly discerned that Brahma in the *saguna* aspect still dwells within the illusion of apparentness and semblance; in other words, the forms, names, and predicate "is" are all subject to death and can be discarded as aberrations of the mind which conceal the genuine nature of the Absolute. Brahma Nirguna is described through sequentially cutting away all attributes, forms, and words. In our case, thus, we are talking about Shiva Nirguna in his supreme aspect.

Is the Shiva literally sitting on Mount Kailash an anthropomorphic being? No. Is Shiva actually horrible or good? No. And so on — one can list an infinite number of negations, or one can take the wise path and take note of the fact that all attributes and descriptions belong to the order of beings (what there is). We can thus immediately ascend in our questioning to pose the question in the following manner: Shiva — is he who there is? No, Shiva "isn't." According to our habitual logic, it turns out that Shiva "is" the one who "is not," i.e., he "is" only the one who is absent and non-existent. But let us ask thusly: Is Shiva absent and non-existent? Once again, no. Para-Shiva's way of being is inexpressible and indescribable. Linear logic and discursive speech yield to him. Paradoxically, "apophatic" does not mean "absent." Nirguna Shiva at once neither is nor is not. The everyday procedures of the mind and logic, severed from the vitality of poetry and mystical experience, break down and fail. Nevertheless, we see that it is speech itself that leads us to this paradox, which is also to say that we have arrived at this boundary by way of reasoning and reflecting, i.e., thinking. The *Shatapatha Brahmana* describes thought as the original element that is neither existent nor non-existent. Speech is governed by thought and is directed either outwards (manifestation, creation, *saguna*) or inwards to the self (extinguishing, destroying, *nirguna*). Speech, led and coming to be known by thought, brings forth itself and all beings that it expresses to its own end — this is like self-sacrifice in language-speech. Kashmiri Shaivism maintains that the Saguna and Nirguna aspects of the Divine, which manifests—itself-in-concealment-and-play, are simultaneously present. This is described through the term *spanda*, that is the flickering, inextricable vibration of both modes of manifestation-and-concealment. In *spanda* and Advaita, there is no border between subject and object, between the one who utters and what has been uttered — the Cartesian dualism of the Enlightenment so familiar to us Europeans is overcome. This is analogous to how *mythos*-speech generates the sayer, the said, and the hearer in different directions. The Utterer himself is split in *spanda* into Speech addressed to the world and Speech addressed to itself — and this is always, at once, the very same Speech and unconcealment-in-concealment.

When the stream of Speech flows about something, *mythos* is speaking forth and affirming the cataphatic manifestations of the Divine, assigning to its manifestations the predicate "is" in various forms. The said is the visible (confirmed to be true) and the done (speech awakens to action), and this means that it belongs to duality, for what is said is always a veil covering the unexpressed and the unsaid. Passage 4.2.2 of the *Brihadaranyaka Upanishad* says that "the gods are fond of the cryptic, as it were, and dislike the evident."[15] This explains the abundance of hymns of praise decorated with poetic flourishes, epithets, and metaphors that frame the ineffable nature of the Divine, which is not directly named.

15　*Brihad-Aranyaka Upanishad* 4.2.2 in *The Thirteen Principal Upanishads*, trans. Robert Hume, (Oxford: Oxford University Press, 1921).

Thought is on the border. The predicate "is" is applicable to it, but through the predicate we can also recursively and reversely turn to the "is not" of thought, i.e., to that instance that lies beyond forms and names, which gives rise to speech about itself and drowns out speech within itself. Such thought is intrinsic both to atman as well as Brahman (Shiva), for it is one thought. This is not always obvious, but if thinking is affected by language and is directly connected to speech, then speech itself can, in its stream of speaking, in its stormy flow, point to that which in principle cannot be expressed in words, images, or forms.

Kashmir Shaivism teaches of several rungs that Speech has in its return ascent from the crude periphery of manifested beings, from the depths of *avidya* and *tamas*, to the center or pinnacle of the Divine One, to the awakening and unconcealing of higher Being. Speech is like a ladder which one climbs up. In iconography, Speech is represented as the white cow Vach (*vāc, vāk*[16]), on which sits Shiva — a symbol of his supremacy over manifested speech and his superiority over Maya and over any poetic means as such (as "means"). The cow nourishes the whole beingful world with speech, like the veins deliver fluids to all the tips of leaves. The cow's four legs are the four rungs of ascent.

The coarsest form of speech, corresponding to matter and objects, is *vaikhari*. This level of speech pertains to mere talking, vocalizing, pronouncing phonemes, syllables, and words, which from the perspective of Shabdabrahman are like readymade phenomena and objects — as if, instead of sounds, things themselves immediately flew off his tongue. On this level we also have spoken languages and writing scripts as the visual embodiments of Speech.

The level of inner speech corresponds to *madhyama*. Madhyama-speech is thought, the space of noesis and imagination. In the terms of modern semiotics, in this space

---

[16] From the Proto-Indo-European root *wek-* ("to speak"), cognate to Latin *vox* ("voice," "speech"), Proto-Slavic *větь* ("to speak," "to proclaim," "thing"), and Greek ὄψ ("word," "voice"), which is connected to ἔπος ("epos," "tale," "speech").

we are grasping and holding the word "cow" along with the idea of "cow" and its image. Madhyama directs the world of ideas into the world of the word and speech by naming them and summoning their forms in the mind. Madhyama is associated with the notion of *vimarsha*, or "consciousness," which is to say that the mind (and speech) can reflect upon and operate with only what is already consciously cognized.

Even subtler is the *pashyanti* stage, of which Baljinath Pandit writes:

> *Paśyantī* is known as the "beholding speech" because through its medium enlightened people can behold all objective existence within themselves. Since *paśyantī* is found within the pure being of a person, beyond mind and everything mental, the tendency to make distinctions among words, word-meanings, and the idea of both, has little or no effect in this form of speech.[17]

In other words, the level of *pashyanti*-speech is such that it dwells beyond any conceptualization in the likes of ideas, images, and notions in language. On this level, the sage contemplates (*pashyanti* literally means "seeing") the manifest world as thisness, as "this-am-I," and thus, rising above any division, approaches the One.

The most accessible *pashyanti* experiences are described as the I radiating between two thoughts, or as the illuminating insight when an artist or poet is struck by some radiant inspiration and knows that something has appeared to them, but at the same time knows that actually turning this insight into images, words, and the final work lies still ahead. This swiftest instant is often described as a flash or excitation at the crown of the head — known in antiquity as the Muse's playful touch upon the poet's head. In our case, this is the very same *sphoṭa*, that is a message, a bestowing, given from above as a pure idea.

Finally, there is the so-called fourth stage or state of consciousness and form of speech — *paravach*, "supreme speech."

---

17 B.N. Pandit, *Specific Principles of Kashmir Śaivism* (New Delhi: Munshiram Manoharlal Publishers, 1997), 55.

In supreme speech, there is no thisness, no manifestation, only the pure One I of the Absolute, *Para Shiva*. If consciousness is a prerequisite condition for speech as the principal of the unconcealing of Shabdashiva as the myriads of worlds within which he is discursively conscious of himself in concealment, then *paravach* is self-consciousness without discourse, concealment, or unconcealment. Nevertheless, it is the subtlest form of speech and is one of the four legs of the cow Vach.

This four-part structure fully replicates the four levels of the Upanishads and Brahmanas, but the Kashmir sages offer the most harmonious and complete metaphysical picture. None of the levels of Speech is separate or independent, but rather, as it were, absorbs and includes the preceding one. We cannot take away one of the cow's legs, for then it would no longer be the whole cow, and one of its legs would not take us anywhere. In precisely the same way, all forms of speech are to be thought in organic unity.

The teachings of Kashmir Shaivism point out the path of ascent and return, of recognition and awakening, along three rungs towards a fourth, returning from atman to Brahma Nirguna, from the world of crude forms towards the apophatic state that is not subject to any image or word, but which generates all as its own manifestation-in-concealment. Hence, the nasalization of the maha mantra Ōṃ proceeds from the chest, where air is inhaled, through vibration up to the crown of the head, and up beyond to the point of Paravach, to exiting the wheel of rebirths.

If *Ōṃ* is exteriorly uttered as a sound, then it is reduced to *tamas*, to dying down in language, and therefore corresponds to the cosmos' passing into the domination of this *guna* in the Kali-Yuga. But this very same path harbors the return to the silent consciousness of *Para Shiva* beyond the spoken word — that is, if we direct the vibration inside and up the head. Then there is no longer the contradiction that we initially discovered, for the dying of the phenomenal world itself is the embodiment of the Divine utterance.

If we direct the vibration of Oṃ down into the chest, then we take the all-syllable to Indra dwelling in the central part of the body, and if we take a new breath, we reinitiate the creation of the worlds. It is not without reason that Abhinavagupta testifies in his treatise *Paramarthasara* that:

> 50. Even in the absence of the body and sense organs, it is I who am the one seeing, hearing, and smelling, although the I [in essence] is not the agent, it is I who am the one who tells of the diverse philosophical teachings, religious traditions, revelations, and logical systems.[18]

Proceeding from the image of speech as the Vach cow and acknowledging the great number of languages, speeches, and traditions in the worlds, we can now look at one of Shiva's names from a sharper metaphysical angle: Shiva is Pashupati, the shepherd of cows. Thus, the plurality of cultures, language-traditions, and natures is affirmed on the sacred level.

The *bija* under the letter ṃ is interpreted as meaning the oneness of Shiva and Shakti, motionless like the stump of the Absolute and the wheel of energy and manifestation, the *Shaktichakra*, whirling around it. This is the intercourse of motionless Shiva with his *lingam* and Shakti as the material, receiving womb. All the worlds are dynamic manifestations of the erotic play (*Lila, Maya*) of the Divine spouses. It is noteworthy that one compound, interconnected set of metaphors used for their union and intercourse, the semantic string of "play—theater—war—sex," is found in many Indo-European languages and widely known cultural themes. The syllable Oṃ figures as the first breath, the erotic moan of the spouses, and the last breath of the fallen.

The first and highest form of speech is poetry. The Divinities create the world with songs, and people respond to them with poetic hymns. The metaphor of the Divine as the creator is widely known, and so too is that of the great painter creating

---

18 [Translated from the author's Russian with reference to *An Introduction to Tantric Philosophy: The Paramarthasara of Abhinavagupta with the Commentary of Yogarâja*, trans./ed. Lyne Bansat-Boudon and Kamaleshadatta Tripathi (London: Routledge, 2011)].

the world out of himself. Here we cannot afford to neglect the metaphor of theater and the associated poetic, artistic, and aesthetic concepts of language and speech. Theater is the stage of the world, its mythohistory, its plots, actors, and masks together with its great director, who is at the same time the viewer and the author of all the librettos. The whole beingful world and all beings unfold as one total theatrical production within Shiva's consciousness.

The aesthetic and poetic theoreticians of India, having studied the manifold techniques of metaphors and linguistic embellishments for poetic text, maintained that the intention of the author is present in any work whatsoever, that this intention should be conveyed to and understood by the listener, and, moreover, that when the listener (or viewer) understands the author's message, it transforms their essential nature. The author's message hidden within the work is called *rasa*, that is the flavor (emotion, hue) that the listener must taste for themselves and recognize.

Any poetic work contains multiple levels of meaning. Some are generated by the decor, the tropes, and the exclamations, others by the deliberately ambiguous or polysemantic lines and terms. In addition, a given word itself has its evocative, provocative power that gives rise to meanings and significations that lie beyond the literal and figurative meaning of the line. This power of the word is subject to gifted poets whenever a completely unexpected, independent, new meaning arises. The closest analogy would be the case of idiomatic expressions whose meaning is not obvious or is tertiary to the literal meaning of the phrase, which outside of its idiomatic context might be completely absurd or utterly opaque.

Finally, in each and every work there is an altogether indirect meaning, or indirect message, embedded in the words and sounds, in the general rhythm and dictation, that does not strictly coincide with them. In relation to this indirect meaning, any poet acts, to draw an analogy with music, not so much as the composer as the musical instrument upon which the meaning plays its own melody that is mysteriously interwoven into the poet's work. Moreover, it is believed that indirect meaning is intrinsic to all speech, even prosaic and everyday speech. Indirect meaning does not cancel out all other meanings and possible interpretations, but rather permeates them like the veins of a leaf. This meaning is called *dhvani*.

Dhvani is of interest to us because it, like *rasa*, can be found not only in the work of a poet or playwright, but throughout the work of the Divine art that is the entire universe. After all, the one *Aum* is at once the lowest atman and the supreme Brahman. The listener must taste the indirect meaning, understand it, and thereupon he will be transformed. But who is the recipient of such indirect messaging encrypted in everything? This person is the *sahridaya*, the "heartfelt listener," the "one of like heart" (whose heart can therefore hear my message). The heart of the listener, the heart of the one who recognizes the deep *dhvani* amidst all the other meanings and flavors of *rasa*, is akin to the heart of the one who wove this ontological meaning into the lines of all verses, melodies, and all speech in general. This is Brahman seeking an interlocutor. *Dhvani* is his voice and speech which he hides within all other speeches and poetry, calling for the heartfelt listener to respond and enter into dialogue. But only the Divine can converse with the Divine, therefore the atman that responds to *dhvani* experiences self-recognition and merges with the One.

Amongst all the manifold metaphysical patterns of teachings on Speech, the most important is the orientation of the heartfelt listener, for it is the one that, among other things, affirms the primacy of the unexpressed over the expressed. Let us once again recall the words of the *Brihadaranyaka Upanishad*: "the gods are fond of the cryptic, as it were, and dislike the evident." Heraclitus echoes this: "Nature loves to hide."

Speech is the principle of unconcealment. Myth is the tale with content, the cataphatic form of speech-manifestation that proceeds from pure radiance to the coarsest and dirtiest forms. Woven throughout and everywhere is the indirect meaning and the Divinity's call to enter into conversation. One needs only to catch the vibration (*spanda, sphoṭa*) of Shiva's voice. Discursive speech generates space and time — the continuity of the phrase, the direction of the sound, the length of the line, and the time needed to read it. Accordingly, the reverse movement from the manifest world to its apophatic Divine source is a folding up, a collapsing of discourse back into *spanda*, to the point of dissolution into silence. For this, there is the *maha mantra* and the archetypal, root formula of awakening: *tat tvam asi* — "thou art that."

The phrase "thou art that" is already discursive, yet it affirms the identity between the "thou" and the "that" which in language are nevertheless different pronouns and parts of a sentence. Pronouns themselves are special indicative signs, a kind of linguistic masks that hide a name or something that cannot possibly be named, but which still must be put into speech. But let us leave this for now and focus on the collapsing of the phrase.

The meaning of the formulation *tat tvam asi* must be grasped without moving through it as if step by step (such is merely the manner in which the distinction between the pronouns is established), but as something whole and merged together. If a person on the level of *pashyanti* experiences the world as "thisness," as an embodiment of the "I-am-this," and the whole world upon which he reflects in his mind is perceived as a macrocosm with corresponding analogies, then "thou art that" directs his attention away from the world of multiplicity (phenomena, objects, and experiences) and back to the source of Divine consciousness that is Shiva, that is from atman towards Para-Shiva. Note how the determinations of the sides change and are (re)structured around the verb "is," whereby the level of *paravach* corresponds to pure Being without names and forms, where there is no "I," "you," "this" and "that," only pure bliss and liberation.

On the level of language, this means ascending from everyday chatter to poetic speech, and then to mantras, words, syllables, phonemes, the imagination, and ideas. This is the becoming of *sahridaya*, *spanda*, and, finally, silence. The silence of Silence is the *dhvani*, the womb and grave of Speech, the space between thoughts, the backdrop to the unfolding of the whole beingful world and being in the manifest world. Silence, as the deictic sign of Nothing, is left out of view, but it is that special part of speech that gives speech the space to unconceal out of itself as well as conceal within itself.

Shiva Nirguna comes to be known namely in Silence alone.

Odin's Sacrifice

The Germanic-Scandinavian tradition is one of the most thanatocentric traditions of Europe. This was beautifully grasped in the leaden works of the British artist Arthur Rackham, which were based on the *Nibelungenlied* and the *Edda*.

We have repeatedly pointed out that the Germanic-Scandinavian tradition — namely its mythology as its self-telling of what there is and what shall be — reaches its apex on the horizon of Ragnarök, the fulfillment of the fate of the lords, and comes down to the death of the whole cosmos, the Divinities, the Thurs monsters, and humans, followed by regeneration in a new cycle, as foreseen by the Völva (*Völuspá* 59-66). But until this happens, the being of Germanic man is a life on loan from the imminent end. This is repeatedly reflected in the military ethos, epics, sagas, and the entire history of the warlike Germanic peoples and Scandinavians, as well as in their philosophy, which conceived of and posed the very question of its own exhaustion and end.

Let us turn our attention not to Ragnarök as fate, but to Ragnarök as the very principle of the world, the sacred violence inlaid on the cosmogonic level. The first myth that we encounter is the story of the killing and dismemberment of the giant Ymir, out of whose body parts the Aesir created Midgard. We encounter a similar plot in the Indian myth of the killing of Purusha. Georges Bataille expands our understanding of this motif to the level of the sacred killing of the leader or king in archaic societies, whose victimhood was meant to lay down the solid foundation for a new cycle and the good of society. In the myth of Ymir's dismemberment we also find a typically shamanic element: the renaming of each detached part of the body, which imbues each of them with a new quality within the structure of the cosmos.[19]

---

19 *Vafthruthnismol* 21, trans. Henry Adams Bellows (1936).

Vafþrúðnir kvað:	Vafthruthnir spake:
Ór Ymis holdi	Out of Ymir's flesh
var jörð of sköpuð,	was fashioned the earth,
en ór beinum björg,	And the mountains
himinn ór hausi	were made of his bones;
ins hrímkalda jötuns,	The sky from the frost-cold giant's skull,
en ór sveita sær.	And the ocean out of his blood.

Responding to Gylfi's questions, the High One clarifies that the killing and dismemberment of Ymir and the creation of Midgard were carried out by the three sons of Borr, that is the brothers Odin, Vili, and Vé. But the myth leaves us with one of this tradition's enigmatic mysteries: What became of Ymir's heart and where did it go?

The first war in the world is waged between the two lineages of the Deities, the Aesir and the Vanir. The war ends in reconciliation and, according to ancient custom, the exchange of prisoners taken from among the divine aristocracy. The Vanir send to the Aesir the patron of the seas, Njörðr, and the fecund Freyr, while the Aesir send the Vanir Hoenir and the wisest Mimir. That Hoenir quickly becomes the leader of the Vanir underscores his Odinic trait as an Áss, and indeed Hoenir is described as either a brother or hypostasis of Odin. A quite different fate awaits Mimir: suspecting that something is not right, the Vanir decapitate him and send his head to the Aesir.

Wishing to keep this wise interlocutor, Odin uses magic and sacrifices his own eye to save Mimir's life, and places his head at the source of the roots of Yggdrasil.

The name Mímir is translated as "Remembering" or "Thinking," which corresponds to the Old English word *mimorian*. Mimir is also often classified as a giant, which lends altogether lucid meaning to the refrain in the Völva's prophecy of the beginning of Ragnarök:[20]

---

20 *Voluspa* 45 in *The Poetic Edda: Stories of the Norse Gods and Heroes*, trans. Jackson Crawford (Indianapolis: Hackett Publishing Company, 2015).

Leika Míms synir,	The giants are at play,
en mjötuðr kyndisk	and the gods' fate is kindled
at inu galla	at the blast
Gjallarhorni;	of Gjallarhorn;
hátt blæss Heimdallr	Heimdall blows that horn hard,
horn er á lofti,	holds it high aloft,
mælir Óðinn	Odin speaks
við Míms höfuð.	with Mimir's head

Here we can see how "Mimir's children" (*Míms synir*) is a kenning for the Jotuns who wage war against the Æsir and Vanir. "Play" is a classic metaphor for war and strife, such as the German *Endspiel*. Gjallarhorn is the horn of wisdom from which Mimir's head drinks for the Lord's pledge. An altogether similar motif can be found in another Eddic song in which Odin engages in a competition of wisdom with the giant Vafþrúðnir — there, too, a head is at stake. Finally, Odin himself talks to Mimir's skull before the battle on Vígríðr Plane, which emphasizes the significance of this mythological figure.

Here, once again, we encounter Odin in the semantic context of violence and the establishment of the world. The Russian word for "world," *mir*, is positively helpful here, as it simultaneously encompasses the semantics of *mir* as cosmos, order, and law, and *mir* as the absence of war, i.e., peace. The exchange of prisoners establishes the world-peace between the two great lineages, and even Mimir's execution does not break it. Mimir's skull figures right at the point where the twilight of the world sets in: the destruction of the harmony of order and the flash of the final battle.

The apotheosis is one of the greatest Odinic myths: the myth of Odin's self-sacrifice, his completely monistic act of sacrificing himself to himself. In essence, the phrase *sjalfr sjalfum mér* ("himself to himself") can be placed on par with the great sayings *tat tvam asi* ("thou art that") and *soham* ("I art this"). They are fully consonant down to the letter, as each case uses a pronoun indicating a single person or principle, and they are even more consonant in spirit. There is also an echo to be heard in one of Odin's names, *Alföðr*, "All-Father," as well as other heiti which extol his status and glory, as is always typical of the supreme and monistic heads of pantheons.

The mystery of Odin's self-sacrifice mirrors the cosmogonic event of Germanic-Scandinavian mythology. The acquisition of the runes as speech, as a writing system, and as magical signs is the final accord in the creation of the cosmos ad the establishment of the cosmic law of *Wyrd*. It is not surprising, and indeed it is completely genuine, that Odin's act is once again bound up with violence and killing, but this time the overall configuration is different: instead of the three brothers led by Odin in killing the primal titanic being, now the All-Father — the supreme Divinity — now kills himself. Even furthermore, he does not simply kill himself, but sacrifices himself. This is the fundamental point, for not every killing is a sacrifice.

There are two kinds of sacrifice: that of exchange and that of bestowing oneself. Ritual exchange has been known since archaic times as, among other things, a form of the gift economy bound up with the spirits of things. Such exchange does not imply a monetary equivalent, and it can be carried out not only on the horizontal plane between people or the spirits of places, forests, mountains, and lakes, but can also be addressed to the other world, such as the netherworlds of the departed ancestors or to the Deities in the higher worlds. The rule for respectful offerings to other worlds is that the thing must be destroyed. It must be broken, drowned, burned, thrown away, or in some other way excluded from everyday life. This destruction is a bridge over which the thing is transported to the dead and the Divine. The souls of ancestors, the beings inhabiting various natural spaces, or the Divinities respond to the offerings made by their descendants and people with the gift of abundant game, animals, fish, fruits, rains, and harvests, or by thwarting pestilences and storms. Life is a cycle of sacrifice-gifts between all the worlds and all beings; everything lives by the gifting-through-dying of another.

Quite another matter is sacrifice as bestowing oneself, when the offerer brings to the altar something of such extreme value as their own life, as a symbol and gesture of faithfulness, reverence, and surrendering their fate into the hands of their elected Deity. This is a one-way gift which the offerer sends to the Deity without asking for anything in return, without any hope or expectation that the Divine will respond and grant something (for which one does not even ask). In such an act of sacrifice, there might be no response whatsoever, or perhaps only a laconic "the sacrifice has been received," or the response might even be a hundred times disproportionate to what was given, such as when the Divine responds with the gift of absolute and final prosperity, which in the East is regarded to be liberation or awakening. But neither this nor anything whatsoever is guaranteed. Sacrificing oneself is a gesture *immer Treue*.

Rituals of sacrificial offering or sacrificial passage through trials, violence, pain, and symbolic death (with the possibility of literal death) are often associated with initiation, i.e., consecration into a new status, being reborn, and ascending to the next level and next revelation of a certain sacred mystery.

In archaic cultures, the leader or another figure claiming the high status of elder must sacrifice all his property, whether by dispensing of it at ritual feasts, in gifts, or even by literally destroying it in front of the entire tribe, leaving him the morning after with literally nothing.[21] Moreover, in some cults the leader himself becomes the promised offering, killed as the highest gift to the Deities or killed because he could not guarantee rains, harvests, or upholding the peace. In some cases, such as in the story of the king of the Nemean Forest, acquiring royal status directly means immersing oneself into being-towards-death.

---

21 See Marcel Mauss, *The Gift: Forms and Functions of Exchange in Archaic Societies*, trans. Ian Cunnison (London: Cohen & West, 1966); Georges Bataille, *The Accursed Shared*, 3 vols.; Karl Jettmar, *The Religions of the Hindukush: The Pre-Islamic Heritage of Eastern Afghanistan and Northern Pakistan* (Bangkok: Orchid Press, 2023).

We see many of these motifs inlaid and intertwined in the cosmogonic myths of the Germanic-Scandinavian peoples, such as in the dismemberment of Ymir, the murder of Mimir, and especially in Odin the All-Father's self-sacrifice. Odin sacrifices the greatest "thing" of all possible things: himself. He thus passes through initiation, through death-towards-rebirth, while at each and every step and in all hypostases he is the supreme Konung, the All-Father, the leader of the Aesir.

In this incredibly intense act of the myth, we see the elements of sacrifice-as-bestowing-oneself monistically closing in on the very essence of one's selfhood. But "the gift awaits an answer," as the High One instructs, and this answer comes with the acquired runes. The question remains open: Is Odin giving himself as a gift in response to his own sacrifice? Or is this gift the gift of Being itself?

Let us look at the songful lines of the *Hávamál*:[22]

Veit ek, at ek hekk	I know that I hung
vindga meiði á	on a wind-battered tree
nætr allar níu,	nine long nights,
geiri undaðr	pierced by a spear
ok gefinn Óðni,	and given to Odin,
sjalfr sjalfum mér,	myself to myself,
á þeim meiði,	on that tree
er manngi veit	whose roots grow in a place
hvers af rótum renn.	no one has ever seen.
Við hleifi mik sældu	No one gave me food,
né við hornigi;	no one gave me drink.
nýsta ek niðr,	At the end I peered down,
nam ek upp rúnar,	I took the runes —
æpandi nam,	screaming, I took them —
fell ek aftr þaðan.	and then I fell.

---

22 *Havamal* 138-142, trans. Jackson Crawford.

Fimbulljóð níu	I learned nine spells
nam ek af inum frægja syni	from the famous son of Bolthorn,
Bölþorns, Bestlu föður,	the father of Bestla,
ok ek drykk of gat	and I won a drink
ins dýra mjaðar,	of that precious mead,
ausinn Óðreri.	poured from Othrerir.
Þá nam ek frævask	My imagination expanded,
ok fróðr vera	I became wise,
ok vaxa ok vel hafask,	I grew, and I thrived.
orð mér af orði	One word chased another word
orðs leitaði,	flowing from my mouth,
verk mér af verki	one deed chased another deed
verks leitaði.	flowing from my hands.
Rúnar munt þú finna	You will find runes,
ok ráðna stafi,	runic letters to read,
mjök stóra stafi,	very great runes,
mjök stinna stafi,	very powerful runes,
er fáði fimbulþulr	which Odin painted,
ok gerðu ginnregin	and which the holy gods made,
ok reist hroftr rögna.	and which Odin carved.

The tree whose roots are hidden in the unknown depths is, of course, Yggdrasil, the world tree of the Scandinavian tales of Germanic myth. Despite the fact that the sources clearly indicate that this tree is an ash, there also exists the version that the world tree was previously regarded to be a yew. Indeed, the Germanics revered the yew tree for the strength and straightness of its branches, from which bows and arrows were made. This is spoken to in the Icelandic rune poem's verse on the rune *ýr* (ᛦ):[23]

(Ýr) er bendr bogi	The yew is the bent bow
ok brotgjarnt járn	and jagged iron
ok fífu fárbauti.	and giant arrow.

---

23 [Translated from the author's Russian, based on the translation of S. Grabovetsky].

Even more importantly, the strongest spear shafts were made from yew. The spear is an attribute of Odin and figures as his first weapon, Gungnir. On the lesser scale, the spear is also an allegory and symbol of the world tree itself. Even more archaic is the worship of the yew as the tree of war. Myth connects both versions: the branches of both the yew and the ash are interwoven into one pattern, both species having their allotted place in the mystery of the All-Father.

It is very likely that the roots of Yggdrasil are lost somewhere in the darkness of Ginnungagap, the enchanting and deceiving gap of the primordial Abyss. At the depths of the roots dwell the three Norns, Urðr, Verðandi, and Skuld, who at the source of Wyrd decide the fates of the world, people, and the Aesir. The celestials also gather at Yggdrasil for the Thing. From its roots flow forth the many rivers that run through all nine worlds. Mimir's skull lies hidden there.

Upon first approach, we thus have Odin sacrificing himself to himself on the altar of the entire cosmos, the world ash, and using as his weapon a spear, which at once refers to the wooden shaft made of the sacred yew. In his status as the supreme Áss, the leader and All-Father, Odin covers the entire cosmos, becoming immanent to it in his sacrifice.

A second approach requires of us more attentive reference to the very name of the world tree. Yggdrasil is a poetic kenning consisting of two words: *Yggr* means "the Terrifying," which is one of Odin's heiti, and *drasil* means "steed." Yggdrasil, thus, is Yggr's steed. This kenning is often deciphered to mean the "gallows tree," but this is not entirely correct, for Odin did not hang himself by rope on a branch, but pierced and pinned himself to the entire tree with his spear. The epithet "steed" refers us to Odin's horse, the eight-legged Sleipnir, that is "the Slipping one," the horse that transports Odin between the worlds — and such is a common epithet for the shaman's drum. If the Scandinavians were familiar with the latter instrument, then it most likely came from their Laplandish and Finnish neighbors, among whom the drum's handle was believed to be the *Axis Mundi*. The ecstatic rhythm of drumming resonates with beating one's shield with a spear, or dancing with and rattling spears, which is reflected in the famous bronze bas-relief of dancing berserkers from the Swedish island of Öland. It is obvious that Yggdrasil as the world tree figures in the act of Odin's sacrifice not only as an altar, but also as the guiding steed.

That the world tree is named after one of Odin's heiti is another question. *Yggr* is the one who terrifies, who instills the gravest fear. The cosmogonic terror of the leader of the Deities gallops and sways on the ash tree. Experiencing the sacred is an experience of "re-living through" the greatest horror as well as the astonishment that is inseparable from such, that seizes a person and calls upon them to put their very life into question. It is not for nothing that myths repeatedly emphasize that a mortal is unable to bear the sight of a naked Deity in its true form. Such is Yggr in the act of self-sacrifice: the terrible guise[24] of the mad Heavenly Father who appeared in the silhouettes of clouds in a stormy sky, from where he looks down upon his children in Midgard and their mother, Jörð (*Erde*, Earth).

The verb "to terrify" in this case should be understood not as being overwhelmed by fear of something external, something that instills horror, but rather as a verb of emanation, of pressing out, of cutting through, i.e., as "terrifying-into," "terror-tearing-into-the-world." Terror embeds the sacred into the entire cosmos for eternity. The whole beingful world is an agonistic vision of the Divine in its self-sacrifice.

Yggr's steed is the ash tree, which in Icelandic is *aski/askur*, from the Old Norse *askr*, and in German is *Asche/Esche* from the Proto-Germanic **askaz*. We find this very word as a proper name in the case of the first man, Askr, "Ash," and his wife

---

24 *Grimr* is another heiti of Odin which means "mask" or "the mask-wearing one." Its modern meaning is associated with "dark" and "wrathful."

Embla, "Willow," whom the trio of brothers Odin, Vili, and Vé found on the shore in the form of uncut logs. The Germanic words for ash are regular homonyms or differ only by one or two phonemes from the word for "ash," *aska* in Old Norse, *Asche* in German, from Proto-Germanic **askǭ*.

The tree is also a metaphor for the human being, reflecting the human's link to the earth and rising up to the sky. The tree is the middle world, the mediator and the path between the two poles. Aristotle used the term ὕλη, "wood," to denote the whole category of matter in ancient philosophy. If Yggdrasil is the world tree, then the metaphor of ὕλη-matter only strengthens this state of affairs, and the very same motif is repeated in the myth of the origins of people. We thus arrive at the understanding that the symbol of the tree has several sequences at different levels, all of which are interconnected: the cosmos, matter, man, altar, and steed. In the kennings of the *Younger Edda*, man and woman are called "maple," "forest," and "ash." All of these references to Yggdrasil can be read cosmogonically as well as anthropologically. The pictures turns out to be even more intense, as it directly affects us humans.

Odin spears himself to man. Man is the altar on which the Deity sacrifices himself to himself, furiously terrifying himself. The Deity cuts his own being like a wicker pattern is cut into a board, framing it with the poetic word-weavings of skalds. Yggr's steed is a kenning of man, man bearing the Terrifying One, man open to the downwards movement to the bottomless source of Wyrd and up to the apophatic selfhood of the All-Father — *zum apophatischen Selbst des Allvaters*.

The theme of solitude is also subtly touched here. The High One describes his self-sacrifice as the ritual act of a loner: "no one gave me food, no one gave me drink" during his nine days and nights on Yggdrasil. Thus, in order for a person to be Yggdrasil, that is an altar for the Divine, one must endure in solitude the terror of their self-sacrifice as the cutting of the specific "death of God" into the human inner-worldly being. This moments gives us hints as to one of the possible explanations of the theology of the ensuing "flight of the Gods" in the tragic history of the West.

The Deity sacrifices himself in an act of pure volition, freedom, and solitude. Man is the factical agony of the Divine in the casting out of Beyng into here-being through the renunciation of oneself, the oblivion of oneself. How does Odin's consecrated endowment of himself end? What do the cosmos, man, and Odin himself get in the end? Scholars of the Scandinavian oral tradition have noted that the following verse's line, "*fell ek aftr þaðan*," uses a special verb for falling.[25] The word *fell* (an obsolete form) is the very same as the Proto-Germanic **fallaną*, which has been preserved in all of the branches of the Germanic languages with stable semantic continuity in phrases as well as idioms whose meaning encompasses "going down," "falling down," "collapsing," the felling of trunks and stems, the falling of a waterfall. "Fallen" is also used to mean the one who has been struck down, killed in battle. This meaning connects "*fall*" with the Valkyries and Valhalla, the chosen ones who fell in battle, and the Hall of the Fallen. Finally, in English, "Fall" is also an idiom for autumn, the time of falling leaves and the dying of nature. In Russian translations, "fell" is often translated as *rukhnul*, which reflects "falling down" (*padenie vniz*) but leaves out all the semantics associated with death. Now, in these verses and in this line, we hear that Odin fell as a victim of his own hand and that he fell down to the roots of Yggdrasil covered in yellow foliage, where at the source of Urðr the Norns are cutting and carving away.

In the instant of the maximal tension and ascetic exhaustion of his self-sacrifice, Odin picked up the runes, "*nam ek upp rúnar*." "Runes" comes from *runen*, which means "to speak,"

---

25 Joseph Harris, "*Speak Useful Words or Say Nothing*": *Old Norse Studies by Joseph Harris*, ed. Susan E Deskis and Thomas D. Hill (Ithaca: Cornell University Library, 2008).

"to utter," "to mutter." The word later took on the meaning of "secret" or "mystery" in connection with the magical practices of using runes as a system of signs and writing. "I picked up the runes" means "I picked up words" or "I picked up speech, screaming…" In return for his sacrifice, thus, Odin acquires not just magical signs and letters; first and foremost, he obtains speech and language, in which he will tell his tale about himself. Odin's self-sacrifice is the final act in the creation of the world. He plays out this act alone, unlike the case of the trio's dismemberment of Ymir and the creation of humans. Speech and language are the only equivalent gift in return for the Deity's sacrifice of his lone self.

This line is continued in the next verse, where Odin tells of how he learned nine songs from his uncle (who is unnamed). A brother's patronage of his sister's son was the classical avunculate practiced among the Germanics as mentioned by Tacitus. We believe that this practice reflects the period of transition from matriarchal to patriarchal law. Indeed, with Odin's establishment on the throne we actually see many female figures and mothers shifted to a lower register, to the titanic[26] or to the borderline space between the underworld and the middle world, and we see the establishment of patrilineal inheritance along with the listing of genealogies in which the male heads trace their lines back to the All-Father himself. Nevertheless, we hear that an unnamed one from the lineage of the giants taught his nephew, the High One, powerful songs. We encounter a similar motif of gaining wisdom in the riddle competitions with the Jotuns that take place on several occasions in the *Elder Edda*.

Here, at this point, it is no coincidence that the Mead of Poetry appears, that magnificent drink of Óðrerir, the blood of Kvasir. Things and crafts are designated by proper names when they are especially sacred, when they have their own spirit and

---

26 Thor's mother, Jörð (Earth), figures among the Thurs giants, but in the *Younger Edda* she is counted among the Goddesses.

destiny. The name of Óðrerir's cauldron comes from the root *óðr*. In Icelandic, *óðr* is a homonym for two words which have different but closely converging roots. *Óðr* is poetry and thinking, and *óðr* is rage, frenzy — from this root and meaning comes the name of Odin himself (*Óðinn*). *Óðr* is inspiration and poetic ecstasy in the sense of going beyond one's limits. Proceeding from this point easily allows for disclosing the meaning of the line "*ok gefinn Óðni*" as "given unto, consecrated to, or initiated into the Inspiring and the Poetic." The suggestiveness of poetic signs only intensifies with the repetition in different rhythms of such densely intertwined semantics as songs, rune-words, Odin, Óðrerir, and the Mead of Poetry, culminating in the stanza "*orð ér af orði orðs leitaði*" — "the word yielded the word from the word." This is pure poetry, the creation of the world by the word, playfully articulated in the rearrangement of the letters in the roots *óðr-orð* (in later German *das Wort*). And then, fully in the spirit of the *Shatapatha Brahmana*, after the words come "*verk ér af verki verks leitaði*," that is "deeds yielded by deeds."

The Mead of Poetry is of special interest, as its story is intimately bound up with all the characteristic aspects of Germanic-Scandinavian myth: war, sacrifice, violence, descent into the chthonic regions of the cosmos, salvation from the Jotun giants, and the bestowing of the gift upon man.[27] Germanic *poiesis* is Θάνατοποίησις.

This story is told in detail in the *Younger Edda* by Aegir Bragi. For the sake of consolidating peace after the Aesir and Vanir exchanged hostages, they came together and spat into a cauldron, and their collective saliva created the wisest man in the world, Kvasir, whose name very likely refers to an alcoholic drink. Through evil cunning, Kvasir was lured and killed by the dwarfs Fjalar and Galar, who poured his blood into three cups: Óðrerir, Son, and Boðn. They told the Aesir that Kvasir had died by choking on his own wisdom. Ever since then, one of the

---

27 See Askr Svarte, *Gods in the Abyss*.

constant kennings for poetry was "Kvasir's blood" or "Óðrerir's drink."

When the Dvergar lose the Mead of Poetry as a payoff to the giant Suttungr for their other wrongdoings, Odin takes an interest in it again. Changing his appearance and engaging in a cunning act that costs the lives of nine slaves, Odin made is way under the rock where the Mead was guarded by the giant's daughter, Gunnlöd. He spends three nights with her, for which she offers him three sips, but Odin drinks the whole cauldron and turns into an eagle and soars away with Kvasir's blood. In the final act, Odin in the guise of the eagle, pursued by Suttungr, also in the guise of an eagle, spits the the Mead into a cauldron in Asgard, but a small portion fell behind him, which anyone could collect. This is how bad poets, "rhymers," came about. Hence, the kennings "Odin's spoil," "Yggr's drink," and "gift of the Aesir" became appended to poetry.

Bragi calls language and meter the two components of the poetic art. Language is the first. At its sources lies the Deity's sacrifice and all the wealth of the expressive means of language, as well as the inseparable hierarchy and structure of grammar. Poetic language is threefold. First, there is the name that defines or reflects the essence of the thing it names. Secondly, there are the heiti, the poetic synonyms or substitutions for a name. In most cases, the heiti are not distinguished from a name or are simply used as a name. If we are attentive, we will notice an obvious and extremely terrifying thing: we do not know Odin's name, we know only dozens of his heiti. In principle, Odin is known to us only under word-marks, under secondary means of poetic naming. Thirdly, there are the kennings, more complex metaphors which include allegories and signs connoting completely different things and different Deities, which in especially complex cases brings them closer to idiomatic expressions. Metaphors, allegories, metonymies, deixis, and other tropes are essentially the expressive tiles and decorations of poetic speech that can be found among many peoples. This is the breath of *dhvani*.

The second component of poetry is meter, i.e., the different variations for constructing alliterative verse — which, unlike ancient rhyming, was an authentic expression of Germanic-Scandinavian poetic rhythm. Meter yields the tonal suggestiveness of the dictation, the hypnotic rhythm of the enchanting telling. There are two main types of Germanic-Scandinavian poetry: Eddic and skaldic. Eddic poetry is more ascetic in form, but it tells us the Germanic-Scandinavian *mythos*. Skaldic poetry, on the contrary, is riddled with patterns and is overly pretentious, but in its content it is factual and to the point. Poetic meters like the *fornyrðislag, drottkvett, ljodahått*, etc., specify different orders and tact for the coordination of repetitive consonants and/or vowels. This is the basic rule of alliteration: lines and stanzas must repeat certain phonemes at the beginning of words, which is reinforced by the stress on the first syllable that is inherent in the Germanic languages. This is glaringly obvious in the Icelandic original of the *Hávamál*, especially in verse 141. Alliterative alternation connects lines, quatrains, and even entire verses. Thus arises the pattern of "spinning" with the spoken word, with sound. Moreover, the form of expression of myth itself is part of the myth and its message. What is important is not only what is said, but how it is said, and such is an integral semantic and structural part of what the said is. The extensive use of heiti, kennings, and refrains is dictated by the scale of the alliteration, which requires one or another structure of repretitions of the vowel and consonant sounds in the stanza. The skalds of the past knew by heart, created, and told entire epics in different poetic forms, and they wove together different *vísur, niðar*, and *drápur*.

We follow Gangrad to verses 142 and 144:[28]

---

28 *Havamal*, 142, 144, trans. Jackson Crawford.

Rúnar munt þú finna	You will find runes,
ok ráðna stafi,	runic letters to read,
mjök stóra stafi,	very great runes,
mjök stinna stafi,	very powerful runes,
er fáði fimbulþulr	which Odin painted,
ok gerðu ginnregin	and which the holy gods made,
ok reist hroftr rögna	and which Odin carved.
[...]	[...]
Veistu, hvé rísta skal?	Do you know how to write them?
Veistu, hvé ráða skal?	Do you know how to read them?
Veistu, hvé fáa skal?	Do you know how to paint them?
Veistu, hvé freista skal?	Do you know how to test them?
Veistu, hvé biðja skal?	Do you know how to ask them?
Veistu, hvé blóta skal?	Do you know how to bless them?
Veistu, hvé senda skal?	Do you know how to send them?
Veistu, hvé sóa skal?	Do you know how to offer them?

Of interest to us in the line "*ok gerðu ginnregin*" is the last word, which is composed of two roots: *ginn* and *regin*. This word is usually translated simply as "gods," but the original tells us much more. The first root, the mysterious *ginn*, we find in the complex name of the abyss, *Ginnungagap*. According to Jan de Vries' theory, *ginn* means "to bewitch," "to deceive," just as the original, non-romantic sense of the word "to enchant" meant to deceive, to mislead. Another theory traces this root back to the Proto-Germanic **ginnaną*, which means "to begin," "to originate," "to ascend" (cf. *physis*) and "to be open," "to open up," "to reveal." In the Icelandic language, the root *gin* means mouth, or rather open mouth. Thus, the primordial abyss is immediately given as something hidden within the most visible place. Mythopoetic thinking can easily understand how something can manifest itself in concealment, can be "hiding in the open," like all the variations of poetic tropes.

The second word goes back to the Proto-Germanic **raginą*, whence *regin*, the Divinities, are literally "the ones who rule," "the reigning ones." Analogously, *Ragnarök* is the fate of the lords, the fate of the reigning ones. In this case, *regin* is a classic epithet for the power and authority of the Aesir. But on an even deeper level, *raginǫ* means "to give counsel," "to establish the law," "to get the truth straight," "to make a decision." The discussion and adoption of laws and the holding of council take place at the Thing and involve verbal speech. The law is what is said by the Aesir or that which is decided by the worthy men gathered at the general assembly.

The runes are made by those who, in their openness or by the power of their enchantment, make decisions and rule the law with speech. Hence, "Rúnar munt þú finna, ok ráðna stafi" is "Words shall you undoubtedly find, and [thereupon] you shall comprehend the signs." In the German translation, *stafi* is *Stäbe* (from the German *Stab*, English "staff"), that is the ancient wooden stick on which signs were carved, and which could be used as a cane, a staff, a walking support for the traveler. Runes were originally carved on wooded sticks, hence the persistent question "Do you know how to cut them, do you know how to paint them?" To this day, in German *Stab* is used to mean a letter in the alphabet or the letters of a typeface. "Staves" is the habitual name for complex combinations of runic signs made for magical purposes. In this domain, the metaphor of speech and action manifests itself as spinning, cutting, carving.

It is extremely telling that the German verb *lesen* ("to read") literally means "to collect sticks," to gather together. This coincides with the Greek *logos*, which as we know means "gathering," "speech," and the written word. In one of the enigmatic passages in his *Black Notebooks*, Heidegger points out that the writing of signs, and writing as such, should not be elevated to the rank of absolute, because they can rest content only with beings; instead, one should keep their focus on Beyng, which he calls "the rupture of the difference and the *Rune* of its strife."[29] This is the only instance in which Heidegger ever mentioned this specific Germanic word, which is taken to mean "speech of strife" or "secret of dispute." Knowing the great

---

[29] Martin Heidegger, *Zametki I-V (Chernyie tetradi 1942-1948)*, trans. Aleksei B. Grigor'ev, ed. Mikhail Maiatskii (Moscow: Gaidar Institute, 2022), 510.

reverence which this German thinker held for the creative role of the word, as well as to *polemos* as the principle of the distinction and differentiation of the plurality of beings, we can grasp and pick up a dense bundle of additional meanings for *runa*.

The Germanic languages have a diverse palette of verbs and names for "speech." In German, *Sprache* is language as such, and the derivative verb *sprechen* refers to the capacity to speak. The medieval form of short, edifying verse was called *Spruch*. A similar distribution can be seen in the Icelandic *mál*, which is both language and speech/speaking, the naming of sayings, telling tales, as well as the grand verse constructions like the *Hávamál* or *Vafþrúðnismál*. Yet, *mál* is also an affair, a subject, a topic for conversation or a matter for judgment. The magical verse often used by men is called *galdr*, from the Proto-Germanic **galdraz*, which means song and lamentation. In modern German, *Leid* is the word for both "song" and "sorrow." The Germanic word *runo* was adopted by the Finns, Karelians, and Estonians as a common name for their epics. The last chapters of the *Younger Edda* list dozens of direct and indirect heitis for speech, word, and mind.

In the next verse, the meter changes abruptly into a hypnotic refrain, the essence of which boils down to an affirmation of the elite nature of language and speech. Runes should not be cut and sung by someone who doesn't know them, who doesn't know how to address and treat them, or how to pain them in the color of blood. For those who do know, Odin lists the spells he knows and sips out of Óðrerir. Then:

> Now the words of the High One
> in the home of the High One,
> needed by people,
> not needed by Jotuns.
> Health to the one who speaks them!
> Health to those who know them!
> Joy to those who recall them!
> Health to whose who hear them![30]

---

30 [Translated from the author's Russian, based on the translation of N. Topchii.]

Here, the All-Father strictly distinguishes the knowledge that is unnecessary and useless to the Jotuns, the greedy, and beggars, with the exception of the most ancient, mostly stupid and crude creatures.

The runes, thus, are in essence the only equal return for Odin's sacrifice of himself to himself. As we have pointed out, this sacrifice is the last accord of the cosmogony, the point at which the cosmos acquires and is endowed with speech and words. The runes are the incisors with which Yggr carves and interweaves the most complex and intricate patterns into art, poetry, myth, the mind, wisdom, and the fate of the world. They are the incisors for Yggdrasil, the yew, the ash, and the willow. Carving, dyeing, and singing the runes and *galdr* is the direct embodiment of Odin in the middle world. The voice of the singer, the chorus, and that which is sung literally blend together with the voice of the *Runatyr*, the All-Father, the High One himself.

The Icelandic *Rúnakvæði*, the runic poem in which each of the sixteen rune signs is explained through a verse, shows how the runes correspond to things, phenomena, and mythological semantic series:[31]

ᚠ (fé) er frænda róg ok flæðar viti ok grafseiðs gata.	Wealth is source of discord among kinsmen and fire of the sea and path of the serpent.
ᚢ (úr) er skýja grátr ok skára þverrir ok hirðis hatr.	Shower is lamentation of the clouds and ruin of the hay-harvest and abomination of the shepherd.
ᚦ (þurs) er kvenna kvöl ok kletta búi ok varðrúnar verr.	Giant is torture of women and cliff-dweller and husband of a giantess.
ᚨ (óss) er aldingautr ok ásgarðs jöfurr ok valhallar vísi.	God is aged Gautr and prince of Asgard and lord of Valhalla.

---

31 Bruce Dickins, *Runic and Heroic Poems of the Old Teutonic Peoples* (Cambridge: Cambridge University Press, 1915).

R (reið) er sitjandi sæla
ok snúðig ferð
ok jórs erfiði.

Ƴ (kaun) er barna böl
ok bardagi6
ok holdfúa hús.

❋ (hagall) er kaldakorn
ok krapadrífa
ok snáka sótt.

ᚾ (nauð) er þýjar þrá
ok þungr kostr
ok vássa lig verk.

I (íss) er árbörkr
ok unnar þak
ok feigra anna fár.

ᛆ (ár) er gu na góði
ok gott sumar
algróinn akr.

ᚼ (sól) er skýja skjöldr
ok skínandi röðull
ok ísa aldrtregi.

↑ (týr) er einhendr áss
ok úlfs leifar
ok hofa hilmir.

ᛒ (bjarkan) er laufgat lim
ok lítit tré
ok ungsa ligr viðr.

Ƴ (maðr) er anns gaman
ok moldar auki
ok skipa skreytir.

ᛚ (lögr) er vellanda vatn
ok víðr ketill
ok glömmunga grund.

ᛦ (ýr) er bendr bogi
ok brotgjarnt járn
ok fífu fárbauti.

Riding is joy of the horseman
and speedy journey
and toil of the steed.

Ulcer is disease fatal to children
and painful spot
and abode of mortification.

Hail is cold grain
and shower of sleet
and sickness of serpents.

Constraint is grief of the bond-maid
and state of oppression
and toilsome work

Ice is bark of rivers
and roof of the wave
and destruction of the doomed.

Plenty is boon to men
and good summer
and thriving crops.

Sun is shield of the clouds
and shining ray
and destroyer of ice.

Tyr is god with one hand
and leavings of the wolf
and prince of temples.

Birch is leafy twig
and little tree
and fresh young shrub.

Man is delight of man
and augmentation of the earth
and adorner of ships.

Water is eddying stream
and broad geysir
and land of the fish.

Ý is bent bow
and brittle iron
and giant of the arrow.

Weaving and spinning are thus another metaphor associated with speech, corresponding to the feminine pole of metaphysics and associated with the Norns. The main sanctuary of the Aesir is by Yggdrasil, where each day they administer their judgment, i.e., utter their decision-pronouncements. In the *Younger Edda*, the Aesir tell Ganglier that the Ash has one of its roots up in the sky, and under it flows a source revered as the most sacred: Urðr. The root in the sky refers to the widespread motif of an inverted tree growing from up above and spreading its leaves on the ground. This symbol reflects man's rootedness in his heavenly homeland. However, confusion might arise over where the roots of the Tree of Limit are hidden, i.e., where the source originates and where the Norns gather — are they underground or in the heavens? From the mythopoetic point of view, looking for one reliable version of the myth is a pointless and absurd affair, because both variations are true and the tree is always one and the same.

The name of the source of Urðr, *Urðarbrunnr*, means "Fate." Through the Proto-Germanic root *wurdiz*, it is connected to the Old English *weorþan* ("to become," "to happen") and the notion of *Wyrd*, "that which shall happen." The latter is one of the most important existential verbs in Germanic mythology. The source of Urðr is the source of fate, the fate that is prescribed as the due for humans, the Aesir, the Vanir, the cosmos, and all other beings. This is the cosmic, universal law. It is at this source that the Aesir gather for the Thing. Moreover, we are confident that this is the site of the hall from which emerge the three Norns: Urðr, Verðandi, and Skuld.

We have already examined the name of the first Norn, Urðr, to which is fixed the meaning of the past. This Norn is responsible for what has already happened and appeared, what has already been. That which is due was prophesied in advance in ancient times and has been cast forth as something that is to become true in the coming future, like the continuity of fate.

Verðandi's name means "becoming" or "happening now," formed from the Icelandic verb *verða*, "to be," "to become." This verb is derived from the Proto-Germanic *wértti or *wert, meaning "to turn," "to turn around," "to rotate" — and this directly refers us to the solar Year-Wheel.[32]

Skuld's name means "Coming," the root literally meaning "debt," a loan that is to be repaid. Despite this synonymity with *Wyrd*, Skuld covers the whole cosmos and its history as a prophecy told in advance about the future which shall be fulfilled. In this sense, the future is not merely that which is coming to meet us tomorrow, something that simply will be, but rather something on loan whose fulfillment we live. As a result, we live only when we are fulfilling and embodying what was prophesied before. When we deviate from Wyrd, we lose the complex, intertwined thread of the pattern of life, i.e., we get lost in intricacies and forget about what is due.

Besides the three Great Norns, there are also lesser Norns who come to newborns and weave the pattern of their fates. If good ones come, then their fate (*örlög*) will be bright, but if the baby is visited by evil Norns, then their life will full of tribulations. The great horizon of the due facing the whole cosmos, woven by the weavers of being, is Ragnarök, the world fire, death. Everything that exists in Germanic-Scandinavian myth is taken on loan from death.

> I know an ash tree
> named Yggdrasil
> a high tree, speckled
> with white clay;
> dewdrops fall from it
> upon the valleys;
> it stands, forever green,
> above Urth's well.[33]

---

32 The Year-Wheel and its associated sacred phonetics are discussed in detail in Askr Svarte, *Gods in the Abyss*.

33 *Voluspa* 19, trans. Jackson Crawford.

Let us go back to the beginning. The High One says *"nam ek upp rúnar,"* which word-for-word sounds like "I took the runes up," i.e., raised them from down below, and then *"fell ek aftr þaðan,"* "I fell back down." The All-Father raises the words and speech of the runes up from the roots of Yggdrasil and falls unto them. This marks the end of his sacrifice and initiation. There, at the roots, the source of Urðr flows and the Norns spin. One could put forth the cautious hypothesis that they weave the fabric of fate precisely with prophetic words/speeches. This is indicated in the 20th verse of the Prophecy of the Völva:[34]

> Þaðan koma meyjar
> margs vitandi
> þrjár ór þeim sæ,
> er und þolli stendr;
> Urð hétu eina,
> aðra Verðandi,
> — skáru á skíði, —
> Skuld ina þriðju;
> þær lög lögðu,
> þær líf kuru alda börnum,
> örlög seggja.

> Thence come the maidens
> mighty in wisdom,
> Three from the dwelling
> down 'neath the tree;
> Urth is one named,
> Verthandi the next
> — On the wood they scored —
> and Skuld the third.
> Laws they made there,
> and life allotted
> To the sons of men,
> and set their fates.

The original word *skíði* means logs, wood. They are cut by the Norns, hence the Russian translation directly speaks of "runes" where the English speaks of "wood." In the German translation, *skíði* is turned into the *Stäbe* with which we are already familiar. Thus, fates, runes, words, and wood are all linked together into one, and the leading metaphor is not spinning the fabric of fate, but cutting the "lots" out of wood or carving the "lots" into logs.

The roots of the Tree of Limit are lost in Ginnungagap, the primordial void out of which all beings, the first sparks, winds, and creatures appear. Regardless of whether we trace the roots of Yggdrasil back up into the heavenly heights or deep

---

34 *Voluspa* 20, trans. Henry Adam Bellows.

underground, the deeper we go we arrive at *gap var ginnunga*, the gaping opening, emptiness, or chasm, as the word "gap" means in the Scandinavian and English languages. Deeper than Mother-Earth and deeper than the Mad Father, the roots of Yggdrasil lead to the Void. Man is the middle plexus of the uranic and chthonic principles[35] stretched out from abyss to abyss, and our nature is being-in-between, *in-Mitte-sein*.

Our myth tells yet another story of the origin of people and their acquisition of speech. The overall plot differs between the *Elder* and *Younger Edda*, so it should be considered in its entirety. In the *Elder Edda*:[36]

Unz þrír kvámu	Then from the throng
ór því liði	did three come forth,
öflgir ok ástkir	From the home of the gods,
æsir at húsi,	the mighty and gracious;
fundu á landi	Two without fate
lítt egandi	on the land they found,
Ask ok Emblu	Ask and Embla,
örlöglausa.	empty of might.
Önd þau né áttu,	Soul they had not,
óð þau né höfðu,	sense they had not,
lá né læti	Heat nor motion,
né litu góða;	nor goodly hue;
önd gaf Óðinn,	Soul gave Othin,
óð gaf Hænir, lá gaf Lóðurr	sense gave Hönir,
ok litu góða.	Heat gave Lothur
	and goodly hue.

---

35 It should also be mentioned that, according to his genealogy, the All-Father himself descends from the chthonic powers, but he achieves his selfhood and supreme dignity as a Deity, not a Jötunn.

36 *Voluspa* 17-18, trans. Henry Adam Bellows.

In the *Younger Edda:*[37]

Þá mælti Gangleri: "Mikit þótti mér þeir hafa þá snúit til leiðar, er jörð ok himinn var gert ok sól ok himintungl váru sett ok skipt dægrum, ok hvaðan kómu mennirnir, þeir er heim byggja?"	Then said Gangleri: "Much indeed they had accomplished then, methinks, when earth and heaven were made, and the sun and the constellations of heaven were fixed, and division was made of days; now whence come the men that people the world?"
Þá mælti Hárr: "Þá er þeir gengu með sævarströndu Borssynir, fundu þeir tré tvau ok tóku upp trén ok sköpuðu af menn. Gaf inn fyrsti önd ok líf, annarr vit ok hræring, þriði ásjónu, mál ok heyrn ok sjón, gáfu þeim klæði ok nöfn. Hét karlmaðrinn Askr, en konan Embla, ok ólst þaðan af mannkindin, sú er byggðin var gefinn undir Miðgarði…"	And Hárr answered: "When the sons of Borr were walking along the sea-strand, they found two trees, and took up the trees and shaped men of them: the first gave them spirit and life; the second, wit and feeling; the third, form, speech, hearing, and sight. They gave them clothing and names: the male was called Askr, and the female Embla, and of them was mankind begotten, which received a dwelling-place under Midgard…"

Of significance to us in the lines told by the Völva is the gifting of spirit, *óð[r]*, to the first people. This gift is bestowed by Hoenir, but from the very same root comes the name Óðinn. Hoenir does not simply give any kind of spirit, but gives people the spirit of frenzy, the possibility of ecstatic madness.

The High One speaks of the three brothers, Odin, Vili, and Vé, who created people out of wood and gave them names, faces, speech (*mál*), hearing, and sight. The name of the third brother, Vé, means sanctuary, the abode of the Divinities, which means

---

37 *Gylfaginning* 9, *The Prose Edda*, trans. Arthur Gilchrist Brodeur (1916).

that his gifts are inherent in his essence and bear his imprint. In other words, the faces, speech, hearing, and sight bestowed upon man are sacred. That Vé gifts all of them at once is quite similar to the distribution of these senses and qualities in the *Shatapatha Brahmana*. The word *mál* is used as the second root and ending in the names of many Eddic songs, guidances, and speech polemics, such as the *Hávamál, Vafþrúðnismál, Alvíssmál, Grímnismál*, etc.

Mythopoetic holism and monism are intrinsic to the Germanic-Scandinavian tradition. This is especially clearly said in the *Younger Edda*, when the noble King Gylfi, well-versed in spells, heads to the Aesir to test and learn their power. He changes his appearance to that of an old man. Coming to Asgard, of which the Aesir had sent him a vision, he introduces himself as Gangleri ("tired on the road"), which we also find among the lists of Odin's heiti. In Asgard, Gylfi-Gangleri engages in the traditional competition of wisdom with the trinity of Deities: the High One, the Equally High One, and the Third One. The wager is his head. Having asked everything about the origins of the world, language, poetry, people, orders, and morals, and having also learned the prophecy of the Deities' fate, Gylfi-Gangleri reaches the limit of possible wisdom. The High One responds to him: "But now, if thou art able to ask yet further, then indeed I know not whence answer shall come to thee, for I never heard any man tell forth at greater length the course of the world; and now avail thyself of that which thou hast heard."[38] Gylfi's subsequent fate tells us what is most important:[39]

---

38 Gylfaginning 53, *The Prose Edda*, trans. Arthur Gilchrist Brodeur (1916).
39 Ibid., 54.

Því næst heyrði Gangleri dyni mikla hvern veg frá sér ok leit út á hlið sér. Ok þá er hann sést meir um, þá stendr hann úti á sléttum velli, sér þá enga höll ok enga borg. Gengr hann þá leið sína braut ok kemr heim í ríki sitt ok segir þau tíðendi, er hann hefir sét ok heyrt, ok eftir honum sagði hverr maðr öðrum þessar sögur. En æsir setjast þá á tal ok ráða ráðum sínum ok minnast á þessar frásagnir allar, er honum váru sagðar, ok gefa nöfn þessi in sömu, er áðr váru nefnd, mönnum ok stöðum þeim, er þar váru, til þess, at þá er langar stundir liði, at menn skyldu ekki ifast í, at allir væru einir þeir æsir, er nú var frá sagt, ok þessir, er þá váru þau sömu nöfn gefin. Þar var þá Þórr kallaðr, ok er sá Ása-Þórr inn gamli.

Thereupon Gangleri heard great noises on every side of him; and then, when he had looked about him more, lo, he stood out of doors on a level plain, and saw no hall there and no castle. Then he went his way forth and came home into his kingdom, and told those tidings which he had seen and heard; and after him each man told these tales to the other. But the Æsir sat them down to speak together, and took counsel and recalled all these tales which had been told to him. And they gave these same names that were named before to those men and places that were there, to the end that when long ages should have passed away, men should not doubt thereof, that those Æsir that were but now spoken of, and these to whom the same names were then given, were all one. There Thor was so named, and he is the old Ása-Thor.

In the beginning, we see how Gylfi, who is described similarly to Odin, replicates the latter's patterns of behavior: changing guise, wandering for wisdom, calling himself by a different name, competing in wise words. This is *imitatio Dei*. Gylfi-Gangleri is a figure of the Odinic ethos, and he tests the All-Father himself, who appears before him under the name "The High One."

At the end of Gylfi's visions, we see lucidly that the myth told itself to itself, giving birth at once to the seeker of the tale, the tellers of the tale, the listeners of the tale, and the whole world, the world being the content of the storytelling itself. The myth loops back to itself: having moved away, it returns along a Möbius strip to itself as its own source. Myth reveals itself as the oneness of the form of expression and the content of the storytelling that it itself tells. The High One "recognizes" himself as a character in the tale that he himself is now telling. Or, in other words, Beyng unconceals itself through him as the storyteller and as the storytelling.

Poets and Philosophers

All peoples have their poetry. Poetry, so it seems, has since the most archaic times been the model form of speech, or speech as such altogether. Yet, as Martin West notes, the Indo-Europeans apparently did not have a singular word for designating the poet.[40] The different words for naming the poet refer to the different roles and functions that poetry encompassed as a special and central activity in the ancient mythopoetic vision of the Indo-Europeans. These words most often pertain to "singing" (the Vedic *sāman* and numerous later European variations), "saying" or "telling" (the Greek ἔπος, the Indo-European root **wek*, whence we have the Indian *vác*, "speech" and Latin *vox*, "voice"), as well as lexemes which later came to mean "word," "speaking," and "singing." Herein lies the key status and, according to West, the primary function of the poet: the poet is the one who sings the sacred hymns, myths, and invocations. One important trait of the ancient singer is his altered, ecstatic state, which is described as "mad," evidently induced by the singing itself and the wisdom inherent in it, which is to say the gift of expressing the sacred in hymn.

Another facet of poetry is expressed in thinking, in recollection, in the function of remembering and recalling many tales, sagas, and legends, which the poet knows by heart and in which tradition itself is kept, including knowledge of the cosmogony, the origin of people, and the glorious deeds of the Divinities and the heroes. We encounter this feature in the frequent refrain of the Völva, "She remembers...," whenever she refers to herself in the third person in answering Odin's questions about the past.

The next manifestation of poetry is direct creativity, i.e., the creation of poems, sagas, hymns, songs, and the pro-ducing of being through the word. It is here that we encounter the terms that became definitive of European culture: τεύχειν и ποιεῖν.

---

[40] See M.L. West, *Indo-European Poetry and Myth* (Oxford: Oxford University Press, 2009).

The first is the *tekhne* of tricks, cunning, and craftsmanship with matter, which we can correlate with the poetic meter, vocalization, articulation, intonation, and the form of a myth. Heidegger translates the second as "pro-ducing," i.e., bringing-forth-here as bringing-into-existence. West also mentions the association of poetry as a craft with magic, spells, and witchcraft. Poetry is at once bringing-into-being through telling (*mythopoetic*) and telling of how things come to be (*mytho*-poetic).

Coming very close to the latter understanding is the metaphor of poetry as the spinning of words, as a special metrical skill, which is often placed in the feminine semantic context. Another metaphor of the same order would be that of carpentry, carving and making products out of wood (matter *par excellence*). West also points to the Old Norse word *smiðr*, referring to a master craftsman of wood, stone, or metal ("smith" in English), which is found in such words as *lióðasmiðr* ("songsmith") and *galdasmiðr* ("smith of magical spells").

There are two other images that come from the association of crafts, but which are more associated with the motif of wandering. Poetry is compared to a boat of song or ship full of hymns and praises of the Divine. The poet directs his song like a ship whose sails are filled with the breath of the Muses. The second image replaces the ship with a chariot driven by the Muses or the poet, a chariot on which prayer or praise ascends to the higher worlds or exalts and raises up the poet himself. The poetic word has wings and is associated with the element of air. Semantically, this comes close to the primal element of war in the metaphor of utterances as arrows. For example, we hear in the *Mahabharata*:

> Weapons, such as arrows, bullets, and bearded darts, can be easily extracted from the body, but a wordy dagger plunged deep into the heart is incapable of being taken out. Wordy arrows are shot from the mouth; smitten by them one grieveth day and night. A learned man should not discharge such arrows, for do they not touch the very vitals of others.[41]

---

41 *Mahabharata* 5.34, trans. Kisari Mohan Ganguli (1896).

All of the above aspects, as well as many others, are essentially manifold decorations that make speech lofty even in prose. The poetic studies of the Indian grammarians and aesthetes, and on the other end of the continent, Snorri's poetry textbook, all speak of the decor of speech that pleases both people and Deities. Bearing in mind that a tale's form of expression is an important part of its content which creates the proper suggestive effect and reflects the guiding principle of the manifestation of the sacred, we could argue that beauty is of fundamental importance to the venerable traditions of polytheism. At the same time, this beauty is not only that of the bright well-being of a life "far from affairs," but is also the beauty of tragedy, which equally fascinates and evokes the numinous sense of astonishment.

The poet is the co-creator of being, the literal voice of the *mythos* that constitutes the poet for being told. Poetry is — and not only in the Indo-European context — bringing-forth-here and bringing-into-presence, which is to say that the poet leads words and being by the hand to meet each other, bringing together in hymns and prayers Heaven and Earth, humans and the Divine, and preserving the eternal glory of worthy deeds. The poet rules, not as *Rex* or *Dux*, but as the guardian and cupbearer of ἀρχή, the source, the authoritative principle of the sacred language of the existence of the whole beingful world. Hesiod, Homer, Bhartrihari, the Vedas, the Upanishads, the *Elder Edda*, and other traditions' texts with their unknown singers, are such rulers.

We see a characteristic counterpoint in Europe in the treatment of poets in Plato's iconic *Republic*. In this dialogue, Plato presented as a given a notion that had already come into its own in his time but which he would take to the extreme in the spirit of his idealistic philosophy. Plato proposes to expel poets and tragedians from the state, accusing them of blind verbal imitation (*mimesis*) of things, crafts, and occupations of which they know nothing, yet about which they compose epics and poems. For Plato, poets are harmful inventors and epigones who "create phantoms, not being," i.e., they have no relation to truth. The criterion of truth for this disciple of Socrates was counting, weighing, and measuring the benefit which selected types of poetry and poets might bring to the state in their hymns to the Divine and praise of virtuous men.

Plato is a striking figure of disharmony and bias in favor of the rationalizing trait of *logos*. He is the milestone along the descending trajectory of generations of which Hesiod sang. Although Plato's *Republic* reflects some classical Indo-European, aristocratic traits, it is overall the product of a mechanical approach, which means that it is stillborn and unviable in its very outset. In a distant echo, in our era, Theodore Kaczynski wrote that any attempt to build a planned and rational society is tantamount to engineering a technology that is obviously doomed to failure and in its essence is a form of concealed tyranny and alienation.[42]

Plato does not understand poetry and therefore dismembers it. The dominance of the *logos* inherent in Plato leads to the final disintegration of poetry into several weakly connected or altogether disconnected activities and phenomena subordinated to the utilitarian needs of the State. In this respect, Plato is revealed to be a complete bearer of modern thinking. Plato's *logos* is opposed to *mythos*, and instead of harvesting growing tales into sheaves, he uproots them and ultimately prohibits any unauthorized growth apart from what has now become δόγματος (dogma).

The apogee of this de-mythologization would come in the 20th century in the works of the Protestant theologian Rudolf Karl Bultmann and the structuralist Paul Ricoeur. Their approach is characterized by a conscious and consistent desacralization of Biblical tradition. The different miracles,

---

42 See Theodore John Kaczynski, *Anti-Tech Revolution: Why and How* (Fitch & Madison, 2020). Kaczynski associates a "planned society" with left-wing ideologies of control. In the context of our study, we are not interested in placing Plato's *Republic* anywhere on the political spectrum.

visions, prophecies, etc., are declared to be the presence of myth that hides from the reader the main plot of the life and death of Christ that is purely moral and adaptable to the modern and scientific picture of the world. These authors' method strives to extract the pure *kerygma*, that is the rational part of the Biblical message, cleansed of everything supernatural and mythological. Kerygma is contrasted to structure, which is the sum and "precipitate" of everything non-rational, metaphorical, and miraculous.

Logos, like kerygma, grows out of *mythos*, but at some point it begins to fiercely oppose and suppress *mythos*. In this lies the noetic structure of the fulfillment of decline. *Logos* strives to rationalize *mythos*, to perform analysis upon it in the etymological sense of dismembering it into parts. Being is reduced to history, and living speech gives way to the dominance of text. Hence arises the strictly profane tendency and aspiration of searching for the most reliable or consistent version of one or another myth. That is, *logos* approaches the entire array of differently told myths, legends, and tales with the method and criterion of identifying which version is the most consistent, useful, and optimally fits the picture of the world of Modernity. Such a version is taken to be the main one, the proto-historical one confirmable by archeological finds, historical sources, etc. This also serves apologetics for the content of the Old and New Testaments in attempts to scientifically confirm the reality of the events and characters described therein. From the mythopoetic point of view, of course, this approach absurdly reduces all the diversity of myths (which is always centered around the main mythological core, the leading narrative, which prevents the ideological variations of texts from deviating too far) to dry analytical dogmatics. On the contrary, it is the different tellings of one (hi)story that form the fields and landscapes of myths in their totality. It is not just one version that is true but all versions at once, creating as they do the semantic, intellectual, and imaginative space of symbols. Apparent contradictions do not cause turmoil or affect the truth, but rather enrich the canvas of the tale with all sorts of patterns.

Nevertheless, despite all his disdain for poetry, Plato himself was a myth-maker who created and positioned philosophical myths throughout his dialogues — such as the myth of Atlantis, the Cave, the Chariot of the Soul, the Androgyne, and the posthumous fate of the soul at the spindle of Ananke.[43] In his discussions of the role of myth in Plato, Reinhardt casually remarks that "myth is the language of the soul," which is to say that the soul annuls the contradictions between ideas and myth. "The task of myth is to remind us of our roots," Reinhardt says, and this means that myth is associated with anamnesis (ἀνάμνησις), the recollection of the soul's original dwelling in the heavenly world. This includes the midwifery art of maieutics as well as the illustrative and pedagogical functions of myths in Plato — myth and idea are the co-creation of a form and its contemplation. But we can go further, not only to the "time" of the soul's dwelling in the world of ideas, whose structure the soul recollects while being embodied within ourselves, but to the deepest or highest source of all being in general.

The priest, the shaman, the poet, and the philosopher are the key figures associated with sacred speech in traditional societies. One especially interesting example of the matrix of shamanism and the shamanic use of language and poetry has been examined by Claude Lévi-Strauss.[44] He draws attention to a special song performed by a shaman in the South American Kuna tribe to help a woman in difficult labor where even the midwife cannot cope. The rhyming text consists of 535 lines and has a complex structure. Lévi-Strauss proposes an analysis of its structure and how it actually helps the woman. According to the latter shamanic beliefs, the problems faced by a woman in a difficult childbirth consist in that the special force of *Muu*,

---

43   Karl Reinhardt, *Mify Platona* (Moscow: Vladimir Dal': 2019).

44   Claude Lévi-Strauss, *Structural Anthropology*, trans. Claire Jacobson and Brooke Grundfest Schoepf (New York: Basic Books, 1963).

which is responsible for procreation and is identified with the vagina and uterus, oversteps its limits and seizes the "soul" or life force of the women, her *purba*. Because of this, the lesser or individual purbas of the separate organs and parts of the body are rendered inactive and numb, which on the physical level results in the difficult childbirth that threatens the life of the mother and the child.

The task of the shaman and his assistants is to bring the Muu back to its normal state, to moderate its excess, and return the purba to the woman in labor's whole body, thereby allowing for the child to be born and eliminating any danger in the situation. To this end, the shaman summoned by the midwife performs a complex song which, as is to be expected, is thoroughly equipped with tropes, metonymies, and metaphors, over the course of reciting which the shaman and his assistants embark on a long journey to Muu and defeat its evil assistants, rescuing the purba and sealing all the road and paths so as to keep Muu from going beyond her boundaries. Muu is not an evil spirit, but is the excess, disharmony, and maliciousness (hubris) of the behavior of specific organs and forces associated with childbirth. Lévi-Strauss classifies this technique of healing by chants, the text of which at first glance bears no relevance to the problem at hand, as one of those effective shamanic practices that remain inexplicable (for modern man). The anthropologist selects an explanation that might be called "psychosomatic affectation," whereby the plot and forms of the song are transferred through its tempo and rhythm into the state of the woman in labor. By way of words and dense, meticulous descriptions of his arrival, steps, equipment, path, etc., the shaman repeats the path of childbirth alongside the woman until the moment of meeting and dueling with Muu, which is described altogether briefly before proceeding to a long description of his return. The shaman's singing of his return coincides with the delivery of the fetus delivered the healing of the woman's vagina.

Thus, by way of suggestive dictation, the shaman annuls the boundary between the agony of the woman in labor and the myth he sings. His song and its narrative lead the woman's physical condition to the point of complete healing, childbirth, and the overcoming of her suffering. As a person who is an outsider to traditional society, Lévi-Strauss seeks a psychological explanation, but at the same time he makes an important qualification:

> That the mythology of the shaman does not correspond to an objective reality does not matter. The sick woman believes in the myth and belongs to a society which believes in it. The tutelary spirits and malevolent spirits, the supernatural monsters and magical animals, are all part of a coherent system on which the native conception of the universe is founded. The sick woman accepts these mythical beings or, more accurately, she has never questioned their existence. What she does not accept are the incoherent and arbitrary pains, which are an alien element in her system but which the shaman, calling upon myth, will re-integrate within a whole where everything is meaningful.[45]

The anthropologist's qualification that all societies (in this case, he is an external observer of the archaic Kuna tribe) are sufficiently hermetic loci for the diverse manifestations of the sacred that is beyond, yet which is empirically reliable, effective, and true for those who are within it. It remains only partially explicable to those who not only stand outside it like a member of another tribe, but outside of it as members of another paradigm for describing the world, one in which there is no sacred.

Besides the language of psychoanalysis and psychosomatics, whose value for myth is questionable, the anthropologist also points out that the shaman's song gives myth to the suffering woman in labor as a language for describing her otherwise inexpressible state. The monsters and creatures described in the verses are internal names for the torments and physiological difficulties that the woman in labor is undergoing. Lévi-Strauss indicates that the monsters of the song act as signifiers for the

---

45 Lévi-Strauss, *Structural Anthropology*, 197.

pain, as symbols for things, yet they remain within a singular order of expression, because there is no border between myth and the manifest world.

In this example, poetry is directly associated with birth, with genesis and the art of maieutics, and it is noteworthy that the male shaman and his verbal method assume the role of the final midwife. On a higher level, this once again illustrates the principle of *poiesis* and how its actual manifestations can be traced even in remote, archaic, non-Indo-European tribes and societies. Thus, the shaman is not simply a local healer searching for a person's soul in different worlds or telling where to find game and fish. Rather, the shaman's roots are in the deep lingual-ontological and mythopoetic foundations of the manifestation of the authoritative power of ecstasy and the word.

In Europe, poetry has for a long time been increasingly pushed into the periphery, the functions of mythopoetics have been divided up, and the main authority was redistributed between theology and philosophy. Instead of *mythos* and poetic form, there is *logos* and its rational, privative relationship towards preceding tradition. On the whole, in the mind of church theology it is quite rightful that philosophy took the reigning place, because the philosopher is the one who understands ideas, expresses them, formulates them, and rules through ideas. In this lies the power of thought and the thinker, for absolutely everything within the world is understood through the prism of one or another philosophical system and sets of concepts which, according to Roland Barthes, settle even in the most inert layers of the broad masses in the form of stereotypes, clichés, and socio-political mythology. What seems to be objective and given by nature is always originally but a consequence of the philosophical work of the minds of a few. The last Lydian king, Croesus, probably imagined himself to be a great and bright ruler, but his state was swept away by the Persians and his memory faded into history. Standing on one of his palace's balconies, he hardly could have thought that some Heraclitus living in his city of Ephesus was the true ruler whose thinking about being would lay the foundations for all of Western European thinking for thousands of years to come. Heraclitus' fragments would come to be analyzed and interpreted by the great German classics all the way up to Heidegger, who saw in Heraclitus one of the most important flashes of light at the end of the First Beginning of philosophy. Thus, philosophical power may be inconspicuous or completely detached from worldly government, but it is fundamental, because it is closer to the Divinities, to Being, and to the sources of beings and the beingful world. Philosophy is like an acorn which already contains in its compacted form all the power of a centuries-old oak or a whole forest, for philosophy contains everything without exception and it unfolds into all spheres of human life, even in the extremes of rift and self-denial. Philosophy's departure from poetry and the sacred *arkhe* was long-running and far-fetched, ultimately entailing full-scale rationalization, positivism, logic, logistics, and the disenchantment of the world. But it is also in this respect that philosophy inherits, picks up, and appropriates the heritage of *poiesis* as the rule of the word, as the bringing of beings to presence, to structuring, to interpretation, and to the questioning of Being overall.

Poetry's high status was restored within European philosophy in the works of Friedrich Nietzsche, but it received its rightful laurel wreath from the princely hands of Martin Heidegger. Hölderlin, the "poet of poets," exerted an essential influence on the "Turn" (*Kehre*) in Heidegger's philosophy from the phenomenological analytic of Dasein to the hermeneutics of language and the questioning of Beyng (*Seyn*). Together with Novalis, Rilke, Trakl, George, and Celan, Heidegger actively restructured the German language in his philosophy so that it would be capable of expressing his key ideas. Heidegger incorporates anachronisms and rural dialectisms in order to emphasize the "old" and deeper accents and emphases of words, expand the palette of associative semantic connections, and avoid certain connotations. His texts come to abound in complex repetitions and refrains, and his thought becomes intertwined with language in a hermeneutic circle under the "spell" of the guiding question of the Truth of Beyng. This has led some commentators to deem Heidegger the "Black Forest shaman" or accuse him of deliberately striving to remain obscure and incomprehensible.

Heidegger recognizes poetry to be the sister of philosophy, for which he offers the image of two equal mountain peaks — on one peak stand sphilosophy, on the other poetry. Both poetry and philosophy relate to truth, have access to truth, and express truth. The poet hears, bears, and carries the call of Being cleverly concealed within songs. In some sense, the poet is a particular link in the chain of manifestation unfolding from the source to beings and taking on the form of the holy (*das Heilige*). The philosopher rises up from beings towards the source of being that is not reducible to the beings of the world. To do so, he can be attentive to poets and songs, recognizing in the fabric of their patterns the call of Beyng. The passage from one peak to the other lies not down in the valley between them, but in the leap from peak to peak, in mastering poetic saying and dwelling within it, like making one's tale one's own and becoming one's own for the sake of this tale. With Heidegger's method, this means a passage to the hermeneutics of language, to the affirmation that "language is the house of Being." With respect to *logos* and *mythos*, Heidegger accomplishes a friendly, loving turn from the former to the latter: *logos*, which once grew out of *mythos* and contrasted itself to the latter, once again returns to *mythos* and discovers its origins and power. This partially correlates with the structure of the hermeneutic circle which Heidegger deemed to be the normative way of thinking: an ordinary pre-understanding of meaning → immersion into studying a text, speech, tale, word, or language as such → a new understanding.

In questioning Being within the poetry of the German classics, Heidegger is interested in the following key questions and essential expressions that lift the curtains over the History of Being (*Seinsgeschichte*). With respect to Hölderlin, he emphasizes five most important leitmotifs:

1. Composing poems: "This most innocent of occupations." (Ill, 377)
2. "That is why language, the most dangerous of goods, has been given to man ... so that he may bear witness to what he is...." (IV, 246)
3. "Much has man experienced.
   Named many of the heavenly ones,
   Since we have been a conversation
   And able to hear from one another." (IV, 343)
4. "But what remains is founded by the poets." (IV, 63)
5. "Full of merit, yet poetically, man Dwells on this earth." (VI, 25)[46]

The apparent contradiction between the first and second leitmotifs is what preoccupies Heidegger. How is "this most innocent of occupations," essentially a game, at once the "most dangerous of all goods"? How can a good be dangerous? The philosopher determines that the danger of language lies in the threat it poses to Being happening in terms of beings. Words do not guarantee that a being is not a delusion. But in this danger, in the strife and dispute of the word, language is what first makes it possible for dwelling in the midst of the openness of beings. We can recall the line from Hölderlin's *Patmos*: "But where danger is, there is the saving power."

Heidegger writes of the third motif: "Man's being is grounded in language; but this actually occurs only in *conversation*."[47]

---

46 Martin Heidegger, *Elucidations of Hölderlin's Poetry*, trans. Keith Hoeller (Amherst: Humanity Books, 2000), 51.
47 Ibid., 56.

Conversation brings closer, brings together, unites, because in it two are at once one. Heidegger even highlights the role of the ability to hear one another as a manifest need for the word: we hear something not because it was first sounded and thereupon we caught it. Not at all — rather, the word is born towards an open listening that is awaiting and anticipating dialogue.

The Black Forest wanderer then casually remarks that it is the Divinities that draw us into conversation. In language, people name the dwellers of the heavens, greet them, or turn away from them. All of this is painfully familiar to us, for it is known in the Kashmir valley as *dhvani*, as the Divine call for dialogue hidden in words and speech, as the call for the *sahradaya* who will hear and respond.

In the fourth saying, in almost direct and straightforward text, without the expected and perhaps superfluous references, we behold the restoration of the primordial mythopoetic status of the poet. Heidegger writes: "Who takes hold of something enduring in torrential time and brings it to stand in the word? Hölderlin tells us this with the secure simplicity of the poet," for it is the poets who found what endures.[48]

In the original German, the word used for "found" (which in the Russian sounds closer to "building," "creating," or "establishing" — *sozidaniye*) is *stiften*, which also means "to lay a foundation," "to pin something down," and "to offer up." These are quite recognizable Germanic motifs. Giving the gift of the word to the Divinities or to things is the enduring founding (*Stiftung*) of human here-being (Dasein), the establishing of Being. This is why and how man dwells "yet poetically," being in the presence of the Divinities and in shock at the essential closeness of things which he, as a poet, generously gives names. Heidegger says that Being itself is poetic and is acquired not by any merit, but as a groundless gift. He completely rejects interpretations which hold poetry to be an embellishment of life

---

48 Ibid., 58.

or a means of emotional sublimation, which would be close to Plato's delusions. The poet communicates and communes with the Divinities, intercepting their signs and transmitting them to his people. The poet becomes a Dionysian figure on the borderline between the people and the Divinities, wholeheartedly open in both directions, to Earth and to Heaven.

Hölderlin wrote the lines of the final leitmotif in a state of darkened consciousness. In his 31st year, he was overcome by schizophrenia with which he would live locked up in his "tower" for more than 40 years. Madness is often the price that the poet pays, living with an exposed nerve stretched out between Heaven and Earth, between the Divinities and mortals. As he wrote in "Bread and Wine": "Only at times can mankind bear the full weight of the gods." The very same price was paid by Nietzsche, for such is the mark of Dionysus. As Rilke once wrote, "We risk more than one life, for one breath risks much more…" The risk and danger lie in the fact that we live in the desolate and disastrous time of the World Night, when not only have the Divinities left the world, but the Divine radiance itself has faded. We live in a time of scarcity, a miserable time. The longer it drags on, the muddier and denser the tribulation becomes. Heidegger asks with Hölderlin: "What are poets for in desolate times?" In the World Night, only the poets can catch the subtle trace of the Divinities, for which they must reach the very bottom of the groundless, bottomless abyss (*Abgrund*). This is the task of man, the fate and history of Being. In "Mnemosyne," Hölderlin says something essential:

> For the gods in the heavens
> Cannot do everything. Mortals indeed
> Reach sooner to the abyss.[49]

For poets (and for Hölderlin), the experience of the abyss exposes the barely perceptible, nighttime traces of Dionysus. The poet responds to himself via the lips of a friend:

---

49 Friedrich Hölderlin, "Mnemosyne (second version)" in idem, *Selected Poetry*, trans. David Constantine (Eastburn: Bloodaxe Books, 2018), 172.

> But they [poets] are, so you say, like the wine god's holy priests
> Who wandered from land to land in holy night.⁵⁰

The philosopher then summates: "Poets are the mortals who, singing earnestly of the wine-god, sense the trace of the fugitive gods, stay on the gods' tracks, and so trace for their kindred mortals the way toward the turning."⁵¹

Humans — in the face of poets and philosophers straying through the night, calling out to teach other from equally high peaks — must prepare the dwelling-place for the return, for the coming, or for the passing by of the Divinities. Man must attentively and poetically prepare the here-place, the *da* in Da-sein, so that the Divine might come into this *da* and gather the Thing around Being, the *Sein* in Da-sein.

Heidegger turned primarily to the German poets and their language, but the lyrical landscape of Europe is much broader and more diverse. Hugo Friedrich highlighted the situation of modern poetry by turning to the great French poets, Baudelaire, Rimbaud, Mallarmé, as well other French, English, German, and Spanish poets, and illustrating the ensuing peripeteia of 20th-century lyricism.⁵²

The rays of night sparkle in their dark light here, too, nourishing Baudelaire's work as a classic of symbolism and decadence. The poem *"Le coucher du soleil romantique"* is a bridge between the aspirations of romanticism and the sobering realities of the epoch of intense Modernity:⁵³

---

50 Ibid., "Bread and Wine," 97.

51 Martin Heidegger, "What are Poets For?" in idem., *Poetry, Language, Thought*, trans. Albert Hofstadter (London: Harper Perennial, 2001), 92.

52 Hugo Friedrich, *The Structure of Modern Poetry: From the Mid-Nineteenth to the Mid-Twentieth Century*, trans. Joachim Neugroschel (Evanston: Northwestern University Press, 1974).

53 English translation from Cyril Scott, *Baudelaire: The Flowers of Evil* (London: Elkin Mathews, 1909).

> How beauteous the sun as it rises supreme,
> Like an explosion that greets us from above,
> Oh, happy is he that can hail with love,
> Its decline, more glorious far, than a dream.
>
> I saw flower, furrow, and brook... I recall
> How they swooned like a tremulous heart 'neath the sun,
> Let us haste to the sky-line, 'tis late, let us run,
> At least to catch one slanting ray ere it fall.
>
> But the god, who eludes me, I chase all in vain,
> The night, irresistible, plants its domain,
> Black mists and vague shivers of death it forbodes;
>
> While an odour of graves through the darkness spreads,
> And on the swamp's margin, my timid foot treads
> Upon slimy snails, and on unseen toads.

The solar explosion of the East finds its grave in the West, which in German is directly called the "land of sunset," *Abendland*. The slide and fall into the World Night is its fate — yours and ours. For Baudelaire and the decadents, the World Night is quite concrete: it is their contemporary world of Modernity, of galloping scientific-technological progress, in the face of which Victorian morality stumbled and could not keep up — the era of steam engines, the first electrically lit streets and salons, the replacement of wood with concrete, the dominance of the city and the bourgeoisie, social alienation stretched vertically and horizontally. For the decadents, Modernity is the "atrophy of the spirit," the dissolution of the soul, the triumph of matter and squalor, the sewers of Paris and Marseille. The romantic intensity, rush, and astonishment are preserved along with rejecting the mechanical spirit and progress, but they are turned inside-out. Nevertheless, the collapse of the old and the rise of the new fascinates the decadents — they are the witnesses of a rapid fall, the falling-setting of the sun below the horizon of the garbage dump, its disappearance in the soot and stench of factory chimneys. Abnormality, marginality, the sprouts of nihilism, absinthe, opium, immoralism, and negative aesthetics are the essential sources of inspiration and the only adequate form of poetry as a mirror of the era. The decadent poet contemplates the world as it falls, and he falls with it: he himself is the pattern of the era and the sign of decay. He is the contemporary modern, but he knows this and even glorifies it. The verses of the Russian imaginist Sergei Yesenin only slightly, yet aptly echo this maxim:

И теперь даже стало не тяжко	And now it's not even hard
Ковылять из притона в притон,	To hobble from brothel to brothel
Как в смирительную рубашку,	Like in a straightjacket
Мы природу берём в бетон.	We take nature into concrete.

In this verse we encounter manifold themes of decline and a tight connection between alcoholic oblivion, alienation, and being tired of women, all of which are reflected in the outside world in the clinical, psychiatric prison of nature in concrete banks, canals, and the construction sites of the new Soviet government. Oblivion, the twilight of the mind, the collapse of the semantic and structural content of avant-garde poetry — this is the route of lyrics in the new time of Modernity.

Hugo Friedrich quotes Paul Valéry: "My poems can be given any meaning." For others, it would have been important to convert a form, but for Mallarmé it is the suggestion, the methods of tonal and verbal captivation of the reader, that play the important role. In an article from 1896, the poet wrote: "To name a thing is to almost entirely poison the pleasure of poetry, because this pleasure consists in a gradual guessing, an uneasy reflection of a thing, a suggestion — that is the goal." In this approach we can intuit the archaic roots of the formula known both to Heraclitus and the Indian grammarians: "the gods are fond of the cryptic, as it were, and dislike the evident." Mallarmé speaks forth the spirit of (mytho)poiesis, pointing out that in his era the road to it runs through suggestion. But form already prevails over content, hence Valéry could generally discard the semantic content and the reader could come up with whatever meaning he wished. Mallarmé wishes to evoke resonance, to convey to the listener a mood. For example, a poem can and wants to touch the absolute only in the future and hypothetically, and likewise to touch the absence ("nothing") only by semantic darkness.[54] Friedrich argues that the poets turned their lyrics to irrational themes and forms and played with phonetics for the sake of preserving some kind of miracle that would differ from the "miracles of science." Others would go further, indulging in the desire to completely kill the creative process. According to Friedrich, such an aspiration is a reflection of the technologizing era's devastating blow to the essence of poetry. Metaforms and images begin to mix with terms from the scientific and technical sphere; poems are reformed "synthetically," and boring everydayness penetrates them. The surrealist André Breton argued that "poetry must become the disintegration of the intellect," which leads to a flight from any norm whatsoever, even decadent, and towards avant-gardism, vocalism, and composing poems out of only verbs or only nouns, or only out of vowel sounds, in order to demonstrate the possibilities of languages fitting into mathematically calculated dimensions for playing around. Such poems and verses are not written — they are fabricated in workshops and laboratories. Poetry can make language quite flexible and can overcome the rules of grammar, syntax, etc., while the overall restraint of the diction redeems and sacrifices such liberties. But the zealots of the "new language" in modern poetry proclaim the need to destroy grammatical and other linguistic forms out of the desire for "a language without a word and a word without a language," that is for *zaum*, "transgressing the rational," for glossolalia, and even syllabic schizophasia.

Concluding his lively journey, Hugo Friedrich acknowledges that the descriptive language of modern lyricism is entirely negative. If the pioneers (Baudelaire, Rimbaud, Valéry, Poe, etc.) experimented with and transgressed boundaries in rebelling against Victorian morality and its lies, against the noise of machines, and sought refuge for beauty in new forms inspired by the decay and universal collapse of history into the abyss, then subsequent epigones and charlatans left only the grotesque,

---
54 Friedrich, *The Structure of Modern Poetry*.

kitsch, scandal, and the thunderous void of surrealism and futurism (*casus Mayakovsky*).

The rarer poets are, the lonelier are philosophers in this World Night.[55] The ever-rising destitution oppressing them is the unfolding need of the abandonment and refusal of Being.

> But friend, we have come too late. It is true the gods live
> But over our heads, above in another world.
> Work without end there and seem to care very little
> Whether we live, so much and so well do they spare us
> The vessel is weak and cannot always contain them,
> Only at times can humanity bear the gods' fullness.
> Life is a dream of them, after. But wanderings
> Help, like sleep, and need and the night give strength
> Till in the brazen cradle heroes enough have grown,
> Hearts of a strength, as they were, to be like the gods.
> They come in the thunder then. Meanwhile it seems to me often
> Better to sleep than be so without comrades
> Waiting thus and what to do in the meanwhile and say
> I don't know nor why be a poet in a dead time?
> But they are, so you say, like the wine god's holy priests
> Who wandered from land to land in holy night.[56]

---

55 See Askr Svarte, *Gods in the Abyss*.
56 Hölderlin, "Bread and Wine."

We, Nothing

"Language is the house of Being" — such is the rightful verdict of Martin Heidegger. The task of the philosopher and the poet, the few, is to question Being, and within this questioning to dwell in the world, to turn oneself into one's own, to be local, native, at home — on the earth, under the sky, surrounded by other people and in the presence of the Divinities. This dwelling comes about in language, speaking, and thinking.

Heidegger's next saying is: *das Sein ist das Nichts* — "Being is Nothing." Being radically differs from all beings. The Black Forest philosopher tells us: "You can go through all beings, but you won't find any trace of Being." In this lies Heidegger's fundamental perspective: the ontological difference between beings (*das Seiende*) and Beyng (*Seyn*). Beings are beings-in-being-as-a-whole (*das Seiende-im-Ganze*), that is literally, totally everything to which the predicate "is" might be applied, everything of which it can be said that it in one way or another, materially or ideally, thingly or in the imagination, somehow "is." Everyday thinking regularly replaces Beyng with the idea of a supra-being, a certain being that is the source of all beings, of the essence of being. Later Heidegger refers to such a supra-being as *Sein* (the normative spelling of the word "Being" in German) in distinguishing it from pure Beyng, written as the archaic form *Seyn*, which does not become something extant. This is what Heidegger has in mind with the phrase "*das Seyn ist das Nichts*." The Nothing is the total opposite of everything that exists in general, being-as-a-whole, everything that it is. This opposite paradoxically allows beings to be as beings, but it itself never becomes a being. How can we be — and can we be? — involved in Nothing, and what are the interpretations of it that come down to us from traditional and metaphysical doctrines? How can one possibly gain any kind of access to that which in no way is, which is not?

If Western metaphysics is the *adaequatio,* the correspondence, between some kind of ideal form and an always variable thing, or the correspondence of knowledge to certain criteria (however diverse) of truth and correctness of method, then there can be no metaphysical approach to Nothing. Something cannot correspond to Nothing like an imprint to a matrix, an embodied thing to an idea, or a notion of "ought." Nothing simply is not —- not in any way that it could be corelated to any being like a blueprint for establishing a measure of the accuracy and competence of the master. Thus, the problem of Nothing and any reasoning about it leads us purely out of metaphysics, either to incomprehensibly high levels of transcendence or to considering the problem in the light of the purely immanent world. In any case, even these criteria of transcendence and immanence fall away as metaphysically loaded.

A being is something that covers and conceals Nothing, thereby consigning the Nothing to complete oblivion: "being is, non-being is not." Such being is often identified with matter. Imagine a lavishly set table that is covered with a thin yet opaque veil whose folds replicate the contours of the dishes and cups in detail. This is being(s), the beingful world of nature in the diversity of its landscapes with its mountains, valleys, rivers, oceans, steppes, dunes, and plains. Yet, such an image can give rise to the false interpretation that the Nothing really represents some kind of landscape which is merely covered and replicated by the beings thrown on top of it. Obviously, this cannot be the case. Any attempt to cut a tunnel into a mountain or dig down in a depression will not lead to a breakthrough into Nothing, but will only form a depression and fold in the very same being. Thus, the natural harmony and continuous diversity of local landscapes are not, as it were, subtly given by the topology of Nothing, but are immanent to the present being itself as its self-covering. In monistic theologies, being in the form that it is presented in nature, including the animal world, the worlds of spirits and humans, etc., is a direct manifestation-in-unconcealment of the Divine. The veil cast over the Nothing does not take on any form, it simply falls upon and covers. The landscapes of beings are not only natural, but are all those possible beings that "are," that are created, manifested, and maintained by the Divine principle. Matter turns out to be altogether close to the Nothing, but it is still qualitatively, infinitely far from it at the same time. The triumph of materialism, which in European culture was bound up with nihilism towards the high culture of the spirit, is something other than the ontological problem of the Nothing. The Nothing "is" something so hyper-infinitesimal that it is not even neglectable as insignificant. "Insignificance" (in Russian, *nichtozhnost'* misleadingly contains the *nichto*, "Nothing") and any sense of scale or dimensionality should be disassociated from the word "nothing" in order to grant it its power to indicate the abyss of Beyng.[57]

Speech is always speaking something; the stream of speech is always the stream of something being spoken. But what about Nothing in speech and language? Language is the house of Beyng, and in it we encounter Nothing, even when only by saying the word itself. Indeed, the word itself is a clear threshold on the verge of the question under study. The "*chto*" ("what," "that," "something") in the Russian word *nichto* consists of the Proto-Slavic **čьto*, which acts as a broad pronoun for anything, which means for being-as-a-whole. Absolutely everything of which we can say "it is" can be placed under the pronoun "*chto*." But before this "something" is the strong negational prefix "*ni-*," hence the word itself indicates a negation of the totality of being. A similar situation is found in the English language, where "nothing" consists of the negational prefix "no-" and the negated substantive noun "thing." In the German "*Nichts*" there is also a negation of the Proto-Germanic root **wihtą* ("thing"), which through the Proto-Indo-European root **wekti-* is cognate with the later Church Slavonic **veštĭ* (also meaning "thing").

---

57 See Heidegger, *Contributions to Philosophy (Of the Event)*.

The German word is also comparable to the Old English *niht* ("night") from Proto-Germanic **nahts*.

Thus, the word "nothing" immediately leads us into a fundamental context, one that is intelligible even on the everyday level: "nothing" means "apart from the veil of being." This word is literally the boundary of language and thinking, because it is a casting out from some-thing towards absolutely no-thing. The word "nothing" is a deixis (from the Greek δεῖξις — "indication," "pronoun"), a classic gesture whose essence lies not as much in itself as in the direction or thing to which such a gesturing points, to what it "points out." In the case of "nothing," however, there is no referent or reference, such as from a pointing finger to the moon. The ordinary word "nothing" demands of us a fundamental, unimaginable shift and translation in view and thought. The Nothing "is" inaccessible to us within discursive thinking and language. "Nothing" "is" paradoxically more primordial than any "not," any logical negation. The word "nothing," which appears to us to act as a certain object, something objectifiable in language with which we can carry out almost tangible manipulations, is in point of fact none other than a conceptual and logical casting out from the Nothing that always whispers to us: "apart from being."

From words we can move on to symbols, because a symbol is not a strict sign, but is always a cross-section of a certain order of ideas and semantics. As a sign or thing, a symbol is concrete, yet it does not merely refer to one direct signified, but rather places it within a broader context of an idea, a semantic field. In the space of such semantics, the sign, thing, and word itself might shift to mean others which also belong to the same semantic sequence, for example, spear, sword, staff, mountain, tower, bowl, depression, cave, spinning wheel, etc. Replacing one symbol with another can underscore and accentuate new nuances or eliminate other features of a phenomenon, but they will always belong to a single field or gesture, e.g., feminine or masculine symbolism, the symbolic orders of Deities and traditions, symbols of war, craft, earth, sky, etc. A symbol is always broader than the Aristotelian law A=A, because a symbol does not only show itself, but always refers to a higher category or idea of which it is an emanation or sequence. A symbol is always something else, something more, entailing an openness to movement along semantic threads.

In sacred texts and hymns, in the depictions and evocations of the Divinities in poetry, there is a specific set of epithets and words: night (Νυκτός), darkness (Ἔρεβος), ocean, abyss, nameless, inexpressible, beyond words, etc. Such can be either independent images in poetry as well as decorations and words of praise addressed to the immortals. This would be one level of meaning, yet an even deeper one awaits disclosure. Between such epithets one can trace the symbolic connections of deixis. For instance, the symbol of the cup refers us to the feminine principle and feminine semantics, while a sword refers us to the masculine principle, which indicates that it is specifically something masculine being revealed here. But epithets and superlatives of darkness and obscurity do not refer us to anything; their eidetic threads are lost in the void. We recognize their common semantic field to be a definite form of *dhvani*, a concealed message, which points us to what is, in principle, impossible to think directly, of which one can speak solely with hints, symbols, and indications. Hugo Friedrich cites Mallarmé's commentary on his own sonnet to illustrate how the poet can employ the semantic obscurity of a verse: "An open window at night; a room with no one inside; a night made of absence and inquiry; no furniture; at most, a hint of indefinite sideboards, with a dying mirror in the background, astrally and incomprehensibly reflecting the Big Dipper and thereby linking the deserted home with the sky."[58] These lines offer an excellent illustration of utter absence, in this case the absence of a witness, a person, the human that in modern times became the subject substituting for the Divine. And yet there is absence.

---

58   Friedrich, *The Structure of Modern Poetry*, 96-97.

Friedrich remarks that in all of Mallarmé's poetry "absolute being cannot reach language." A similar maxim was expressed by Ernst Jünger: "Perhaps obscurity presents the inexpressible rather than an inability to communicate."

Such descriptions and, at first glance, sheerly aesthetic decorations are cataphatic expressions, symbols, tropes, and metaphors which come close to apophatic semantics. One of the proper characteristics of cataphatic expression is its desire for finitude, for restraint, for strictness of expression. In other words, when it comes to Nothing, language tries to build a strict sign structure, as Frege would have it, or give a clear, prosaic definition. The word "definition" comes from the Latin verb *finio*, meaning "to close a boundary," "to prescribe," "to set a limit." In Russian, this directly corresponds to the notion of *opredelenie*, that is positioning a limit around an entity by way of describing it and assigning it to one or another category. Similarly, the Latin word *terminus* means "border," "limit," "border stone." Speaking of any definitions of Nothing would be a stretch, but we might speak of the "infinitions" of Nothing (from the Latin *infinitus*, infinity), that is "definitions" which contain an indication of the impossibility of any final definition, indications which speak to limitlessness and the elusive evasion of any description.

The ordinary, prosaic language of everyday communication does not lack infinitions and tropes, as it is thoroughly structured by various metaphors, their intersections and insertions. This means that the potential for entering poetic horizons is always preserved in close proximity, already interwoven into any form of speech. For the sake of this, however, according to Heidegger, the word must resort to violence and renounce any kind of ἰδέα or φύσις.

If language always says something, then deictic words, symbols, and infinitions are cataphatic beings pointing towards the apophatic instance beyond being. From Being-as-being we turn our gaze to non-Being. But simple "non-Being" is not yet

Nothing. The apophatic negation of Being, as it were, puts "non-Being" into our hands as a logical antithesis, but the negation is applicable to it as well. The negation of non-Being does not lead to a logical return to Being-as-being, since it has also been negated. In such cases, sacred texts say that something "neither is nor is not," which forms a paradox, a koan, and conveys the impossibility of expressing this extreme instance. Nothing is not simply no-thing, a negation of any "is," but is also the negation of any "is not." Apophaticism tensely pushes us towards a different way of thinking and language, towards being-on-the-border of being and Nothing. This border is language as the primal element that generates speeches (*mythoi*, discourses), and the borderline nature of Nothing is immanent to language.

Let us recall truth as ἀλήθεια, un-concealment, in which resounds the root λήθη —"oblivion," "concealment." In language, this means that speech also carries with it, or is even about, the un-said, the ά-λεκτο (from the verb λέγω, "to speak," *logos*, and the Latin *lēctor*). The unsaid is not something that really was or something about which one prefers to keep silent, as if a being whose expression was bypassed in speech. The unsaid is that which is in absence, the apophatic part of speech, or perhaps, albeit conditionally, the "background," the "backdrop," like the white sheet of paper behind a text or the still silence at the threshold of a tale about to be told. The unsaid is an echo of the silence that gives space, that is mixed in with and among words, and some words implicitly and delicately draw sensitive attention back to this "source," to the Nothing.

Let us return to *poiesis* again. Ποίησις is bringing-into-the-light-of-the-world, bringing-forth-here (in the word), but from where is a being brought forth, out of what darkness? Ontotheology speaks of words and beings brought out from the sacred, the source of which is the Divine. But the Divine in and of itself also belongs to the register of "is," which means that the Divine also conceals Beyng-as-Nothing. For Western metaphysics, this is a variation of absolute idealism, as Beyng is substituted by some supra-extant source, even a Divine one.

Following Neoplatonic henology, which lies at the heart of Rhenish mysticism, as well as the analogous Advaita, we are brought to speak of making a theological distinction[59] between the Deities (*Götter*) as the ground (*Grund*) and their groundless ground that is the Abyss (*Abgrund*) of ineffable Divinity (*Gottheit*). The apophatic dimension in theology places the Nothing in the hidden depths of the Deities as the ineffable One and *Selbst* (which neither is nor isn't). The Nothing of the Divine, as the source of the intertwined, innerwordly phenomena of speech, language, poetry, and philosophy, immanently transmits, translates, and speaks forth itself within them, like the veins running through a leaf, like the *dhvani* always present in any speech utterance. Language is the gift of the Divine through which we enter into dialogue with the Deity and, even deeper, recognize within it and through it the always presencing Nothing. Heidegger says that Beyng "is" as the juncture, the in-between, in which the Divinities and the human being discover themselves and which they question from their own perspectives.

In the passages where Heidegger speaks of thinking coming from Being, we can interpret such to be an originary happening, an eventing ("...*das Denken vom Sein ereignet...*") of thinking from Nothing. The premonition of Beyng comes to the human being not from a being, but from that which alone is equal in rank to Beyng itself, that is the Nothing, the excess of pure refusal which purifies Nothing and renders Beyng simple. Heidegger insists that any sense of "negligible" must be removed from the word "nothing" so that it can point towards the abyss of Being.[60]

---

59 There is also the discursive and linguistic distinction, following Shankaracharya's maxim that "the gods are fond of the cryptic, as it were, and dislike the evident" and Heraclitus's saying that "Nature loves to hide."

60 See Heidegger, *Contributions to Philosophy (Of the Event)*.

Within the world, the telling and thinking presence is the human, Da-sein, concrete here-being, a special being that is open to thinking and experiencing Beyng, which is not a being. The *da* in Da-sein is the human being itself, for man is the here, the place of Being. The complex, multidimensional, all-encompassing relation between the human being, the Divine, language, beings, Beyng, and the Nothing can be summated in the following series of retentions and interpretations:

I. The human as a being can be open or closed in relation to the Nothing. In its present being, a being (*Seiende*) converges with nothing (*Nichts*).

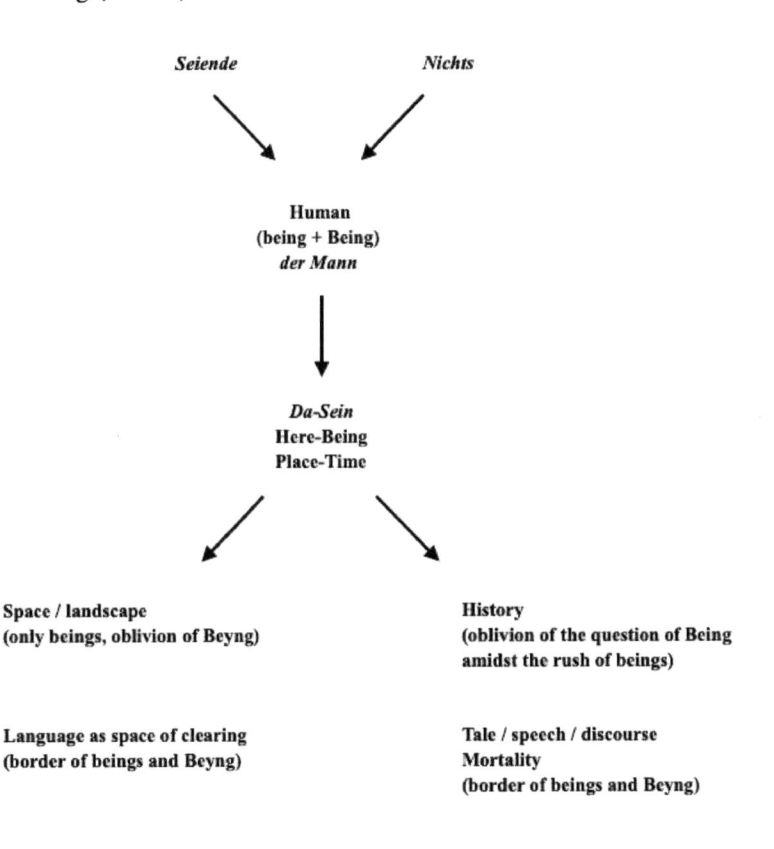

```
    Seiende              Nichts
        \                /
         \              /
          ↘            ↙
            Human
         (being + Being)
           der Mann
               │
               ↓
            Da-Sein
           Here-Being
           Place-Time
            ↙      ↘
           ↙        ↘
```

Space / landscape   **History**
(only beings, oblivion of Beyng)   (oblivion of the question of Being
                                      amidst the rush of beings)

Language as space of clearing   **Tale / speech / discourse**
(border of beings and Beyng)   **Mortality**
                                     (border of beings and Beyng)

109

II. The human is the uttering one (cf. μῦθος) who, thanks to the Divine gift of language, determines the names of things (λόγος) and brings them into Being (ποίησις). Language always bears an intermixture of the unsaid and tropes which point to the Nothing. In Heidegger's second saying, *Sein* can be understood equally validly as *Seiende-im-Ganze* as well as *Nichts* depending on the attuned intentionality of thinking presence.

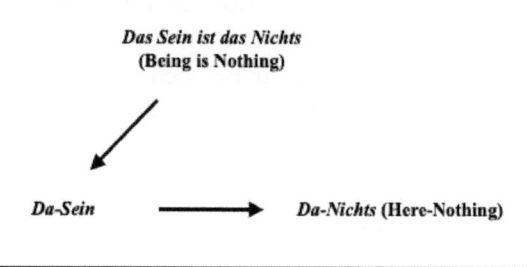

Das Sein ist das Nichts
(Being is Nothing)

↙

Da-Sein ⟶ *Da-Nichts* (Here-Nothing)

Das Haus des Seins ist die Sprache
(Language is the house of Being)

↓

Das Haus des Nichts ist die Sprache
(Language is the house of Nothing)

III. The human being is defined by his mortality (*Zeit*, "time," and *zum-Tode-sein*, "being-towards-death") and language (*Sprache*). Language is the gift of the Divinities, who themselves converge around the fire of Beyng-Nothing in their questioning.

```
                            Human
                              │
                              ▼
              Language is the house of Nothing
                 ╱            │            ╲
                ╱             │             ╲
               ▼              │              ▼
        Nihilism              │         Nicht-Selbst
  (intraworldly orientation,  │         (Nothing-Self)
   gigantism of the negligible,│       Groundless ground
   decline, eschatology)      │         of here-being
                              ▼
                    Language and thinking
                  ("Thinking born of Nothing")
```

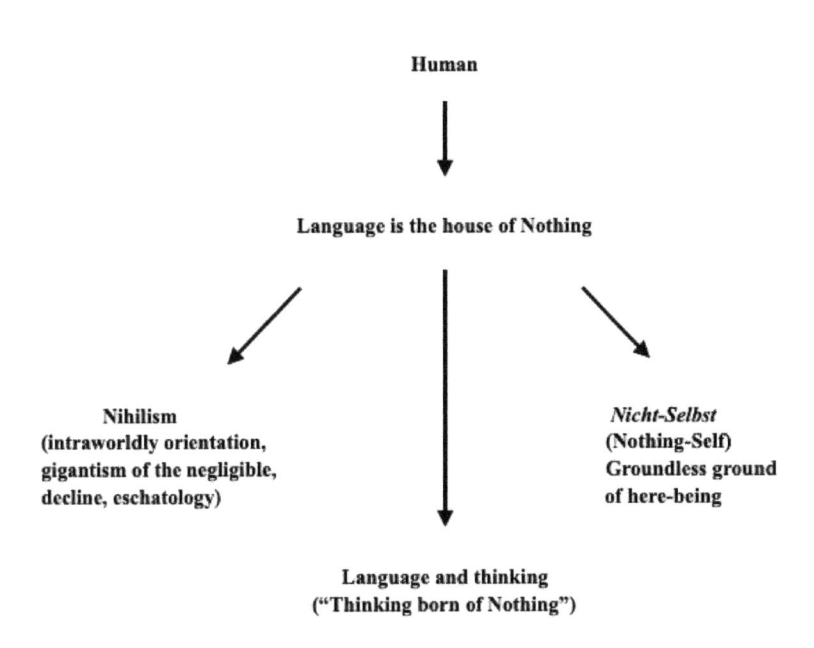

IV. In this case, nihilism has nothing to do with Nothing, with thinking about Nothing. The essence of nihilism lies precisely in the complete oblivion of the Nothing, in absorption into the mechanistic nature of beings and the bored agitation of machinations (*Machenschaft*, τέχνη) upon beings. Nihilism is the need for, yet refusal to turn to, Beyng in the situation of its furthest oblivion, the end of metaphysical thinking, over the course of the general degradation and unfolding of eschatology. Nihilism is the reign of emancipated beings abandoned by Beyng.

V.

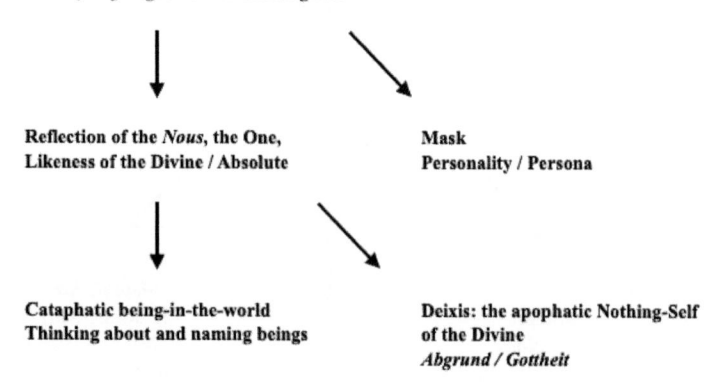

Mind (νοῦς) / ego / human thinking is...

↓ ↘

Reflection of the *Nous*, the One,　　　Mask
Likeness of the Divine / Absolute　　　Personality / Persona

↓ ↘

Cataphatic being-in-the-world　　　　　Deixis: the apophatic Nothing-Self
Thinking about and naming beings　　　of the Divine
　　　　　　　　　　　　　　　　　　　Abgrund / Gottheit

VI. The Divinities around the truth of Beyng are a circle of masks around the Nothing-*Selbst* of the Divine.

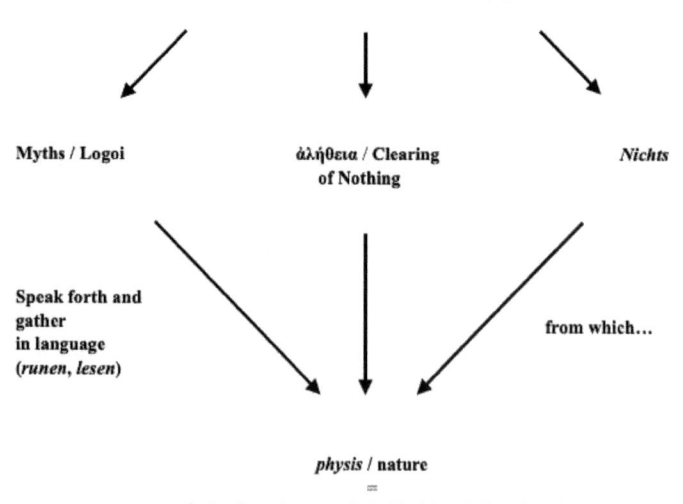

Divinities around the truth of Beyng

↙　　↓　　↘

Myths / Logoi　　　ἀλήθεια / Clearing　　　*Nichts*
　　　　　　　　　　of Nothing

Speak forth and
gather
in language　　　　　　　　　　　　　　　from which...
(*runen, lesen*)

↘　↓　↙

physis / nature
=
circle of masks around the Nothing-*Selbst* of the Divine

↙　　　　　　　　　　　　　　...of what?
　　　　　　　　　　　　　　　　↘

Symbol / Circumpunct　　　　　　That which is not
Year-Wheel　　　　　　　　　　　identical to the center point of
Thing / Veche　　　　　　　　　Nothing

Having traversed a circle around this semiotic and ontolinguistic path of tropes, we discover the Nothing as the addressee of deixis, the unsaid, and the "source" of language and thinking. Language is the house and *topos* of the Nothing, and man is the one who tells the tale in language.

Having ascended through ontotheology, we return to the apophatic Nothing of the Divine groundlessness. If "atman is Brahman," then man "inherits" the Nothing along this same line. But this "inheriting" is burdened by the primary emphasis on the cataphatic "is" and descriptions of a supreme Divinity. In other words, very few traditions draw this most profound distinction between Nothing and the being(s) within the abyss of the Divine; the majority of traditions are satisfied with equating Being with the cataphatic aspects and theophanies of the Divine. If we can say something of the sort at all, then we shall say that there is no Divinity within the Nothing, but this does not mean nihilism or atheism. Hence Heidegger's altogether specific affirmation that the Divinities need Beyng as something that does not belong to them so that they might be themselves, i.e., immortal Divinities, the Divine ones.

According to the analytic of the Being of our here-being, our thinking presence, we also discover the immanent and substantially intrinsic — intrinsic to us — borderline openness of and to the Nothing (the neither is nor isn't) that is interwoven into our existence.

The Nothing is not some kind of distant something, the path to which is so difficult and concealed that we exclude this something up to the point of denying it Being. The Nothing is not merely something unimaginable and unthinkable from our innerworldly and contemporary cultural vantage point, but it is something concealed behind the impenetrable veil of obscure expressions, stanzas, and infinitions.

We ourselves are the Nothing. We bear it within ourselves. We ex-press it, speak it out. We think it out and we are always open to it, even though we can turn away from it and lose ourselves among beings. Furthermore, the Nothing is an enigmatic and problematic instance for the Divinities themselves. Just as man is *tat tvam asi,* so it is that *da-sein ist da-nichts*. The Nothing is always we ourselves.

Tradition as Language

It is not so much the case that tradition, understood as the unfolding of culture initiated by the sacred, is reducible to language, as it is the case that the very notion of language is extendable to all of culture as the foundational metaphor and structure. Everything is language: specific speech practices, gestures, rules, laws, taboos, everyday affairs, the material culture of crafts, hunting, plowing, and harvesting, the structures of kinship, marriages[61], estates, and hierarchy, styles of speech, notions of space and time, systems of numbering and accounting, the events and life course of surrounding nature[62], etc. All of these are semiotic spaces, and therefore lingual. Outside of language and semiotics, which can be brought together as a whole, there is no world.

Tradition acts as a language, as a grammatical and poetic (in the sense of bringing beings-into-Being) system which ensures the coherence and correctness of the most diverse expressions and discourses. Language does not pronounce judgments on the truth of one or another expression; it only gives them the space, structure, meaning, and time for being told. An expression or utterance within a tradition can be any individual theological or philosophical school, a series of jewelry-like ritual objects, a *Männerbund* warrior campaign, a dynastic union, the architecture of a cult site, ritual laments and songs, etc. The song form reigns supreme among sacred texts and addresses to Deities because songs and poetry are essentially the language of the Divinities, the ones who sing and dance. There are as many traditions, as many manifestations of the sacred, as there are languages and divine songs.

Language gives the space for different discourses to be and to affirm themselves in the world. Rising up to a broader

---

61 See Lévi-Strauss, *Structural Anthropology*.

62 See Eduardo Kohn, *How Forests Think: Toward an Anthropology Beyond the Human* (Berkeley: University of California Press, 2013).

vantage point, we can see the plurality of languages as structured by different grammars (metaphysics) and yielding the infinite diversity of noetic, discursive universes. In other words, we are dealing with the open possibility of inexhaustible mythopoiesis. Like a wanderer between lands, moving between language-traditions demands of us the subtlest and most sensitive art of translation, if it is possible at all, as well as a handy meta-language with which we might correctly correlate different and distant tradition-cultures and, no less importantly, formulate the question of the ultimate sources of lingual diversity in the manifest world. Such a meta-language must inevitably be philosophical and Traditionalist.

Earlier, we drew a fundamental distinction between the Deities (*Götter*) and the Divine (*Gottheit*) that is the apophatic ground of the former: the Deity concealed in self-revelation is the ground (*Grund*) of the world, and it itself rests on a groundless ground (*Agrund, Nichts*). The situation with languages is analogous: every language is the ground and all-pervading structure of culture and thinking, but languages themselves have their roots in the *Abgrund*. The path of the emanation of language can be mediated by a Deity that gives the gift of a tale about itself, about man himself, oe about language itself (the turning of language towards itself). The ensuing branching out into languages and their respective discursive, social, political, cultural, and material manifestations resembles a single tree.

In mythopoetics, the tree is a symbol and metaphor not only of the human being, but of tradition as a whole. Its roots run into the earth and its crown reaches up into the havens. Earth is the mystical soil, the topogenesis and surrounding landscape, climate, and nature in whose bosom a people lives and which is reflected in a people's culture and imprinted in their thinking. This is Mother Earth. The heavens are the patrimony of the Heavenly Father, the vertical spiritual principle of a people, its sacred myths and traditions, the upper world of the Deities, spirits, and ancestors. It is sometimes said that the Tree has its roots in the sky and its leaves spread across the earth. This emphasizes that the single root of tradition is up above, growing toward the earth and branching out into numerous spiritual paths, the cults of different Deities, and the traditions and legends of various estates and families, etc. The leaves are the immense abundance of manifestations of one or another path (the Slavic *vervi*) within a specific culture, of all its music, songs, spiritual poetry, architecture, crafts, smithing, decor, styles of embroidery and drawing, typical gestures, postures, corporeal plasticity, etc. Each particular people lives in the middle world between its earth and its heaven, sprouting out of one root with the generous sweep of a branching crown. All peoples together form the forest of traditions. The totality of the forest, its forestness as such, corresponds to language as the common element that unites the manifold within its oneness. The branches and leaves subject to the winds of history and seasonal fall in the lead up to winter best reflect the temporariness and mutability of the forms of the manifestation of the sacred in the world and in particular things. But the deep foundation that draws and transmits the fluids that nourish the entire tree, the roots that run into the impenetrable darkness of the *Abgrund*, are authentic thinking in its innermost bond with language.

Bearing in mind the plurality of language-traditions, it bears examining in detail the connection between language and thinking, how language affects the thought process itself as well as, consequently, culture. The very affirmation of such a connection and of the influence upon thinking exerted by language, with its grammar, syntax, semantics, morphology, etc., seems to be well-established, but this was not always the case. The tight bond between language, speech, and thought was pointed out by many ancient thinkers and traditional, often mystical schools, ranging from the Indian subcontinent to Mediterranean and European antiquity. In addition to what has been expounded in the preceding chapters, it is worth mentioning the caste-specific sociolects know in the Indo-European languages with their intrinsic phonetics. Differences in the "professional" occupations, rituals, and social status of various groups within society — the source of which, in sacrocentric thinking, is in the will of the Divine as recorded in a given set of myths — are reinforced by linguistic differences, ranging from knowledge of certain words to literacy and writing systems which exist among the twice-born but remain unknown to the lower varnas. To this should also be added the feminine sociolects that exist among different peoples as well as the special linguistic constructions and discursive forms associated with the structure and hierarchy of the traditional family.

Drawing on the problem of expressing mystical experience in language in the case of Meister Eckhart, the linguist Johann Leo Weisgerber argued that language is "the process of recreating the world in the word," or "wording the world" (*Worten der Welt*).[63] Special attention has been paid to the influence of language on thinking by German philosophers and linguists, although their basic formulations and approaches have undergone significant changes since the first perspectives were offered. This line runs from the founder of linguistic philosophy, Justus Georg Schottelius, to the anti-Enlightenment philosophers, such as Johann Georg Hamann, who was the first to substantiate on the basis of faith in God the thesis that thinking is linguistically relative, and Johann Gottfried Herder, the author of the beautiful maxim "peoples are thoughts of God." Herder insisted on the leading role of language in the human being's formation in becoming human. This line was later continued by Wilhelm Humboldt and the Humboldtians, such as the Russian linguist Alexander Potebnya and the German linguist Leo Weisgerber. Nor can we refrain from mentioning the German philologist and scholar of religion Friedrich Max Müller, the founder of the discipline of comparative religious studies. Müller proposed examining the development of religious ideas by analogy with the development of language and thinking, and he demonstrated the influence that the form of a word and naive etymology play on the development of religious representations.[64]

---

63 Borodai, *Iazyk i poznanie*.

64 Ibid.

This line also includes the German-educated ethnographer Franz Boas, who studied the indigenous population of Canada. Boas was one of the first to insist on the equivalence of all languages and cultures, and thus rejected the division of languages into primitive vs. developed in terms of a singular evolutionary path of mankind. For Boas, "civilization" is a particular case, a relative value, that is not at all necessary for different cultures around the world. The evolutionary criteria of one "high civilization" cannot be applied to evaluate other cultures and people — such would be gnoseological racism and chauvinism. This is partly consonant with the even earlier argumentation put forth by Potebnya, who defended the plurality of languages as a diverse, complex palette of conceptual styles as opposed to universal projections of a single synthetic language or the establishment of linguistic hegemony, which, in Potebnya's opinion, would lead to the degradation of thinking in general. Boas also drew on the works of Müller and Humboldt. Moreover, he proposed that the imperative nature of a grammatical system presupposes a special way of schematizing experience in verbal activity. Hence the thesis that different languages' classification models are unique. Boas also established the now commonplace practice of comparing and contrasting the Indo-European languages with the modern European languages as well as more exotic ones, such as the Amerindian languages. One of Boas' foremost students was Edward Sapir, who went on to become the founder of the entire field of linguistic anthropology, an active defender of the American Indian population, a prolific author and visionary of linguistic science.

As soon as Sapir's name has been mentioned, we already know what theses we are approaching. Appropriating and mastering Boas' main theses, Sapir developed them in his own vein. His absolute maxims include the argument that it is impossible to think and reason without language. Language is present in cognitive processes even where and when it cannot be identified introspectively. Language is no mere isolated and cold instrument for cognition and the expression of thought, as Immanuel Kant insisted, but is an active co-participant in the formation of thought in the very form and content that thought itself manifests. In his book *Language: An Introduction to the Study of Speech*, Sapir cited a number of examples to illustrate the thesis that grammar compels one to express certain meanings and organize thoughts in a specific way. What for European language is necessarily grammatically encoded, i.e., what can be expressed in the language only by sticking to the important accents of thought (the obligatory use of the verb "to be," for instance), might be simply absent in the grammars of non-Indo-European languages, or expressed on the lexical level, or not expressed at all. The converse is also true: the grammatical and lexical structures of the language of North American tribes encode and accentuate as of primary importance certain modes and details which in European languages pertain to supplemental or secondary clarifications of a situation.

Sapir draws a close connection between language and the notion of "meaning." An element of element is a "house" or "symbol" that brings together thousands of different phenomena of experience and is capable of uniting thousands more. The perception of external reality, the "stream of experience," happens through the deep lingual distribution of meanings. A phonetic system plays an important role as the "foundation." Let us cite one of the classic comparative examples:

> In realty, symbolization involves shaping a thought or impression in accordance with the structure of a native language. To substantiate this claim, Sapir refers to a variety of conventional modes of expression. For instance, observing an object called a "stone" flying towards the ground, a native English speaker analyzes this event using the notions of "stone" and "falling"; combining these two representations into English expression, he says: "The stone falls." Speakers of German, French, and Russian would add to this an idea of gender, while the Chippewa Indians would add the idea of inanimateness. A Russian would be puzzled why a definite reference to the stone, coded by the article "the," is needed in English. Meanwhile, a Kwakiutl Indian would consider all of the preceding statements incomplete, since they do not convey information about the visibility of the stone and its spatial relationship to the participants in the situation. To a Chinese speaker, on the contrary, these expressions would seem redundant, since for him there is enough information about the presence of an

object that is in a state of falling (without indicating the gender, time, direction, etc.). The most exotic form of expression is to be found in the Amerindian language of Nootka, in which this situation is described with the use of a verb form consisting of two main elements: the first denotes the general movement or position of the stone-like object, and the second the downward movement. This expression might be conveyed by the artificial phrase "It stones down."[65]

Here, it becomes obvious how the language system of any given people within its culture gives the one and the same phenomenon a unique shape and accentuation. On this basis, Sapir proceeded to proclaim the principle of linguistic relativity, which holds that a given language influences certain formal domains of thinking. As in the case of Boas and Sapir, an important role in the development of this line of ideas would be played by Sapir's talented student, Benjamin Whorf. Mastering the basic principles of his teachers and continuing to study the Amerindian languages, especially Hopi, in comparison to the so-called "Standard Average European" (SAE[66]), Whorf reinforced the argument for linguistic relativity and the influence of linguistic structure on thinking. In particular, Whorf argued that identical physical phenomena do not necessarily lead to a uniform conceptual system for constructing experience out of represented information. This argument entered scholarship and mass culture under the collective name of the "Sapir-Whorf hypothesis." The most widespread version of this thesis has both strong and soft formulations:

> Strong version: Language determines thinking, and linguistic categories accordingly limit and determine cognitive categories.
>
> Soft version: Language only influences thinking. Alongside linguistic categories, thinking is also formed under the influence of traditions and certain types of non-linguistic behavior.[67]

---

65 Borodai, *Iazyk i poznanie*.

66 "Standard Average European" (SAE) refers to the European languages that possess common grammatical properties. The group includes the Romance, Germanic, Balkan, and Balto-Slavic languages.

67 Sergei Borodai, "*Sovremennoe ponimanie problemy lingvisticheskoi otnositel'nosti: raboty po prostranstvennoi kontseptualizatsii*", *Voprosy iazykoznaniia* 4 (2013), 17-54.

Neither of these, however, has anything to do with the real state of affairs. Whorf was in many respects an independent and original thinker (who was even influenced by Eastern metaphysics and esotericism). He was never Sapir's co-author, and, moreover, he did not formulate any "hypothesis" on his own or jointly with his teacher. Whorf greatly developed what Boas had already foreseen as the influence of language on the categorization of experience and the formation of thought (the relationship between form and meaning) up to the point of linguistic and cultural pluralism. He insisted on the need for further research to verify such theses.

The problem with the "Sapir-Whorf hypothesis" is rooted in subsequent linguists' completely erroneous understanding of their ideas. It is to later linguists, following the Chicago conference of 1953, that the "invention" of this "hypothesis" is owed, including its strong and weak versions which are nowhere to be found in the original works authored by Sapir and Whorf. Whorf simply followed his teachers and did not put forth any hypothesis, instead preferring to discuss empirically observed patterns and facts. The completely balanced generalizations he drew on the basis of the material available to him did not need verification due to the obviousness of the very difference between languages. Only later, by dint of a combination of misunderstandings of Whorf's ideas and critiques arrayed against a "hypothesis" falsely attributed to him, were the ideas of linguistic relativity and linguistic determinism "rejected," giving way to the prevalence of linguistic theories that were hostile to "Whorfianism."[68]

Nevertheless, the further development of Whorf's ideas, along with later investigations of the erroneous trajectory of understandings of his project and the essence of the "Sapir-Whorf hypothesis," have exerted a colossal influence not only on linguistics, but also on many related and separate sciences,

---

68 In his fundamental monograph *Iazyk i poznanie. Vvedenie v postreliativizm* [Language and Cognition: An Introduction to Post-Relativism], Sergei Borodai traces in detail the trajectory of the maturation, formulation, perception, and large-scale influence of the ideas of the Boas-Sapir-Whorf line.

including ethnolinguistics, psycholinguistics, ethnopsychology, philosophy, cognitive science, etc.

The discovery of the linguistic specificity of thinking exerted particular influence on the theory of "conceptual metaphor" developed by George Lakoff and Mark Johnson.[69] Proceeding from comparisons of how time is conceptualized differently in SAE languages and some Amerindian languages, Whorf often remarked that Europeans understand time through the metaphor of space, e.g., approaching/coming, passing by, ahead of/behind oneself, etc. Lakoff picked up and developed this idea and discovered that speech and thinking generally, all the way down to everyday, routine speech practices, are thoroughly permeated and structured by metaphors and systems of combinations, insertions, and transferences of metaphors. A metaphor is no mere decoration, trope, or established linguistic construct like an idiom. The conceptual metaphors which have become established and fixed in a culture integrally constitute the organized cognitive models of a given society. Metaphors are not simply descriptions of the surrounding world; they participate in forming the cognitive style, the very thinking and key notions that define the world. From these deep notions grow styles of behavior, actions, evaluations and ideas about the world. Lakoff says that the whole of "social reality" and culture, which is necessary for any society within which systems of hierarchies and relationships to the environment function, is built on an established, corresponding structure of conceptual metaphors.

Also of interest is Lakoff's reference to Quine's idea that there is an "ontological relativity" built into every language. According to this approach, the conditions and very notion of truth cannot be given objectively in universal terms, as part of a universal and common logic, but rather will always be expressed in a specific way within a language and, by extension, a culture.

---

69 George Lakoff and Mark Johnson, *Metaphors We Live By* (Chicago: Chicago University Press, 1980); George Lakoff, *Women, Fire, and Dangerous Things: What Categories Reveal about the Mind* (Chicago: Chicago University Press, 1987).

Different languages divide the world into different categories of perception in a unique way, thereby creating the unique and diverse structures of metaphorical thinking. For example, there are peoples who completely lack any spatial metaphor for "right" and "left" in their language and thinking; for another people, the expression "the stone falls" is impossible if the speaker does not guarantee that that such an event happens; for others, the expression would be meaningless without clarifying whether the event is in the line of sight of the speakers or in relation to a specific landmark, etc. This thesis has enjoyed development in the new anthropology, which recognizes the plurality and uniqueness of different peoples' ontologies and rejects the uniform, Eurocentric, evolutionary, and progressist projects.[70] Thus, not only is there a plurality of different structures and modes of being-in-the-world (*in-der-Welt-sein*), but also the possibility of various intra-lingual and intra-cultural truths.

The role of metaphor is key to thinking and to the capacity of higher abstractions, as going further up requires a greater number of complex, interconnected metaphors. Here, the mythopoetics of language, never fully displaced, still makes itself manifest. In principle, it is impossible to speak of something higher "dryly" or "straightforwardly," without the use of allegories, figures of speech, transference, and systems of references to phenomena of the same or another kind. Conversely, as Lakoff notes, metaphors are less needed, or not needed at all, to describe physical laws and the material slice of being. The rich saturation of ordinary language with metaphors and their leading role in shaping the language-specific styles of thinking constitutes one of the most important matters when it comes to defending and upholding mythopoetic being-in-the-world.

Closely related to the topic of lingual and ontological relativity is the classic problem of the possibility of translating statements and meaning from one language into another, especially if these languages are not related and are even exotic

---

[70] We treated cultural, ontological, and natural pluralism in detail in *Tradition and Future Shock: Visions of a Future that Isn't Ours*.

to each other. From the standpoint of universalism, all natural languages are mutually translatable, i.e., a complete semantic translation is possible and can transmit the objective truth of an expression. This is an altogether naive delusion proper to Modernity in the spirit of objectivism and materialism. Several arguments can be raised against it:

(1) Most modal significations (if not all of them) cannot be divorced from their sociocultural and pragmatic context. In order to convey something said, it is also necessary to convey a person's understanding of what they have said and the circumstances in which something is said.

(2) Meaning is expressed within the framework of a language's grammatical system and bears the stamps of this system.

(3) Every language possesses a unique rhetorical style, including a unique means of reference.

(4) The formation of a semantic field in one language substantially differs from the analogous process in another language.

(5) The cognitive and neural processing of every language is unique.[71]

These quite obvious theses are most glaringly manifest when it comes to that most complex task of translating poetry and its tropes, and especially we're dealing with the words of unrelated and exotic languages. The lexemes that are intelligible and evoke corresponding associative series in their native culture might require several paragraphs or pages of meticulous explanations and examples in the language into which they are being translated. This gives rise to the inescapable dilemma of translation method, i.e., whether to render a translation word-for-word or interlinear, or completely change the structure and words of the original verse in order to convey not the words themselves, but the spirit of the author's expression.[72] Borodai emphasizes that for a more or less successful translation it is

---

71 Borodai, *Iazyk i poznanie*.

72 See, for example, the history of the translation of German poetry into Russian in the 19th century: G.I. Ratgauz, "Nemetskaia poeziia v Rossii" in idem (ed.), *Zolotoe pero. Nemetskaia, avstriiskaia i shveitsarskaia poeziia v russkikh perevodakh 1812-1970 gg.* (Moscow: Progress, 1974).

sufficient to evoke in the reader's consciousness a similar mental model within which the translated statement, text, or verse can function. Yet, it is impossible in principle to evoke a completely identical mental model with all the corresponding nuances, cultural references, implications, emotions, jargon, polysemy, contexts, idioms, dictums, etc. More often than not, translating requires significant changes or updating, expanding expressive means of the recipient language often at the cost of transferring (calquing or borrowing) grammatical and lexical structures and constructs from the donor language. Thus, the conclusion may be drawn that any word that sounds and functions in its native language with its polysemantic links and contexts cannot be fully translated or have complete analogues in another language.[73]

Finally, we can raise the more radical question of the fundamental possibility of translating that which the Indian grammarians, poets, and after them the philosophers of Kashmir Advaita called *dhvani*, that is the hidden voice of Shabdabrahman that is always present in any speech. Ritual and sacred mythopoetics are the space where the subtle play of decorations is a constant indication and gentle transmission, the maieutics of that state in which the mind slips into understanding the fact that in poetic speech it is the the Divine itself telling its tale. This require on the poet-translator's part the highest mastery of their own language so as to transplant the seed of this state into the soil of their native language. The *dhvani* will then resound in this language as well, or more precisely: upon inspiration by another model, a poetry will have been created which gives the Divine a place for its subtle voice craving an interlocutor.

The further development of the theses inspired by Sapir and Whorf, reinforced by a number of field studies and experiments, has led to the paradigm of post-relativism on the question of the mutual influence between language and thinking. The resulting

---

[73] Hans-Georg Gadamer remarked that when two thinkers do not know each other's languages, their conversation is ultimately no more than a dialogue between their translators. See Hans-Georg Gadamer, *Truth and Method*, trans. Joel Weinsheimer and Donald G. Marshall (London: Bloomsbury, 2020).

contours of this cognitive architecture and the role of language (in all its manifestations) therein can be briefly summarized as follows. Language occupies the central and connecting place in the cognitive architecture. It facilitates the formation of an original cognitive style and is the main means of accessing higher mental processes. Language can be understood as the organization and categorization of conceptual representations of significant elements from external experience. The formal system of language is in a state of dependency upon its content. Any natural language represents a unique system of distributions, references, and distinctions among various categories and definitions. Explaining any given category requires referring to other categories which in turn also require a system of explanations and references within one and the same language and culture.

Linguistic specificity begins whenever language interacts with information from a given external experience, construes the semantic sphere, and distributes this experience into categories. Linguistic specificity is manifest at all levels: grammar, morphology, syntax, classification in terms of parts of speech, discourse, and reference. Post-relativism concludes that, in essence, every natural language bears traits that are unique to it in all spheres.

> The main way in which language influences cognitive processes is by implicit verbalizations. Insofar as these verbalizations are genetically bound up with the language of a particular community, they inherit a particular semantic organization. It is for this reason that, in order to clarify the role of language in cognition, it is important to study the particular rhetorical style or conventional manner of speaking, and not abstract grammatical structure. The impact of a certain semantic or formal component will be higher the more often it is found in real speech, which means in inner speech. Conversely, the presence of some exotic grammeme which is almost never used in real speech entails a low relevance for cognition... Behind the linguo-specific structure of a language there must be a linguo-specific semantic map.[74]

---

74 Borodai, *Iazyk i poznanie*.

As a child grows up, their assimilating of a language means not only their immersion into a culture, but also the formation of a new cognitive architecture that is filled by language and permeates the work of other systems. Thus, a linguo-specific style of thinking is assimilated on the deep cognitive level as a fundamental system. Borodai writes:

> It bears highlighting at least three complex factors that heavily contribute to this process: sensorimotor constitution, cultural practices, and language system. These factors are interconnected. Sensorimotor constitution is partly innate and partly discloses itself over the course of the ontogenesis that occurs in socio-cultural conditions. A language system constitutes and transmits the current cultural knowledge as well as previously conventional practices that have undergone crystallization in linguistic form. Cultural practices form the broad field for ontogenesis, but they are partially transmitted through language and are unthinkable outside of language. The combination of these factors gives rise to a unique style of categorization which is in turn reflected in a unique cognitive style.[75]

It follows that language "specifies" memory, visual perception, auditory modality, motor system, gestures, imagination, spatial representations, and the emotional sphere. Moreover, the use of language, even in inner speech and thinking, leads to specific bodily reactions and the activation of the body's sensorimotor systems. In other words, whenever we speak to ourselves in our mind, our speech organs, tongue, jaw, larynx, as well as other parts of the body and individual muscles experience tensions and tones that are recordable by instruments. In some cases, general fatigue of the lips and cheekbones can be observed after intensive thinking just as if a person had been speaking out a whole array of information.

Taken together, the deep penetration of the body by language, the linguistic specification of sensory perception, and the theory of conceptual metaphors led John Lakoff to argue that the mind as a whole is embodied. In other words, the mind is not simply the superstructure, but is rooted in or "mixed in"

---

75 Ibid.

with corporeality. Therefore, speakers of different languages not only interpret corporeality differently, but literally have different bodily and sensorimotor responses and behaviors, and these differences are conditioned by language. These variations are fully accountable, noticeable, and play a role within their culture.

Furthermore, Borodai concludes that native speakers "should be studied primarily in authentic conditions, that is, within the boundaries of their native settlement, since the grounding of cognition is manifest not only in involvement in 'cultural knowledge,' but also in the bodily, experiential, motor attachment to a specific landscape, 'groundedness' in the literal sense of the word."[76] The rootedness of language in the body correlates with its external rootedness in the specific landscape in which its speaker, the tribe or people, dwells. This is connected to, among other things, how some peoples might not have a relative system of orientation (relative to themselves), but instead an absolute orientation centered around unique features of the area (for example, a mountain as the central point of orientation and indication of the position of things and people relative to it). All of this lucidly reinforces those theses and theories which posit the unavoidable and obvious influence of the surrounding landscape, space, climate, flora, and fauna — topogenesis in general — upon the culture of the people that dwells in their midst. The surrounding manifest world is reflected in culture and is linguistically specified in a complex way — all the way to the corporeality of a given person and their cognitive architecture.

This situation leads us to argue that it is impossible for the intertwinement of language, thinking, and environment to be unraveled and disintegrated into autonomous domains. One leading component cannot be singled out between them, because all three factors mutually condition one another in a particular here-being and being-in-the-world. If we prioritize one component out of the triad, then we can speculatively rank

---

76 Borodai, *Iazyk i poznanie*.

and rebuild the whole structure in a certain subordination to this leading component. This is what universalists, materialists, idealists, and cognitivists do in accordance with the principle that their systems hold to be primary. Language is etched into thinking like a complex ornamental pattern is etched into wood or metal.

Proceeding from the linguistic specificity of thinking, we can speak of perspectivism from the standpoint of sacred tradition as language. In turn, we can raise the question of the need to study the role and integral meaning of sacred words, metaphors, theonyms, and taboo systems within the system of the linguistic specificity of thinking. In full accordance with the fact that the elements and styles of speaking play a large role in this specification, it is necessary to devote attention to the dialects of estates, to sacred vocabulary, to the peculiarities of using special sacred names for the Divinities and even avoidances of directly naming them, and to their rendering in poetic tropes and decorations, etc. Their role in the specification of mythopoetic thinking must be clarified. Impetus to this course of study is also imparted by the fact that when Boas, Sapir, and Whorf drew parallels between the Amerindian, Central and South American languages on the one hand and the Standard Average European (SAE) on the other, they virtually ignored the huge, fundamental difference in cultural-epistemological paradigms between still archaic tribes (traditional, sacrocentric, albeit in some cases already severely crippled by colonization and genocide) and the already deeply modernized Europeans, and how such is reflected in their discourses and everyday language.

Despite the absolutely correct rejection of the progressive scale of "primitive vs. developed peoples," sacrocentrism on the one hand and aggressive secularism on the other have not been treated as significant. Thus, it would be more interesting and logical to compare, for example, the Proto-Germanic or Old Norse language before the Christianization of Scandinavia with the language of the Hopi or another archaic tribe, rather than with modern German. Despite the direct kinship between

German and Proto-Germanic, in the former there are reflected and at work secular and anti-sacred discourses, scientific and cognitive strategies, classifications of experiences in terms of different values, morphosyntactic and semantic shifts in terminology and lexemes, etc. Taking this problem into account requires close study at the intersection of linguistics and Traditionalism.

Once again, this time proceeding from yet another scientific paradigm and trajectory of argumentation, we have confirmation of the thesis that there is a plurality of truths as variations of tales within the singular space of language. Concepts dealing with the truthfulness of a statement and truth in general are also linguo-specific in culture, in the sphere of being of a particular people.

Based on the actual linguistic specificity of thinking, we can draw the fully concrete conclusion that there is a need to protect not only linguistic diversity, but also the regional dialectisms of one language within a large culture. Dialects show variations of speech styles and discursive forms, word usages, and whole reserves of archaisms, etc., all of which belong to the larger and unified cognitive style of the language and the colloquial koine. This diversity provides greater material for the scholar and generates the regional map of a particular language's variations. Linguistic specificity is a powerful tool for upholding mythopoetics and cultural autonomies, for affirming the plurality of thinking styles and truths, and for overthrowing modernist universalism.

Another close conclusion that follows from such a position is defending a linguistic pluralism that pays close attention to the semantic fields and connections that are formed when a new lexeme is incorporated into a recipient language. For example, all the words needed in modern society as they pertain to scientific-technological progress, technology, and the IT sector come mainly from English and Latin with modern semantics. Such words should be translated and positioned in a recipient language in semantic domains with negative, dangerous, anguishing, demonic connotations. We can find a textbook example of this in the highly purist Icelandic language. In modern society, a computer is a technology, an instrument which is treated strictly positively. A computer is a source of entertainment, a tool for work, a sign of wealth and social status, and in general a long-established element of a normal, even good life. In the Icelandic language, which doesn't tolerate borrowings, the lexeme *tölva*, consisting of the two words *tala* (number) and *völva* (seeress) was created to denote computer. The nuance is that, in Old Icelandic, as well as in other Germanic (and not only Germanic) societies, a seeress is far from always a pleasant female character. Most often, a seeress is a witch or an isolated women endowed with the negative sacred, her status closely associated with danger and the expectation of deceit. In the *Elder Edda*, Odin even appeals to a dead seeress by raising her out of her grave and forcing her to speak. This motif of necromancy is widely known, as is the general gender distribution of such magic. Feminine forms of divination and magic were either outright taboo or were not welcomed in patriarchal, male society. Thus, translating the notion of computer as *tölva* functions in Icelandic with reference to the witch-like, the feminine, the necromantic, and partially taboo semantic field. Such rigor of interpretation is not always observed in translations, and it does not always function properly within modern society precisely because of the difference in paradigms of thinking that we pointed out above. In the modern society of Iceland, a different episteme and system of values is in operation, one in which the traditional and the religious are regarded as a stage in the development of society long ago overcome and abandoned as the "childhood of humanity," hence references to "digital seeresses" do not invoke the due caution and practices warranted by operating with such a device. They are merely a tribute to established customs, an extravagant translation, and a safe reference to cultural remnants, like "folk comics" (cf. Russian *lubok*).

Borodai speaks of the threat of losing linguistic diversity thusly: "When faced with more 'prestigious' languages, the languages of small peoples are subjected to their influence and are often subjected to their reductions." This is indeed the case, hence the thesis that "language does not degrade, but is constantly changing" should be discarded as naive, narrow-minded, and even ideologically biased. It bears recognizing the obvious degeneration of many languages, including the leading European ones, not to mention the extinction of languages that were and are peripheral to Eurocentric civilization.

The abundance of borrowed words, whole expressions, and styles of speaking and writing is often dictated by altogether mundane considerations for fashion, the imitation of social status within a political or cultural colony (the aboriginal who imitates the language and style of speech of the metropolis thinks that his status is increased), marketing strategies (Anglicism sells better than the usual native word), and general cultural-political hegemony on the global or regional scale. This directly leads to the degeneration of a language and culture. While recognizing that the world at large is moving along a downward trajectory of decay entailing the diminishment of the good and its eschatological source, it also bears recognizing that language within the world is subject to the same decline.

Ferdinand de Saussure argued that "there is nothing in language but differences." Following Carl Schmitt's definition of "the Political" as a matter of differentiating between friend and enemy, we can affirm the immanently political nature of language. In this light, the preservation of dialects takes on a political dimension in contrast to the state center and literary norm of a given language. For centuries, the numerous rebellious peoples of Zomia in Southeast Asia have practiced actively, consciously changing their language so as to prevent themselves from speaking the language of the Chinese Empire or local rulers.[77]

---

77 See James S. Scott, *The Art of Not Being Governed: An Anarchist History of Upland Southeast Asia* (New Haven: Yale University Press, 2009).

A significant contribution to the formation of linguistic standards, even at the intersection with purism, has been made by translations of the Bible into local languages. In the genesis of the English nation, for instance, one of the most significant events in the formation of the English language, as well as in the resolution of confessional problems, was the King James Bible. In the Russian Orthodox tradition, it is believed that distortions in the text of the Bible are introduced by demons who interfere with and misguide the hand of the monk-scribe. Misprints made under the influence of demons or frivolous word choices distort the true meaning of the Gospel, leading people to heresies, erroneous interpretations, and the death of their soul. Hence the sacrally motivated struggle for the purity and uniformity of translations and canons. An analogous example exists in Islam, in the story surrounding the "Satanic verses" allegedly crossed out of the Koran by Muhammad for being inspired by Ibis.

On the flat plane of secular, Western-centric globalization, the uniformization of language is possible only in step with an ever lowering bar. Languages must be replaced or simplified to meet the common version of the hegemonic language (Simple English) or degrade under the influence of global Internet slang and texting methods (1337 speak, Emojis). This facilitates the onset of uniformity and globalization over cultures, whereby all local civilizational-cultural features, including language, are turned into exotic-cosmetic frame for one and the same content.

Recognizing the influence of the environment on the formation and preservation of a language, we can conclude that the global urban monotony of megacities and even more so the virtual environment contribute only to fundamental, existential alienation, degradation, the molding of defective and limited forms of language and speech styles, instilling in natural languages pronounced tendencies and elements from synthetic languages, such as programming languages and the subcultures surrounding them. Ultimately, all three elements in the dynamic interrelationship of language, environment, and thinking are subject to decline, dissolution, and involution.

The counter-thesis from the side of mythopoetic thinking is the affirmation of the strict need to immerse children into the linguistic environment of tradition from the perinatal period, such as songs and lullabies sung to the fetus by the mother and midwives (ποίησις), and over the whole course of their ontogenesis, upbringing, and education. The child ought to assimilate from their surrounding environment and family the local dialect, speech style, vocabulary (including sacred and taboo), etc., which will cultivate a a direct embedding of the linguistic specification into their cognitive structures, and thus render high metaphysics and mythopoiesis even more open and easier to assimilate. This, of course, is a rather big problem that inevitably raises the issue of opposition to the surrounding environment of the dominant culture and separation from society as the bearer of a hostile culture. These problems, which are beyond the scope of our present examination, must be solved at the intersection of philosophy, linguistics, folklore, and pedagogy.

Another conclusion of obvious importance is the urgent need to preserve and study the isolated and archaic languages and cultures that still survive.

Another interesting case study is posed by philosophical language, which is distinguished by a high degree of syncretism: it operates with the most complex spatial, historical-temporal, cross-cultural, and interdisciplinary constellations of terms, metaphors, and images, which are often elevated to the level of highly abstract categories. Philosophical language also has the tendency to generate independent discourses that refer to and operate with respect to other philosophical concepts and narratives rather than donor cultures. In other words, the field of philosophical thought and language within the scope of classical metaphysics has the tendency of becoming detached from the soil and forming a field of "pure thought." However, as studies by linguists have shown, the grammar of language and folk etymologies have exerted a strong influence on the development of philosophical categories of thinking and theological constructs.

This played a definite role in the (onto-)linguistic turn in philosophy in the 20th century. We can speak of a dialectical or hermeneutic approach to the development and disclosure of the philosophical foundations of folk language with excursions into high philosophical metalanguage, and translations made from the latter in the spirit of a thinker's descent from the mountain peak down into the valleys. Discoveries by linguists and the post-relativist project of grounding the linguistic specification of thinking can have a powerful impact on philosophy and the plurality of *logoi*, i.e., paradigms of thought which do not have to be reduced to a universal cognitive model, culture, or fate.

Whorf wrote that metaphysics is implicit in language. It is well known that the grammar of the Greek language decisively influenced the structure of Greek and, consequently, all of Western metaphysics. Émile Benveniste drew parallels between the structure of the Greek language and Aristotle's categories:

> The category of substance corresponds to the noun, the category of quantity and quality to the adjective, the category of relation to the comparative adjective, the category of place and time to adverbs of place and time, the category of position to the middle voice, the category of state to the perfect voice, the category of action to the active voice, and the category of undergoing to the passive voice.[78]

In the SAE languages, "time," "space," "cause," "effect," "progress," "past," "future," "substance," and "matter" are essential segments. According to Whorf, the metaphysics of the culture of SAE languages can be generally outlined in the following way:

> Thus the implicit metaphysics of SAE culture presup poses a uniformly flowing 1-dimensional time-order, a 3-dimensional space- order distinct from it, a universe consisting of a void or 'holes' b substance or matter which has 'properties' and forms island-like 'bodies', an absolute un bridgeable difference between the matter and the 'holes', events 'caused' by 'preceding' events, things happening to matter, nothing happening in the void.[79]

---

78 Borodai, *Iazyk i poznanie*.

79 B.L. Whorf, "Yale Report" (1938), in Penny Lee, *The Whorf Theory Complex: A Critical Reconstruction* (Amsterdam: John Benjamins, 1996), 264.

Furthermore, citing his favorite example of the Hopi language, Whorf shows the contrast between the different structure of metaphysics implicit in the latter and the modern European languages:

> The Hopian metaphysics has no time and space orders like ours has a contrast of two realms; a the causal, or unmanifested which includes the future and the mental-psychic and is dynamic and in a process the end of which is manifestation, and b the manifested, which includes the present, past, and physical or apparent, and does not act causally per se, but contributes to causality by helping as it were to maintain a general well-being that aids the cycle of events. Within realm b there is a contrast of two modes of existence and/or extension; punctual (outlined around a point-center) and tensive (extending more or less indefinitely), which contrast takes over much of the work of the SAE matter-void contrast and is worked out throughout grammar and vocabulary in literally thousands of ways...[80]

Borodai also cites the research project of V.G. Lysenko, whose main thesis says that "the development of atomism in Greek and Indian philosophy was conditioned by reflection on the phonological structure of these Indo-European languages, while the specific phonological structure of the Chinese language and its method of fixing the written word prevented the formation of an atomistic natural philosophy."[81]

Charles Kahn developed Benveniste's ideas to show that an important condition for the development of Greek metaphysics was the specificity of the Greek verb εἰμί, which combines the semantics of existence, vitality, truth, and the matrix of stativity, durativity, and locativity. Greek philosophers used all these shades of the word without specifying its nuances, since such were implicitly clear to them. Kahn thus concludes: "We can say that Parmenides created the metaphysical concept of Being by bringing together all of the aspects and nuances of the Greek verb into a single concept of the immutable Fact or Entity:

---

80 Ibid., 265.
81 Borodai, *Iazyk i poznanie*.

to eon, 'that which is.'"⁸² In this example, we encounter yet another striking feature of the difference between the archaic state of metaphysically, sacredly saturated languages, and the average modern SAE and its culture. This difference lies in fundamental polysemy, semantic richness, and symbolism, all of which are characteristic not only of key ritual and mythopoetic terms, but also everyday verbs and nouns. For instance, the ancient Indian notion of *Rta* (from Indo-European *h_2R-to*, "right") is generally untranslatable into other languages, as it is simultaneously and literally means "truth," "order," "cosmos," "being," "law," "way," "sacred word," "prayer," "hymn," etc., and in other texts its meanings encompass associations with the sun, light, fire, movement, cart, axle, sacrifice, fat, etc.

In deeply sacred, mythopoetic cultures, such words and notions are manifold — ποίησις, τέχνη, οὐσία, το ὄν, λόγος, *runa*, *oðr*, *Sein*. They are irreducible to any single meaning that would be familiar and comfortable for instrumental use and translation by modern man. Such words and their status cannot be algorithmized. In this lies the fundamental difference with the modern paradigm which strives to truncate the polysemy of words and reduce symbol to one strict sign or formula. Key here is the early Wittgenstein's "atomic fact," his project of cleansing language of allegory, and the complimentary project of analytical philosophy, which hedges all stakes on logical-mathematical accounting, analysis, and propositioning about philosophy and the world. In turn, this lays the specific instrumental foundations for creating a basic mathematical language to account for, digitally calculate, and completely digitize the manifest world. Heidegger spoke of this prevailing closing of all access to Beyng as the domination of the *Gestell*, the reduction of all Being to "calculating and calculable beings." In other words, the trajectory of man's alienation from his being has as its horizon a virtual culture in which the only that exists is that which can be accounted for in mathematical language and

---

82 Charles H. Kahn, *The Verb 'Be' in Ancient Greek* (Indianapolis: Hackett Publishing Company, 2003), xxviii.

ultimately reduced to binary technological calculation. Drawing on Lakoff's thought, it could be said that this is a conscious movement away from highly abstract metaphors, philosophy, metaphysics, symbolic culture, complex natural languages and the authentic here-being of man within the world, within his unique language culture and cosmos.

At this point, we cannot ignore the special case of the philosophy of Martin Heidegger, who accomplished a fundamental linguistic turn in ontology with his maxim that "language is the house of Being." Following the event of the "turn" (*Kehre*) in his philosophy, Heidegger turned to the primal matrix of language in which we constantly pronounce and utter Being in the regular verb "to be" — in German *ist, bist, war, waren, wessen, west*, etc. In the Russian language, this verb linkage has practically disappeared, as we can speak without the obligatory indication of "is" without losing the meaning. To Heidegger belongs the important indication that "*die Sprache spricht*" — "language speaks," or "telling tells [itself]" — expressed in his classic manner of forming a verb out of a noun. Heidegger thus called for paying close attention to what language itself constantly says in itself, in its discourse (*Rede*) and talking (*Gerede*) that are existentials of Dasein's dwelling in the world.

The necessity of the turn towards language in Heidegger's philosophizing proceeded from different premises and grounds than those underlying the project of linguistic relativity for Sapir, Whorf, and later post-relativism, but they have a rather close and altogether specific horizon of convergence and mutual enrichment in the sphere of philosophy.

At the center of Heidegger's later project stood the leap of thinking about Another Beginning of philosophy as the Event (*Ereignis*), the eventing of the truth of here-being beyond classical metaphysics, whose decisions and solutions Heidegger held to be erroneous and irrelevant. Such a posing of the question in the light of ontolinguistics demanded that Heidegger create and develop an entirely different style of speaking and expressing philosophy. This language is grounded in a hermeneutic circling, in immersion into words, in rejecting the ready-made concept-words of metaphysics. Heidegger developed a special, non-conceptual language for speaking and clearly embodying his program, at the heart of which lies an interlinking: "another beginning of philosophy requires another thinking, and that means another language." Language as the historical word is the "hail of the gods" of earth and world. For the German "prince of philosophers" and "Black Forest shaman," attuned and rooted in the mountainous provincial landscape, there can be no question of creating some kind of artificial language like Esperanto. Rather, Heidegger developed the language of Another Beginning out of the very same Swabian dialect of the German language, which he began to structure and pronounce in a special way and with sensitivity to archaisms that mark the important distinctions made over the course of his thinking (*Sein* → *Seyn*, *ist* → *west*, etc.).

As we can see, the field of intersections between linguistics, philosophy, metaphysics, the sacred, politics, ethnography, thinking, and education is so enormous and full of examples, projects, tasks, and problems, that even an approximate map of such a continent cannot possibly be described and composed in brief.

To return to the metaphor of tradition as language and as a tree, we can firmly conclude that there is the fundamental possibility, like an open path with no hindrances, of speaking forth another myth, or other myths, and engaging in the mythopoetic and philosophical (philo-mythical) maieutics of planting and cultivating a new tree in the soil of the heavens and the soil of earth.

The Metaphysics of the Mask

A person who goes through an initiation ritual becomes twice-born. Their first birth from their mother and father is not enough; they need to be born not only into society, but also into a name and status in view of the spirits, ancestors, and Divinities. The death of a faceless, nameless boy or girl, still shrouded by suspicion over whether they are humans and the community's own or foundlings left by spirits, is an obligatory part of the trial and path to rebirth. Initiation is the primary social and sacred axis.

A special role in the spiritual realization and, by all accounts, the soteriology of the ancient Greeks was played by the mysteries, the closed sacraments for those who are already initiated. So much has been said about the mysteries that there is no need to dwell on their various aspects here. But it still remains worth emphasizing the extreme importance of being initiated into them, which elevated the neophyte into communion not only with a circle of others like him, but with the fundamental, root myth and literal miracle. The initiate took upon himself the strictest vow to keep the secret of the mystery, so we know very little about the inner aspects and deeds of the mystery apart from reconstructions. In other cases, the mysteries became a phenomenon of such significance that they were completely equated with the cults of Deities and even whole cities, such as Eleusis, or they were subjected to large-scale persecution, like the Bacchanalia in Rome.

Eleusis became the archetype of the mysteries par excellence, and it is Eleusis that is of great interest to us here. The core of the Eleusinian cult was a mystery that is clearly of agrarian origin, connected with fertility, the afterlife and rebirth, and the myth of Hades' abduction of Persephone. The most important symbol was grain, a barley spike or wheat, the fields of which surrounding Eleusis were used to prepare the intoxicating drink known as *kykeon*.

Persephone was the daughter of Demeter and Zeus. When Persephone went missing, her mother, the Deity of fertility, fell into a great sorrow that caused the cessation of growth and harvest in the world. In this plot, we see traces of the archaic motif of a female Deity who simultaneously gives life and brings death, like earth that gives rise to shoots and swallows bodies (like seeds). As the mother mourned her daughter, Eleusis became a place of suffering and sorrow. When a long crop failure and lack of seedlings threatened the world with death, Zeus intervened and brought Persephone back from the underworld, having reached an agreement with Hades that his wife would spend six months with him and six months in the world of humans.

Karl Kerényi honed in on this myth as the most important nerve of the mystery revealed in the central room of the Eleusinian temple that was closed to everyone else. According to Kerényi, the essence of the mystery was a visual demonstration of the miracle of the emergence of life from death, of how "death gave birth." After having become the personification of barren, dead earth, Demeter once again spread her shoot, i.e., death gave birth, just as a grain dies in order to provide space for germination. According to one theory, the initiate was shown the miracle of germination and the swelling of the ear of wheat. Nor should we lose sight of the psychedelic effect associated with ascesis before the mystery and the consumption of the ritual *kykeon* drink, which was brewed from wheat grains and mixed with wine. According to yet another version, ears of corn were an important part of the recipe. In any case, the sacred drink should not be interpreted as a profane or purely "mechanical" explanation of the mystery as something illusory, something imagined only in a state of delirium and intoxication. This approach is completely irrelevant. Sacred inebriation plays a definite and immense role in archaic traditions and often acts as a gate, bridge, or conductor to states and knowledge that have a completely different nature and source than the drink itself.

The Eleusinian mysteries bore a vividly soteriological nature: those who were initiated no longer feared death and knew of the rebirth of the soul. It is no coincidence that one of the main roles played in the mysteries belongs to the Deity of death, Hades, whose actions trigger the chain of events that conclude with the mysterious revelation of the consoled Demeter. Translated from Greek, the name Ἀΐδης means "invisible," "unseen." As already mentioned, it shares the same root as the word ἰδέα, that is the visibility of form, an image. Hades is the unseen Deity whose essence is to hide, to conceal the dead and Persephone, whose mother cannot find her due to her non-presence, her absence from the middle world. Hades was sometimes depicted as having his face turned away, or without a face altogether, which emphasizes his "non-present" nature. Death, thus, is associated with absence — of the deceased and of growth, of new birth, of the juices of life. By kidnapping Persephone and taking Demeter from the world, Hades gained power over the world in holding back the sprouting of all plants, crops, fruits, and the births of all creatures.

But our friend Heraclitus left us with a strange passage in which he attributes the bacchic and phallic rampages of Dionysus to Hades himself, thereby literally identifying the two Deities with each other. In favor of this speak their common epithets, such as Eubouleus ("Good Counselor") and Chthonos ("Underground"). Karl Kerényi adds some important indications: "In general, there was a close tie between the wild fig tree and the subterranean Dionysos: his mask was cut from its wood in Naxos. To this day the Greeks have a superstitious fear of sleeping under a fig tree. A wild fig tree designated the entrance to the underworld in places other than Eleusis."[83]

Dionysus is the son of Zeus and Persephone under the name Zagreus, meaning that Hades is at least his uncle, which brings us close to the avunculate we have already encountered. In the *Sisyphus*, Aeschylus calls him the son of Hades. Dionysus Zagreus is also the patron of the mysteries. It was he who was taken by surprise by the Titans when he looked into the mirror,

---

83 Carl Kerényi, *Eleusis: Archetypal Image of Mother and Daughter*, trans. Ralph Manheim (Princeton: Princeton University Press, 1967), 35-36.

and later in the form of a bull was driven out, torn to pieces, boiled, and devoured by them.

Hades and Dionysus share an even deeper connection than the intersection of kinship and mythological lines, the semantic fields of life, death, and reigning or descending into Hades. They are connected by the problem of appearance, of guise, and of bringing an image to visible presence. In other words, if Hades is Ἀΐδης, the invisible, the unseen, the faceless, then Dionysus is the Deity of metamorphosis who manifests himself in an unlimited array of images and faces (Zeus, Cronus, the bull, lion, snake, baby, toddler, horse, the thyrsus, phallus, etc.) which figure as masks. Thus, the contrast between absence and excess is held together around an absent or inaccessible center. We do not see Hades because of his concealing, withholding nature which leads to fatal lack, and we do not see Dionysus because he has an extraordinary multiplicity of manifestations whose motley, carnival shapeshifting steals and carries away our attention.

Here, we arrive at one of the most important points: classical, ancient, European theater's origin in the mysteries and in close connection with Dionysus. In the multifaceted phenomenon of theater, itself unique in the structure of the cosmos, what interests us is the realm of metamorphosis and the metaphysics of masks. The very word θέατρον is connected to θεωρία, "theory," which means a spectacle, a site for beholding and contemplating.

In folk theater, which is connected with scenes from the mysteries and agrarian sacraments, the setting for the plot is everyday life: scenes were played out on the porch, in the street, in the market, in the yard, or out in the fields. Everyone took part in acting out and reciting the mythical stories and roles. Myth was revealed and reproduced directly in the fabric of life here and now in connection with the calendar cycles. More complex and refined theater is defined by the presence of a special site for the performance of comedy or drama (theater as *topos*) and the emergence of the figure of the spectator, the viewer, who contemplates the performance as a myth unfolding before him. On this point it bears recognizing the presence of a certain degree of alienation between the viewer and the action, unlike the archaic folk festival played out in the middle of the streets.

Normative of mature Greek theater was the location and architecture of the Theater of Dionysus in Athens, located on the southeastern slope of the Acropolis. Thus, in the very center of the *polis*, the focal point of power, there is an orchestra of metamorphoses and Dionysianism. Behind the orchestra and opposite the *theatron* is a special space called the *skene*, the place where, hidden from view (like the mysteries), the Dionysian metamorphoses of the actors' changing masks and costumes took place. A little lower down the slope behind the theater was a separate sanctuary dedicated to Dionysus. A small altar to Dionysus, called the *thymele*, was obligatorily raised on the site of every theater.

Metaphysically speaking, the stage figures as the space for taming the dangerous elements of metamorphoses and *polemos*. In theater, the leading metaphor is shifted from war to play. We know metaphors of argument as play, war as a party, and stable phrases such as *Endspiel*, "theater of war" and the like from many languages and cultures. Through the metaphor of play and theatrical performance, the basic structure of the manifestation of the Divine as *polemos* is transformed into a play of comedy or drama. The Divine manifests itself in the world in a regime of duality and fragmentation into many (πολλα). War, play (the enjoyment of the Divine, cf. Indian *Lila*), and eros are essentially modes of dealing with pairs and multiplicities within the *imaginaire* of the Mind that is at once turned both to the world and towards the One. Here, theater acts as a mirror, or rather a fractal doubling of space where extremely serious plots of drama, tragedy, satire, farce, comedy, and eros play out — a space residing within the absolute Divine's beholding of itself as, all at once, the spectator and the actor, the troupe, the director, and the surrounding world. The absolute Divine is the one that both hides itself and finds itself in the role of someone in the play that it itself imagines. Such, at least, is the structure of the whole manifest cosmos proposed by Kashmir Shaivism with its non-dual aesthetics and high theological metaphysics of theater.

It is worth noting, however, that unlike the authentic and original theater of Greece or the metaphysics of theater in Advaita-Shaivism, the Germanic-Scandinavian tradition never yielded its own theater out of its own soil. All the traveling troupes and later medieval folk-theatrical performances were taken from Greco-Roman culture. The Germanics do not have their own authentic theater and mask, although some moments and scenes from the Eddic ballads are quite amenable to the stage. For instance, scenes of feuds being resolved through fun and games of arguments, such as when Loki makes the vengeance-seeking Skadi laugh, are plots virtually ready-made for folklore productions. Moreover, the Germanics had a Deity who wore masks and concealed himself, and their myths are full of frequent motifs of shifting guises. But this metaphysics was not developed within the Germanic Logos, probably due to the emphasis on war, thinking, and then philosophy as the leading Germanic principles. In philosophy, meanwhile, the metaphor of theater is often used for discussing and identifying the ontological status of the actor and the "subject" as such within the framework of the relationship between actor and the role or mask they play and wear.

The word "mask" comes to us from the Romance languages (French *masque*, Latin *masca*) and from the Proto-Germanic *maskā, which has a common bundle of meanings: to cover, to hide, often with woven fabrics (cf. Russian *maskirovka* — "camouflage," "military deception"). In the Germanic languages, "mask" also refers to dirt or a solution that is literally rubbed over one's face, hence the modern English "grime" (from Proto-Germanic *grīmô), "grimace," and the stable semantic reference to gloom and the ominousness of appearance in the word "grim" (Proto-Germanic *grimmaz — evil, creepy). In the Icelandic language and in Germanic-Scandinavian mythology, Grímnir, "the Mask-Wearer," is one of Odin's heiti. The Latin word *persona*, whose origin is unclear but probably has similar roots, means mask, character, or figure. The latter goes back to the Latin *figūra*, which means to give form, to distinguish contours, to give appearance (cf. linguistic de-finition).

The Russian word for mask, *lichina*, comes from the poetic Proto-Slavic *likъ* ("face," "form," "image"). *Lichina* is a seeming appearance, a substitution for the face. Hence the legitimate interpretation of *lichnost'* ("personality") as a kind of social mask, a set of roles in the family, society, and politics, a place in a hierarchy, or the set and structure of a person's individual characteristics, etc. Our *lichnost'*, our "persona-lity," is our mask for being-with-others on the sociological dimension; it is a social appearance that we don like a mask, like the specific mask-object of folklore. Accordingly, any social personality or guise is always not our very own self, *Selbst*, but a bringing of some qualities to the fore while hiding others, i.e., a conscious caricature of our *lichnost'*. If we follow the path of definition further, then the recognition that the *lichina*, the mask or persona, is always not we ourselves, leads us to what in Eastern teachings is a most interesting conclusion: our ego or mind which we suppose to be our immutable "I" is merely one form of oblivion and substitution, a false selfhood, which in its vanity endlessly drapes over and diverts attention from our true "I." In other words, even what we consider to be "undoubtedly ourselves" might very well be recognized to be one or another form of *masque*.

A character, a personage, only becomes real when the actor puts on the mask, comes into the role, and leaves his own "I" aside to give the persona full ontological status. The self under the mask is concealed, and it would be wrong to address it during the play, for then only the mask-personage is responsible for all the actions, words, and events. This is partly similar to the Advaitist description of the nature of the manifest world. In the theistic monism of Shaivist Advaita, there exists only one absolute reality: Shiva, Shiva's consciousness. Accordingly, the cosmos and the manifold atmans exist only within his boundless imagination, within Maya. Insofar as Shiva is "absolute reality," then everything he imagines is no mere phantasm of the mind, but is absolutely real by virtue of belonging to his consciousness. A special logic is manifest here. The manifest world is extremely authentic and real; it cannot simply be dispelled like mirages of hot air over the surface of a road, as other darshanas teach of the nature of the manifest world. The Divine is present in any moment of time, in any event, in any particular thing, and therefore immanent in each and every thing at once. The position, hierarchy, and status of the sacred, even when defiled, are given according to the plot, hence Advaita does not mean, and is not reducible to, any egalitarian decay and confusion, nor does it contradict the hierarchical structure of the cosmos.

It is precisely this dimension that we are dealing with in the mysteries, in the ritualized celebrations of folk theater as *imitatio Dei*, in the direct repetition of myth, when the living give up their places, bodies, hands, and faces to masks, to the personages and figures of spirits, demons, ancestors, and Deities. A genuine shift and replacement of subjects takes place in the middle world; enthusiasm in the direct meaning of being enraptured by the Divinities descends upon the actors, and the humans-as-actors disappear altogether in offering themselves up as the space for real and present theophany. But in order for this to happen, one must hide himself, put his self into the shadows, and become a clearing for the entry and action of the spirit, the being, the personage, or the Deity in oneself and through oneself. A mask, a metamorphosis, a change of identity is needed. Masks are found everywhere, in all corners of the earth, among archaic tribes as well as in classical civilizations; they have come down to us from the deepest antiquity and are one of the symbols of culture as a whole.

There are several scenarios at play here. First, giving up one's place to the mask means concealing one's personality (*lichnost'*). The personality in and of itself is a social mask which in some way reflects and in some way conceals our selfhood at its deepest core and as a whole. Thus, there is change in masks over the self.

Second, the mask itself has duality, acting simultaneously as the new face of a personage (the one being depicted by the mask, on the obverse side) and as an object, i.e., the mask as a ritual thing which is in some sense like its empty reverse side into which we put our face. The craftsmanship of the mask does not matter — it can be ornamental, realistic, or simply a piece of bark freshly peeled off a tree with with eyeholes poked into it, or a clay cast hardened in the hands.

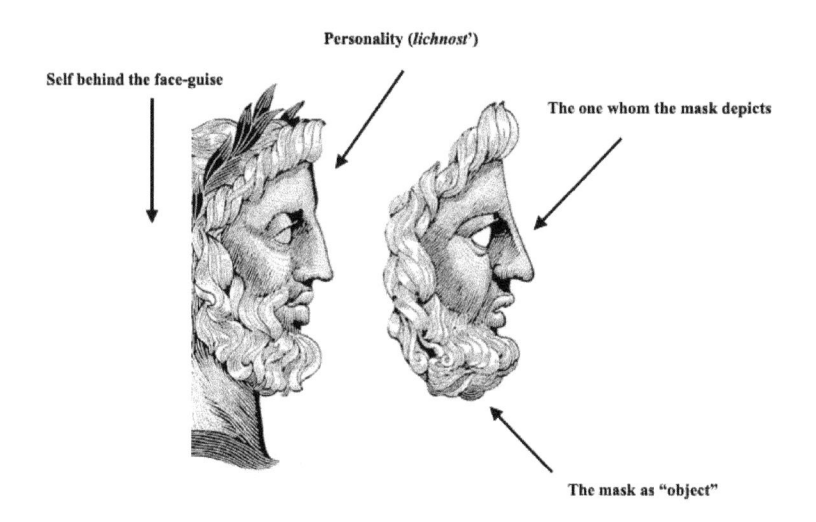

Personality (*lichnost'*)

Self behind the face-guise

The one whom the mask depicts

The mask as "object"

From here on out, the winding paths of the situations diverge. We know from traditional doctrines that a person's deep identity is their Divinehood manifest within them in the middle world: *tat tvam asi* and the indistinguishable fusing of Atman and Brahman. When a person puts on the mask of a Deity, there can be an ecstatic implosion, a complete fitting and coinciding of the deep Divine self and the Deity on the outside, for the being of which man provides himself. But where and what are we ourselves in such a situation? We are in-between, like a permeable membrane, the Divinehood outside and inside. The ego-persona and the social mask-layers fall away, leaving us out in the open possibility of letting and releasing the Deity through us. One literally, physically feels like the reverse side of the mask of the Divine actor into which one inserts his "face."

Metaphors of "nesting," "interlayering," "inputting," reflecting, fractality, aporia, and recursion reign here. The mask acts as both the signifier (the symbol referring unto something) and as the signified (what the symbol refers to). Then, upon taking off the mask of the Deity, we return to ourselves as an individual personality (*lichnost'*), but on an even deeper level the very same Divinehood sees and speaks through us, like an actor through the mask's empty eye sockets and open mouth.

The mask is Dionysus. Not the one who puts it on, and not the one whom it depicts, but the very boundary and event of metamorphosis. The situation is even more interesting when it comes to a mask that only hides, that doesn't express anything, i.e., a faceless mask whose guise does not even refer to any anthropomorphic silhouettes. To whom or what do we present ourselves as *chronos* and *topos* (*Zeit und Da*) when putting on a faceless mask? Obviously, the leading motif here is the absence of any subject whatsoever. This leads us to two things: to the death of the subject, in which case the concealing mask is an alternative symbol of a burial shroud, a grave, Hades (and we might also mention pure corporeality, since the subject-ego is absent, leaving only the corpse), or, in the case of classic deixis, to the apophatic instance of the Nothing.

Finally, in modern conditions, we can raise the question of the metaphysics and ontological status of the person who wears a mirror mask which in form (figure) doesn't express anyone, but which reflects absolutely everything. In this optic, the person and his I are concealed, but to whom and to what, to what personage, are being and subjectivity delegated? To none, for there is no subject, but there is the whole world that converges in the focal point of the mirror mask. Thus, in there is no-one and nothing in the center, but around it absolutely everything is reflected and unfolds.

Classical as well as extravagant masks depicting no-one or a mirror still belong to the register of beings, i.e., they "are," even if only as indications of absence. Moreover, in language and speech we can draw a direct analogy between masks and metaphors, kennings, symbols, and names. On the whole, the word is also a mask, and a mask is a symbol, and it follows that it belongs to the order of language.

The situation is manifoldly complicated in theology, for all the names of the Divinities, all of their theophanies, descriptions, epithets, guises, stories, deeds, and myths are all sets of masks which have been seen, heard, perceived, and placed on altars by people across different cultures. There is no point in drawing any analogy with the vulgar argument that "man invented the Divinities," for the emphasis has already shifted to how the Divinities or the Divine have in all times remained concealed, while on every altar or in every cult and mystery stands a mask, beautifully decorated in *mythos* and with a deictic sign in the form of holes for the eyes and mouth which point to the apophatic dimension.

The pantheon of Divinities is a circle of masks which the ineffable and unknowable Divine tries on and, upon choosing one, in an absolutely credible and fully-fledged way becomes it, i.e., becomes a specific Deity and its *mythos* that fascinate peoples and enchant unions of epopts.

People peer into the masks of the Deities and put them on. The Divine also peers into its masks, but, unlike man, puts it not on its "face," but onto everything exterior, simultaneously creating this exterior and leaving the center empty. This is somewhat similar to the notion of how a Deity manifests itself in the world and in so doing renders itself manifest ($\pi o i \eta \sigma \iota \varsigma$), reflected in nature, traditions, language, and the people who invoke, pray to, and praise it. The Divinities, then, are in essence Being's visions of itself in various *mythos*-generating manifestations. From here we come to the recognition that all being(s)-as-a-whole (*Seiende-im-Ganze*, the cosmos, totally everything) is, in the light of any monistic ontotheology erected around and from any known Deity, none other than the manifestation of one or another mask. The world, nature, and we ourselves are a mask turned around and facing us. The faces and enigmas of the Divine are the manifest world. But this cosmic mask hangs over the void of the Nothing. In Russian folklore, there is the beautiful riddle of the "masked faceless," to which the response can only be recursive: it is an "enigma," a "riddle."

The mask, the concealing-unconcealing play, is, for instance, the faithful conviction in the distinction between atman and Brahman. The metaphor of matter and Maya as a veil attains theatrical dimension not only as the curtain, but as the fabric covering the self. At the same time, everything extant thrown on top of and projected over the Nothing, with all the filigree-carved patterns of natures and the fates of people and peoples, points to the Nothing itself like a mirror.

To return to the image of a reflective mask on this ontotheological and metaphysical level, if we move from exterior "objective nature" to its "subjective" source-center, then we once again discover only its reflection. In the best case, we understand that this reflection is a reflection onto something, and then we'll be dealing with the figure of a Deity hidden by and within the world. All traditions and religions dwell on this point in speaking of a supreme Father-Deity or a Divine Mother and their offspring kin and humans. The light of the glory of the Divine outshines, and thus obscures, any suspicion as to the masquerade character of all being(s), even if it unfolds as a fully-fledged, credible, real and present drama within the world.

When the mask is removed, the world literally disappears. Fear of death is fear of the mask that the Divine removes in order to put it in front of itself and to look (*theoresis—teatron*) into its empty eye sockets where its eyes used to be. Meanwhile, the human being looking into the mask's empty eye sockets sees himself as the Divine contemplating itself from out of the depths.

II
WHERE NO WORD IS

Prolegomena

Evgeny Golovin said that a poet can write only one actually good, genuinely poetic poem in his whole life, after which he might as well either stop writing altogether or rest content with writing unsuccessful works. But the one real work already makes him a poet; the laurels cannot be taken off his head. To Stefan George belong a number of beautiful verses, but we will devote close attention to only one, indeed his most important poem.

Stefan George (1868-1933) began to take shape as a poet very early on under the influence of the French symbolists Paul Verlaine and Stéphane Mallarmé. Experiencing a crisis of identity in his youth, he nevertheless decided to write his verses in German and become a German poet, not a French one.[84] George's unordinary personality, the daring poetic language with which he allowed himself to write in a rather free and experimental style, and his aspiration for pure "art for art's sake" ensured him glory and recognition. After publishing the journal *Blätter für die Kunst*, in the early 1990s he founded a hermetic and influential circle with like-minded thinkers and admirers, the *George-Kreis*.

The George-Kreis brought together a number of Germany's foremost scholars of culture, philosophers, poets, politicians, and public figures, such as Friedrich Gundolf, Ernst Kantorowicz, Ludwig Klages, the Stauffenberg brothers[85], Karl Reinhardt, and others. Many of them passed the circle's ideas on and influenced German culture in the Weimar Republic and the early years of the Third Reich.

Besides the art of the word, at the center of the circle's attention was the philosophy of Nietzsche and, by a later point,

---

[84] Robert E. Norton, *Secret Germany: Stefan George and his Circle* (Ithaca: Cornell University Press, 2002).

[85] Claus von Stauffenberg was one of the organizers and executors of an assassination attempt on Hitler. He was also involved in Ernst Jünger's Parisian circle. Jünger also mentioned George in his journals.

Plato, which they treated less academically and more as Divine figures whose thoughts and dialogues ought to be read aloud in role-playing, acted out in scenes, and venerated.[86] To this end, as well as to read his verses and to examine new candidates for admission into the circle, George paid frequent visits to his students throughout Germany and Europe. Until his final days, George led a nomadic way of life with no constant station.

Within the circle there also ripened the idea of a "Secret Germany," which they called *das neue Reich* and imagined as a complete, purely spiritual transformation of society. Despite the proximity of Stefan George and his circle to the ideas and representatives of the Conservative Revolution, George himself refused to don regalia and rejected offers for a post from the party leadership of the future Reich, including from Goebbels himself, and ultimately secluded himself in Switzerland until his death in 1933.

After the master's death, the circle fell apart, and after the Second World War, Stefan George's legacy fell into disgrace and discarded for having "paved the way for the Reich." Nevertheless, his poem *"Das Wort"* from the *Neue Reich* anthology drew the attention of the "Black Forest shaman," Martin Heidegger, who examined it in detail in his later work *On the Way to Language*.

"The Word" is a poem about the enigma that is the "word" said in poetry itself as the primary form of saying. What is its power, its relation to the thing? What relation can the word have to Being and its truth? This is what interested Heidegger. Moreover, "The Word" is also a penetrating and dense poem about Nothing, which interests us in turn. Everything that is most important is already said in the word and "The Word."

---

86 Mikhail Maiatskii, *Spor o Platone. Krug Stefana George i nemetskii universitet* (Moscow: HSE University, 2012).

Das Wort

Everything that Stefan George wanted to say, he expressed and put into "The Word." In the ensuing, we will embark on our own study, at times wandering off from and at other times closing in on the themes, strings, and images touched upon in this poem as they illuminate the sound and resonance of the master's poetic words. Over the course of this wandering, we will draw on the English translation offered by Peter Hertz, who translated the poem in the context of Heidegger's commentary, but our main excursions will proceed from and unfold around the original German.[87]

Wunder von ferne oder traum	Wonder or dream from distant land
Bracht ich an meines landes saum	I carried to my country's strand
Und harrte bis die graue norn	And waited till the twilit norn
Den namen fand in ihrem born —	Had found the name within her bourn —
Drauf konnt ichs greifen dicht und stark	Then I could grasp it close and strong
Nun blüht und glänzt es durch die mark…	It blooms and shines now the front along…
Einst langt ich an nach guter fahrt	Once I returned from happy sail,
Mit einem kleinod reich und zart	I had a prize so rich and frail,
Sie suchte lang und gab mir kund:	She sought for long and tidings told:
«So schläft hier nichts auf tiefem grund»	"No like of this these depths enfold."
Worauf es meiner hand entrann	And straight it vanished from my hand,
Und nie mein land den schatz gewann…	The Treasure never graced my land…
So lernt ich traurig den verzicht:	So I renounced and sadly see:
Kein ding sei wo das wort gebricht.	Where word breaks off no thing may be.

At first glance, the narrative canvas of the poem is clear: we have before us the peripeteia of a wanderer who longs to bring a miracle to his homeland and needs assurance that it can be conveyed in words. In the first three strophes which end with an ellipsis, he awaits success, joy, and radiance. In the second verse

---

[87] Martin Heidegger, *On the Way to Language*, trans. Peter D. Hertz (New York: HarperCollins, 1971).

consisting of the fourth, fifth, and sixth strophes, he experiences his dream being denied, and the seventh strophe puts a seal and draws a line to the truth of the word. Perhaps this distillation of the "dry" plot re-informs us of its already obvious meaning, but if we let the words and turns of phrase themselves speak, then the emerging picture takes on dizzying depth and a wealth of patterns.

> *Wunder von ferne oder traum*
> *Bracht ich an meines landes saum*

The traveler carries to his country a wonder, a miracle, from afar, or a dream, either a subtle dream in the likes of when one sleeps or daydreams, or a dream in the sense of an aspiration, a vision. It is not yet clear to him what it is, so he hesitates, "*oder*" — is it a miracle, a sleeping dream, or a visionary dream? The difference is tangible. A wonder, a miracle, is something impossible that happens in spite of everything. In a sense, the appearance of a wonderful miracle means the destruction of the world in which it is revealed, as if destroying its very foundations, if such a world resists and denies miracles. Quite another matter are the worlds of dreams, where anything is possible. As Edgar Allan Poe concludes in his poem "A Dream Within a Dream":

> *All that we see or seem*
> *Is but a dream within a dream*

We, too, hesitate in the face of the question as to whether we are talking about a "wonder or dream from distant land?" or a "a wonder from afar or from dreams?" One thing may be said for sure: his land is clearly poor in dreams and wonders, and he cautiously brings them from afar, from a different country than his own. What is this country of his? "*Meines Landes*" — of my lands, country, homeland. This land is clearly either poor in wonders or denies them altogether. Where can we encounter such a *Land*? In the name for Europe, *Abendland*, we hear the "evening land," the "sunset land." Europe is the land where the sun recedes over the horizon and the historical fall (*Untergang*) proceeds with the open possibility of a passage (*Übergang*) into another beginning of fate.

Let us delve sideways into the exterior context. The poem "*Das Wort*" was written in 1919 but only published in the *New Reich* anthology in 1928. This was the beginning of the "short" 20th century, the period of the instability and devastation of the Weimar Republic, in which various aspirations for political transformation and the revival of the German nation were ripening. But crude and straightforward political engagement was foreign to the master poet. The 20th century was also the culmination of the era of Modernity with its total denial, alienation, and uprooting of the traditional — religious, mythological, sacrocentric — paradigm of thinking ("world picture"). The world of Modernity in Europe is a disenchanted world in which man has everything clearly and naturally-scientifically explained to him. Various secret societies turn out to be nothing more than the costume clubs of a bored bourgeoisie and aristocracy flirting with illusionist, technical tricks in the spirit of "spiritualism" and "magic." There are no genuine wonders and miracles, only the industrial landscape blocking beauty and dreams, the noise of machines mercilessly scaring and driving away the subtle Divinities.

Thus, the poem is born in a world of triumphant "reality," hence genuine wonder, miracle, and dreams are alien, astonishing, and far away — perhaps in the ancient East that so fascinated the young George. Bringing genuine wonder into a world that fundamentally and aggressively denies such — in this lies spiritual and cultural transformation.

Und harrte bis die graue norn
Den namen fand in ihrem born —

Arriving at the border between the dreamy afar and his native land, the traveler stops at a well. He cannot pass and bring the wonders any further until they are endowed with names which the gray Norn must find in the depths. The Norns are the three sisters who carve the patterns of fate in Germanic-Scandinavian myth. The first, Urð, cuts what has already happened and passed into the past. The second, Verðandi, cuts out what is becoming, the present. The third, Skuld, measures and cuts the

159

inevitable due, that is death, which casts its shadow from the coming future. The source is also called Urð, or Urðarbrunnr, which is connected with the Proto-Germanic verb for becoming, *wurdiz*. There are grounds to suppose that the gray Norn is the old Norn of the past, Urð, and this is her (*ihrem*) source. Thus, at the border of his homeland, the traveler turns to a very particular figure, Germanic like the author, and a mythological one, the Norn of the past, so that she plunges her gaze into the source of Being and finds there the right names.

Referring to names immediately immerses us into a very broad linguistic context and polemic over the connection between the signifier and signified, between names and things. Traditional, mythological doctrines and thinking insist on the most intimate bond between a thing and its name: the latter expresses the thing's *telos*, essence, fate, or significant aspects. A name is never accidental. In the master's poem, the name is a pledge and a bridge between worlds. Only through the word can the wonder or dream pass into the homeland — this is pure ποίησις, bringing a thing into being present.

The extreme opposite of this point is the argument that signification is of an incidental or conventional character, i.e., that people agree to the name of one or another thing out of convenience or circumstances, or that the name of a thing is completely spontaneous, accidental, and substantiated only post-factum. This opens up the way to tearing the fabric of the middle world into two: there is a supposedly objective, detached, independent external reality, and there is a linguistic, cultural "reality" thrown on top of it in various modes of coupling, linking, and referencing. This rift is strikingly traceable throughout European culture in Modernity; we can see it in just how easily and reflexively we divide *natura* and *cultura*, something which many other "exotic" and archaic peoples do not do, and which ancient people did not do within the framework of mythological thinking. A classic example of this is voiced in William Shakespeare's tragedy *Romeo and Juliet*:

> O Romeo, Romeo, wherefore art thou Romeo?
> Deny thy father and refuse thy name.
> Or if thou wilt not, be but sworn my love,
> And I'll no longer be a Capulet.
> 'Tis but thy name that is my enemy;
> Thou art thyself, though not a Montague.
> What's Montague? It is nor hand nor foot,
> Nor arm, nor face, nor any other part
> Belonging to a man. O be some other name.
> What's in a name? That which we call a rose
> By any other name would smell as sweet;
> So Romeo would, were he not Romeo call'd,
> Retain that dear perfection which he owes
> Without that title. Romeo, doff thy name,
> And for thy name, which is no part of thee,
> Take all myself.

Here, the girl gives voice to the most complex topic of names, particularly personal and family names in the case of belonging to two powerful, hostile lineages. For Juliet, Romeo is a slice of matter, a totality of body parts and a pleasant face — after all, up to this point they haven't even met each other personally. Falling in love requires meeting in the midst of the danger of names. The way to naive happiness is to call on the lover to abandon himself, his family, and his name in order to be with her, or to take her name and family in order to free her from their authority. The whole essence and nerve of Shakespeare's tragedy is inlaid in the belonging of the lovers to different names and lines. If their names were merely a convention, like a dress that one can easily change into and out of, then the tale would end immediately after the scene on the balcony. But this is not the case: contrary to the linguistic and philosophical, albeit erroneous thought put into Juliet's words, the author shows the lot, authority, and essence of names that penetrate fate and history deeper than the flesh and blood to which they are supposedly appended.

The above-cited passage also hosts the textbook case of the rose:

> That which we call a Rose
> By another name would smell as sweet

The famous Russian translation of this line features a contradiction: the girl says that the flower "smells like a rose" even if we call it by another name. Even deeper here, however, is the fragmentation and tearing away of the being of language and speech from the material slice, the accidentalness and non-traumatic change of their relations. More broadly, this topic leads us to the problem of the ontological status of things and the possibility of the existence of an "objective" world outside of culture and the human being's existential presence.

The case of the rose finds continuation in popular folk rhymes, such as in the famous form recorded by Joseph Ritson in the late 18th century. The first line of the original says: "The rose is red, the violet's blue." The rose is red, and "to be red" is "to be a rose," namely the particular rose being said. The correlation between name and thing is taken holistically: the rose exists through redness and its sweet smell. The integral whole precedes all characteristics and is not merely the sum of them. We cannot separate redness from the rose, nor can we separate the rose from its fragrance. Hence the textbook hyphen that indicates indivisibility: the-rose-being-red and the-rose-smelling-sweet. One could even compose a verbal form: the rose "roses" or "rose-smell," which would be understood as modes of being as such. It is not that "the rose is scarlet," as if a correlation of two elements, noun and predicate, but the "rose scarlets," the inseparability of being-scarlet or being-sweet-smelling in the name and flower that is the rose (the thing). Therefore, if we call a rose by any other name, it will no longer "smell like a rose," just as the tragic exposition of Shakespeare's work would no longer work if Romeo were merely a sum of his body parts.

Yet, words are supposed to grow to meet things. Thus, the hero of "*Das Wort*" awaits the name-words that the Norn brings up from the source of Being. "*Graue norn*" refers to the past. The new and wonderful ought to be verily named out of the past as that which is admissible, authentic, not excessive. Where else to look for names for wonders and dreams if not the world where *mythos* ruled and rules?

And now the name is found and given:

> *Drauf konnt ichs greifen dicht und stark*
> *Nun blüht und glänzt es durch die mark…*

Through the naming, the hero is able to grasp them "*dicht und stark*" — "close and strong," in their ultimate, confident presence. But the word *dicht*, translated as "close" or "tight," is clearly not merely used to double the meaning of strong grip. *Dicht* refers us directly to poetry: in German, poetry is *Dichtung* and the poet is *Dichter*. The word *Dichtung* is also used to refer to a dense, thick forest. Martin Heidegger cited his frequent walks along the paths of the Black Forest (*Holzwege*) to collect firewood: walking through dense, dark forest, one comes upon a clearing, and this is an elementarily accessible image-metaphor for understanding truth as Ἀλήθεια. The clearing of unconcealment amidst the dense crowns of beeches, oaks, and fir trees does not assert anything, but rather gives the space for light, rain, snow, and birds to enter it. The density of the forest (the forest of thinking) is the condition for the manifestation within it of the clearing (truth as unconcealment).

The master's protagonist says that he grasped the dreams in their close and tight poetic name, in firm grip in the clearing of unconcealment. They then blossom and overflow in radiance "*durch die mark.*" *Durch* refers to the name and literally means "through," "across," "by," "by means of passing through." The name is not something standing to the side or stuck on like a label; the name is the *durch* through which the dream shines across the border. The *mark* is not only the boundary, like a marking on earth or a demarcating line, but the measure, a measurement, for instance of gold as payment. Wonders do not simply pass into *meines Abendlandes* — they blossom and luminously flash over the border, through the tight grip on the name given by the guardian of fate.

This concludes the first three strophes and the first part of the poem. The tone and mood here are positive, the hero is fortunate, the source of the Norn is favorable, and the impossible wonders now blossom in his country. But then there is an ellipsis.

> *Einst langt ich an nach guter fahrt*
> *Mit einem kleinod reich und zart*

The fourth strophe opens with the word "once": once in the past, our hero was once again returning from his glorious path, carrying some "little prize" or "treasure," *kleinod*. The latter is usually said of pearls or precious stones. Its smallness is very delicate and tender (*zart*), but at the same time it is generous, rich, and priceless (*reich*).

> *Sie suchte lang und gab mir kund:*
> *«So schläft hier nichts auf tiefem grund»*

This time, he waits a long time for the Norn to answer, as she searches for the name in the source of Urð. Alas, even at the deepest bottom — the phrase *"auf tiefem grund"* can be alternatively translated as "at the fundamental, final ground of something" — there is no word. The term *"schläft"* poetically says that a word can gently, quietly sleep in the dark depths, waiting to be called to a thing (which is one of the main functions of poetry). But still, nothing was found sleeping at the bottom of the well of Being.

> *Worauf es meiner hand entrann*
> *Und nie mein land den schatz gewann...*

Without a name from the Norn of the past, without the bridge-*poiesis* authenticated by *mythos*, the gentle treasure (*schatz*) immediately slips out of the traveler's palm, leaving his native land with nothing. The ellipsis ends the second, minor part of the verse, and then brings us to the second and main summary of the whole verse in connection with the first direct speech of the Norn: "No like of this these depths enfold," or "Nothing sleeps here at the bottom." This is already a certain generalization of the poetic-ontological principle. The seventh strophe breaks out of the division into two parts of three strophes:

> *So lernt ich traurig den verzicht:*
> *Kein ding sei wo das wort gebricht.*

Before the colon that presents the verdict, the traveler recognizes that he has not simply learned but has really come to know the sadness of refusal: no things can be where there is no word. Here we encounter a kind of "roll call" of place (*Ort*) as the interrogative "Where?" (*Wo*) and word (*Wort*). The word gives the thing a place to be and to have its "where." But if the word is gone, if it breaks off (*gebricht*), if the world is poor in words (*wortarm*), then this means that the obvious need for Being (*Not des Seins*) is a need for the word (*Not des Wortes*). Without the word, there are no things. Such is the bitter lesson of the refusal of Being: the disappearance of that for which there is no place-name.

In a poem by a completely different author, Poe, who was also entangled in the intersections of dreamlike and lucid spaces, we see the bitterness of precious grains of sand (cf. *kleinod*) slipping through painfully clenched fingers into the bottomless darkness of waters.

> *I stand amid the roar*
> *Of a surf-tormented shore,*
> *And I hold within my hand*
> *Grains of the golden sand*
> *— How few! yet how they creep*
> *Through my fingers to the deep,*
> *While I weep — while I weep!*
> *O God! Can I not grasp*
> *Them with a tighter clasp?*
> *O God! can I not save*
> *One from the pitiless wave?*
> *Is all that we see or seem*
> *But a dream within a dream?*[88]

Of course, it is not the "weight" of the word that is at stake here. In fact, in the final line of George's poem we first hear this "word" itself, *das Wort*, which loops the entire verse and refers to the title.

---

88 Edgar Allan Poe, "A Dream Within a Dream."

Wort is the the Scandinavian *orð* from the 141st verse of the *Hávamál*:

Icelandic:	German:	Russian:	English:
orð ér af orði	Wort aus dem Wort	слово от слова	Word from word
orðs leitaði	verlieh mir das Wort	слово рождало	yielded word

The *poiesis* ("pro-ducing") of word as name is complicated if we bear in mind that in the Scandinavian-Germanic *mythos*, the word is associated with the rune-speeches, which are acquired in the most complex and unique myth of Odin's self-sacrifice, and in intimate connection with this as well as in the light of metaphor, word-speeches are carved by the Norns out of the tree and on wood (*Stäbe*).

An interesting note for consideration has been offered by the linguist Sergei Borodai, who points out that in European and other archaic languages, there is generally no separate, independent lexeme denoting the abstract concept of "word."[89] The concept of "word" is of great significance to linguistics as a science because it is, in all likelihood, of a meta-linguistic character (i.e., used to describe language itself), and yet it can be examined in terms of linguistic specificity, which is to say within different language cultures across which the qualitative content of the abstract notion of "word" differs. What is the word as word? In the European context, the intralingual meaning of the concept of "word" is "to be a name," i.e., nomination is the first and main function of words in European cultures. The various lexemes for "word" derive from the Proto-Indo-European *$h_3 nomn̥$-*, which means "name." Borodai concludes:

> What has not been named cannot be reflected upon, is not a part of reflexive thinking, and is not a concept in operative memory; in the best case, it is simply a bundle of perceptual features. In order for such a bundle to become a concept with a particular meaning and enter into reflexive thinking, it must receive a name.[90]

---

89 Borodai, *Iazyk i poznanie*.
90 Ibid.

Therefore, the direct identity of name and *Wort* in the master's poem is itself organic to language and culture. "The name from the name yielded the name" — and wherever there is a name, there is a deed, a matter, a thing.

In his analysis of George's poem, Martin Heidegger points out that *Wort* is the Greek λόγος, the word and the gathering into a whole in poetic tale. The most tender and richest wonders are brought into one's own land and put into words in the song of a tale, into Being as such, in the poetic word. Yet, Heidegger also has his own poem with the same title opening the volume *Besinnung*[91]:

Das Wort	The Word
Nichts, Nirgend, Nie	Nothing, nowhere, never
vor jedem Etwas,	before every "something,"
allem Dann und Dort	before all "then" and "there"
entragt das Wort	towers the word
dem Abgrund, der verlieh	out of the ab-ground
Was jedem Grund	which granted,
mißglückt,	what every ground failed to grant
da nur der Bund	since only the bond
mit dem Gesagten	with what is said
jeglich Ding zum Ding bestückt	fits out every thing as a thing
und die gejagten	and scatters in a maze
Sinne wirr verstreut.	the hunted senses.

What begs attention here is the complete negation at the beginning of the poem: nothing, nowhere, never, before any "something" in space and time. Heidegger begins his verse radically apophatically. And then, out of the Abyss, *Abgrund*[92], out of the darkness of groundlessness that every time tries in vain to offer a ground, the word arises. The word is also a name, a bond (*Bund*) with what is said (*Gesagten*), that brings out

---

91 Martin Heidegger, *Mindfulness*, trans. Parvis Emad and Thomas Kalary (London: Continuum, 2006).

92 In Russian, the word for "abyss," *bezdna*, is feminine, whereas the German *Abgrund* is masculine, which definitely leaves its mark on perception and interpretation when switching between the languages.

and nourishes each thing as a thing and scatters handfuls of meanings.

On the whole, Heidegger's *"Das Wort"* echoes and is a resonant response to George's *"Das Wort,"* as both poems speak of one and the same: the power of the word-name that brings things into Being. The only difference is that George appeals to mythological context and imagery, while Heidegger's verse openly expresses the imperatives of his philosophy.

The word ascends and rises as a tower out of the absolute Nothing, which coincides with the Black Forest shaman's thought on the rooting and revealing of beings (*Seiende*) out of the different Nothing-Beyng (*Seyn*). The word once again appears as a bridge or gateway to a present thing, and the only "ground" that endures, and upon which the tower of the word can be raised, is the dark groundlessness, the *Ab-Grund*.

Let us once again draw attention to the fifth strophe in George's poem:

> *Sie suchte lang und gab mir kund:*
> *«So schläft hier nichts auf tiefem grund»*

Knowing that the master appealed to words quite freely and ignored the capitalization of nouns that is customary in the German language, the Norn's answer can be translated and understood in a completely different way that yields a different reading of the second part of the verse. The Norn's response would be *"So schläft hier Nichts auf tiefem grund"* — "Here the Nothing these depths enfold," or "Here the Nothing sleeps at the bottom." In this case, the ensuing behavior of the little wonder in the wanderer's hands would be quite natural: the Norn raised from the abyss of the source of Being the name for the thing, the name Nothing, and thus the thing, having received this name, immediately corresponded to it by evaporating and disappearing. Thus, poetry shows us not only the direct dependence of a thing's existence upon its word-name, but also the capacity of the word to be said without a thing.

The word "nothing" exists in language, but the "Nothing" is not present or represented (*Vorstellen*) in consciousness. At the very most, we are dealing with a dense, dark deixis, one which nevertheless belongs to the order of being(s). Mythopoetics perfectly and beautifully points to the Nothing. In this is revealed the power of the word: not only to say and bring a thing into Being, but even to say the Nothing, to pronounce names for which there are not and cannot be things in the world. In this respect, the other side of the coin is the abundance of nicknames and verbal masks for the Divine in the complete absence of a veritably proper name. A line can be drawn from Heidegger's poem to the distinction between Divinity as the ground (*Grund*) of being(s) and the groundless Divinehood (*Abgrund, Gottheit*) in the spirit of the Rhenish mystics, on which point we may take into account Heidegger's high opinion of Meister Eckhart. Both the word and the Divine are rooted in the Nothing, but they are revealed and said in different ways.

The word "nothing" is the boundary of language, the specific place, time, and sound of the passage from no-thing to some-thing. This boundary is in us. At this boundary, we feel neither the wind nor the cold nor our hair standing up before the approaching unknown — we do not feel anything, which means that we dwell near the Nothing.

Stefan George's poem, like the philosophico-poetic echo of its intention in Heidegger's verses, is concentrated ποίησις.

To complete our immersion, let us turn to the lyrical protagonist himself, the unnamed wanderer who seeks wonders and dreams in countries far from his homeland. Just as the master weaves images from Germanic-Scandinavian myth into his poetry, so do we find similar motifs and figures back in Germanic-Scandinavian myth. The cornerstone Deity of the Germanic *mythos*, Wotan, appears before us as a devout wanderer, hungry for wisdom and knowledge of fates, as the one who knows the Norns at the roots of Yggdrasil.

Even more suitable for the role of the wanderer would be King Gylfi, whose travels and visions constitute the core of the *Younger Edda*. Gylfi is an Odinic character who repeats the gestures of Odin himself, sharing with him the name Gangleri and succeeding in feats. He also ends up in the midst of the obsessions and dreams that he longed to find. The hero of George's poem is an analogous character who clearly fits into the Odinic pattern. Perhaps he is yet another unnamed theophany of the giver of Kvasir's blood amidst the poetry of the thunderous 20th century.

III
THE ESCHATOLOGY OF LANGUAGE

The End of Speech — The End of the World

Time is the duration and structure of the telling of what is to be told. The *mythos*-tale is a laying out, an expositing, an unfolding of space and time in language and speech; it is the time of the telling of the tale, similar to how a writing is the length of its lines. Time as tale is the telling-itself, the Divine's speaking forth of itself, which is experienced by man in the middle world as history, as his personal presence, as life heading towards death.

Insofar as the tale is the assertion of space-time, then the tale of the Nothing is outright impossible, since such means ceasing the telling, breaking into silence. Hence to the aid come metaphors, tropes, and deixis. Understanding *mythos* ontologically, the end of the tale means the end of the world, the falling silent and collapse of the *poiesis* of Being; furthermore, it is the conscious bringing of the plot of the tale itself to its conclusion and falling silent — *thanatopoiesis*.

Cyclical time as it is widespread in diverse variations throughout old traditions is a chain of rhymes, alliterations, insertions, and refrains that orient the diction and suggestion of the recitation of a myth, song, or galdr. In the *Younger Edda*, which tends towards prosaic exposition, Snorri loops the plot through the recursion of the creation of all beings as a tale-telling-itself-in-advance.

But eschatology is *telos*, the predetermined place and time of the eventing of the end of the tale. Tales about the withering and dying of the world differ in their vividness, the tortuousness of the path leading to it, and their detail and tragic quality. Nevertheless, nothing under the moon lives forever. The destruction of thinking and language is the anthropological and mental correlate of the end of the world. We can designate historical reference points and branches of the dying and mortification of *mythos* and language.

Linear time corresponds to prosaic discourse, which has a clear-cut beginning and end, as well as to the figure of the author of a text or a specific narrator. Here we are dealing with Platonism and the principle of creationism, where the irremovable ontological dualism between Creator and the creation belonging to him is the basis of the Abrahamic religions. This is already a step down, a downshift in register from the telling of the tale to increasing materiality, hardening, and departing from poetry in the form of presentation even while generally preserving imagery, metaphors, parables, and philosophical myths.

In the Abrahamic religions (which out of an illegitimate synthesis with Hellenic wisdom laid down the foundations and trajectory of the development of European metaphysics down to the Enlightenment, Modernity, and beyond), *mythos* is replaced by history, and the principle of historicity is asserted as a concrete, real certainty. A tale becomes something "one-off," a single item. The world does not die and is not reborn, like a song that sings itself over and over again in the cascades of diction, but is something that was once created by a specific author and given a finite history, after which there will be no new repetition nor any eternal, static being as if frozen at the peak of the world's heyday — there won't be anything at all.

The Abrahamic imperative of preserving the purity and accuracy of translations of the Bible or the Koran, especially accuracy when it comes to copying (where errors or changes are perceived as the machinations of demons or the temptations of Iblis), represents the killing of *mythos* and arranging a vicious opposition between *logos* and *mythos* (the dogma of text vs. the primal elements of the life of the word).

Man's treatment of language as something sheerly ready at hand, like raw material and matter, unfolds into the total rationalization, standardization, and even state-appropriation of language in Modernity. The primal element of language is "tamed" into the cement of dogmatism, from which even linguistic purism offers no salvation. Typically anti-poetic and essentially anti-lingual is the principle of expediency taught to us in school: "whatever variants contribute to clear, unambiguous, convenient expression of thought should be the norm, while any expressions that complicate understanding and are difficult to express should be discarded."[93] For mythological thinking, this principle is the opposite to that of the Divinities and beauty, since it demands that things be named directly, unambiguously, without poetic embellishments and the refinements of speech. Here, the rationalization and standardization of language is exposed as part and parcel of the process of the secularization and disenchantment of the world. Rationalized language gravitates towards the synthetic, towards unambiguous signification, to which reality responds with projects to create artificial, grammatically verified, easy-to-learn languages like Esperanto, languages which are not "burdened" by many thousands of years of history and layerings of semantic and poetic fields among the people. The development of this principle also deals a blow to metaphor, which remains a beacon of poetry and beauty within prosaic and everyday speech. In the absence of the fascinating and ontological power of *poiesis*, all that thinking is left with in the secular and prosaic environment is the possibility of enacting conventional sling effects, i.e., when qualitative leaps in thinking into an ecstatic state are achieved not by rhythm and diction but by the suggestions of deictic signs, tropes, symbols, and decorations of language in prose.

Such standardizing operations inflicted upon language are often based on the political need to contain centrifugal forces and maintain colonization, hence regional dialects, vernaculars, ethnolects, etc., are labeled as violations of the high literary norm of the center and are supposed to be brought into alignment. The variations of living dialects are labeled as belonging to the periphery, to "rednecks" or "hillbillies," as opposed to the urban capital and proximity to the sovereign. Language becomes very

---

93 G.A. Kazakov, *Sakral'naia leksika v sisteme iazyka* (Comrat: Comrat State University, 2016).

much a politicized marker, including on the other end, i.e., in the struggle for local ethnic and religious identities, wherein languages and dialects that present alternatives to the center and the hegemony form the basis for ethnic dissimilation or the mark of a free man (who doesn't speak the language of the emperor or the enslavers).

This is consonant with Oswald Spengler's dichotomy between Culture and Civilization, where the first stage (Culture) is characterized by symbol and myth, and the second (Civilization) means the cooling down and ossification of the vital drive into passive, brittle forms and mechanicism. Civilization is the death of culture, of the plurality of cultures and languages, including the cultural and linguistic core of the hegemonic people itself.

Anthropologists inspired by Marxism have taken a further step to argue that language as such plays a fundamentally alienating function. We encounter such ideas in Claude Lévi-Strauss, for whom language is the border between nature and culture, the latter of which is fundamentally opposed to the former.[94] But language also serves to cover this gap through fairytales and myth, hence *mythos* is attributed various utilitarian and therapeutic functions rather than an ontological status.

In the paradigm of Postmodernity, whose key forerunner was Freudo-Marxism, language is completely reconceptualized to be a repressive authority that restricts and imposes certain ways of thinking and speaking. Language (and in this case Postmodernists refer to the "scholastic" language shaped through Platonism, Judeo-Christianity, and Modernity) is taken to be a cage not only for the mind, but more importantly,

---

[94] In contemporary anthropology, the antagonism between nature and culture is recognized to be a specific, most often Eurocentric trait, as such a division does not exist in principle among many archaic peoples. Either tribes saw themselves as an inseparable unity with the environment in which they live, or what for European man is a space of "wilderness" is inhabited as an equal continuation of the mythic and social reality of the tribe. See Eduardo Viveiros de Castro, "Who is afraid of the ontological wolf?" (CUSAS Annual Marilyn Strathern Lecture, 30 May 2014).

for unconscious desires. Language becomes the elemental space for the realization of power, yet this power is not concentrated in the hands of state institutions or a dictator, but permeates all of society and people themselves.

As part of deconstructing the very structure of modern European knowledge, the center of critique becomes the phallo-logo-centrism that Jacques Derrida and Jacques Lacan treated as the core of European culture with roots going back into deep traditional antiquity. On the cultural-anthropological and socio-political plane, the overthrow and overcoming of phallocentrism turns into a critique and liquidation of patriarchal structures in favor of all possible variations of feminine egalitarianism (sisterhood instead of patriarchy). This affects the link between the noetic, intellectual principle and masculinity that has been classical since antiquity but is now reduced all the way down to belonging to the male sex (or "gender").

The critique of logocentrism is actually revealed to be a critique directed against the power structure of language and against language itself as the primary instance of access to surrounding reality. Representatives of the philosophical trend of speculative realism actively criticize the principle of correlationism, or the dependence of reality on human thinking and language, and argue that correlationism always leaves us stuck within anthropological subjectivity, in a constant representation or even illusion of an objective reality that is independent of human structures of thinking. In other words, the Kantian thing-in-itself (anything at all, even the whole world as such) is inaccessible to us, because Dasein projects the whole structure of reality out of its thinking presence within the human being. The human being is the bearer of privileged access to the assertion, interpretation, ranking, and use of the beingful world of autonomous objects. Language and human thinking play the leading role in projecting interpretations and thereby simultaneously alienating, repressing, and casting into oblivion the objective being of objects-in-themselves. The correlationist project proposes to completely move away from anthropocentrism by essentially turning Heidegger's philosophy upside down, casting out the central element that is Dasein, and seeking to access objects in their pure form, untainted by human thoughts, to know them by non-human methods, for example by mathematics.

Unlike speculative realists, the classics of Postmodernist philosophy in the wake of Michel Foucault, Gilles Deleuze, and Felix Guattari's projects hedged their bets on the emancipation of the individual from language by way of rehabilitating mental disorders and completely revising psychiatry and psychoanalysis as institutions (into anti-psychiatry or schizoanalysis). In language and speech, rejecting the norm of *logos* and grammatical structure brings to the fore speech disorders, or disorders in pronunciation, perception, and semantic coherence, such as aphasia, schizophasia, and incoherence. Schizophasia especially stands out here, since in this diagnosis speech is constructed grammatically and lexically correctly but is empty in content or has the character of outright delirium. Herein lies the subtle simulation work of decay, since in the case of clinical aphasia and speech incoherence we can easily recognize that our interlocutor is incapable of communication and expression in principle, i.e., he is sick. In the case of schizophasis, however, the sick person can exhibit verbal insinuations, gestures, and convincingly pronounce their monologue; moreover, if so desired, they can even read into it some meaning brought from the outside or snatch individual phrases from the general stream of delirium, which can becomes aphorisms of stupidity or recognized cultural artifacts. Through linguistic and speech incoherence, through the disintegration and simulation of signs, the idea of affirming fundamental uncertainty, the freedom of reassembly and flow, and the construction of pseudo-events of uniqueness within the framework of Postmodern project carry out the overcoming of the rigid structures of Modernity. Poetic rhythm and the recitation of *mythos*, once brought down to the level of a closed, prosaic work, are finally upend up to the incoherent stream of delirium without a beginning or end and without any glimmer of meaning in both essence and form.

In the sphere of text, we can speak of an emancipation of the subconscious in such practices as automatic writing, both within modern European spiritualism, where it is a falsification and simulation of the sacred, and in psychiatric practices. Automatic writing is often accompanied by the "invention" of exotic, "esoteric" alphabets and languages. In such cases, we can see how European esotericism and occultism became some of the cultural precursors of Postmodernism.

Nor can we avoid mentioning the event of the "death of the author" in literary criticism, which we owe to Roland Barthes. The latter philosopher proposed completely excluding the biographical and historical context of a work's author from analysis and ultimately completely severing the work from its author. The finished, final text or work of art is taken to be just as alien to the hands of its creator as it is to any casual viewer or even someone who hasn't become its viewer at all. The rejection of the author means the rejection of any initial or ultimate imparting of the work with meaning, i.e., with its own internal teleology. This opens up the space for multidimensional, rhizomatic, intertextual deciphering and the generation of interpretations of any text in any context whatsoever. The "death of the author" clearly figures as a deconstruction of the structures inherited from creationism, that is the Creator, his creation (man, the world, history), and and the meaning and providence in the fates of people (who are akin to puppet characters).

We find yet another extravagant idea advocating the rejection of language in the intellectual space of left-wing anarcho-primitvist theory, namely in the anthropologist John Zerzan. Zerzan advocates a radical rejection of all the benefits of civilization and calls for human societies to return to the state that preceded the Neolithic revolution and sedentary agriculture, that is to scattered tribes of hunter-gatherers. Carrying forth the notion that language plays an alienating role which separates culture from nature, this thinker takes this idea to the extreme and proclaims the need not only to reject the ideas of progress and civilization, but also "human messianism.⁹⁵" This project also includes a conscious and complete rejection of symbolic culture and language, since concepts in language and thinking are the naming and distribution of things in the external world into linguistic categories such as "fruit," "plants," "meat," or more particular designations such as "peach" or "apple," which, according to Zerzan, alienate one from the pure experience of taste. In other words, between tasting a nameless fruit and tasting a "peach" lies an abyss of alienation and predetermined descent into the rut of culture and civilization. Language drastically narrows and limits the experience of the pure perception of nature and gives rise to power relations between its speakers (here we might recall the presence of estate- and caste-specific dialects in traditional societies). On the whole, despite the radical and extravagant character of Zerzan's ideas, they have developed in parallel to the philosophical mainstream and completely coincide with the anti-anthropological intentions of developing Postmodernity.

The deconstruction of the modern constructs and practices applied to language in the 20th-21st centuries opens up the possibility not only for the further, endless process of destruction and decay, even if this fully fits into the eschatological lot, but also for remythologizing our being-in-the-world. But here it is important to qualify that this remythologization cannot be a simple, naive return to telling and repeating old mythologies as if the previous centuries' phases of decline and paradigmatic shifts in thinking and language never happened. Such would amount to nothing more than kitschy theater in whose plots and characters even the actors themselves don't really believe.

Mythos must be re-founded in its deep, groundless ground, i.e., it must be carried forth in silence anew. It will inevitably not be new in the sense that marketing gives to novelty; it will be different, and it will incorporate the installation of the contemporary era as the eschatological nerve and inexorable denouement of its plot, as the existential tension on the even

---

95 On the ideas of John Zerzan, see Askr Svarte, *Tradition and Future Shock*.

of the *Endspiel* of world history and the oblivion of Beyng. The end of speech is the end of the world, which means the falling, curtailing, and breaking off of the tale into silence. There is neither *mythos* nor *logos* in this silence. In the *Hávamál* of the *Elder Edda*, it is said:

> A brand from a brand is kindled and burned,
> And fire from fire begotten;
> And man by his speech is known to men,
> And the stupid by their stillness.[96]

In this passage, we hear that, besides the familiar metaphor for the human being of wood, logs, and cinder, and alongside the identification of speech and knowledge with a flame that is passed along from person to person, silence is called the source of stupidity. But there is a difference in silences. It bears distinguishing between silence as the poverty of utterance, the absence of thought, or the incapacity to say something, and silence as the preliminary gestation, the tale growing and rising up in the silence of the pre-word just ahead of its telling. Silence frames speech before and after its sounding. The moment of silence in which air is inhaled and rises and a resting tale is already held, and the moment of silence of free exhalation after the completion of the telling, should be seen as equally vital parts of speech and language.

In resonance with the High One, let us recall Hölderlin:

> Much has man experienced.
> Named many of the heavenly ones,
> Since we have been a conversation
> And able to hear from one another.

At the border of silence lies the possibility of listening and understanding, and therefore being together along the path of the stream of the speech of language, for we are in essence a conversation.

Speaking is speaking-forth. By analogy, the practice of keeping silent is a carrying out and forth of silence, a speaking-

---

96 *Hávamál* 57, trans. Henry Adams Bellows (1936)

forth of silence in speech and thought in their stillness and refusal. Martin Heidegger has much to say about keeping silent about what is most important in thinking. One must approach what is most important, that is the unconcealment of the truth of Beyng, and preserve it in the silence of the intelligible unsaid.[97] Sometimes, it is worth deliberately keeping silent about what is most important, because speaking (whether orally or in writing) is more likely to lead to a dead end, to mislead, or or to generate false meanings.

According to the doctrine of cyclical time, which implies the death and rebirth of the world like the daily and annual revolutions of the sun, the silence after the end of the tale can be understood as a pause between the already sung *mythos* and the one whose air is only beginning to fill the singer's chest. This is the pause of the River Lethe, into whose bottomlessness the word dives and from which it rises up on the other shore of unconcealment.

---

97 In Russian we can take note of a useful play of words based on the stress: the *neskázannoe* is what has not been spoken, while the *neskazánnoe* is the supreme epithet for amazement, for what is indescribable.

Sacrifice, Chatter, Caesura

The order, addressees, objects, and intended aims of sacrifices within a society can be seen as a system of signs and communication on par with systems of kinship and taboo. In other words, we are once again dealing with language.

By way of sacrifices, mythological man communicates and communes with the Divinities, spirits, and deceased ancestors in other worlds. The world as a whole is the constant and total system of the exchange of sacrifices and gifts-and-responses in return: people sacrifice to the Deities and spirits, and the latter respond to their prayers by filling waters with fish and forests with wildlife; the living sacrifice to their deceased kin on the other side of the manifest world, sending them the things they need, and the ancestors help their descendants by sending them warnings or other forms of aid.

If the orders and hierarchies of sacrifices within the middle world, as well as between the world of humans and the worlds of the dead, spirits, and Deities, are in essence a language, then what is sacrifice within language as such? This is an especially curious question given that sacrifice is the ground of speech itself in the Germanic-Scandinavian *mythos*.

Things, harvests, animals, deeds, enemies, and one's own life gifted to the Divinities figure as the sacrifices offered within the lifeworld. A thing is thus transmitted to the other world or beyond through its withdrawal from everyday circulation, the cessation of its use, and its destruction in one way or another. Breaking, burning, trampling, dismembering, drowning, and burying — in a word, the destruction of a thing, bringing an object to death — constitute the bridge along which a thing passes to its addressee in the other world. In the case of sending things to spirits and the deceased, it is believed that something broken in this world will in the world of the dead appear whole and in good working order, which means that the relationship between the manifest world and the other world is of a reflected, inverted nature. Silence, then, as the antithesis to tale, is a variation of the tale's passage to the other side: while we are silent here, the tale is told there, and conversely they answer us with silence.

Schizophasia, then, is the irruption of the hypochthonic speech of disintegrated souls into the middle world of the living, which means a violation of the border and order between all the worlds demarcated in folk cultures.

Another approach to sacrifice language is the refusal to complete or conclude *poiesis*, the refusal to think a thought-insight all the way through, or to refuse to say it aloud or in text. Keeping the silence of refusal is the preservation of the sacrificial nature of the word as an offering, as a victim, or the ritual and strictly one-time telling of a thought, word, or song as a vocal gift addressed to the Divinities, followed by the consigning of such words to oblivion. Yet another variation of sacrifice in language is withdrawing the name of a thing, i.e., un-naming a thing, which is a direct refusal to give it a name on the threshold of *poiesis*. A similar case is using dry, impersonal pronouns and gestures when dealing with people sentenced to death or under taboo. Withdrawing a name from a thing comes very close to, as it were, the execution of things. Another variation of such would be interrupting the saying of a name mid-sentence.

Heidegger devotes several enigmatic passages to sacrificial offering in his *Black Notebooks*. His approach is developed on the basis of the fundamentally important distinction between Beyng and beings, where the latter is what is-as-a-whole and the former is the source of this whole which is not a being and is not present. Heidegger writes:

> Sacrifice is the departure from beings on the path to preserving the favor of being. Sacrifice can indeed be prepared and served by working and achievement with respect to beings, yet never fulfilled by such activities. Its accomplishment stems from that inherent stance out of which every historical human being through action —

and essential thinking is an action — preserves the Dasein he has attained for the preservation of the dignity of being... Sacrifice is a t home in the essence of the event whereby being lays claim upon the human being for the truth of being.[98]

Thus, the Black Forest thinker offers apologetics for a type of sacrifice that is a disinterested act of giving, a sacrifice without expectation of any response. Heidegger argues that calculation and the presence of any aim distort the very essence of sacrifice, at the heart of which lies readiness for the existential angst of self-sacrifice. Heidegger associates this kind of sacrifice with authentic thinking of Beyng, which does not seek any support in beings. Thinking that is submerged into beings inevitably falls into calculating benefits, causes, and inevitable effects, and in so doing multiplies and reworks beings and itself as one among the latter amidst the machinations of digits and science, for benefit and profit in the world of beings. Heidegger writes that it is precisely such existential angst that opens up the Nothing. Authentic thinking towards Beyng expends itself in Being, in leading a person towards their fate, towards the freedom of sacrifice for the sake of keeping the truth of Beyng. This sacrifice is committed without coercion, for it is the costly expenditure of oneself, born out of boundless freedom, in preserving the truth of Being for all beings.[99]

When man decides to commit such a sacrifice without any guarantee or intention of reciprocally catching generous gifts, then it is accompanied by the secret gratitude of Beyng itself, which out of its "generosity" allows man to become its guardian. This thankfulness of Beyng is primordial, for it is the beginning principle of human word and speech, of the word as a message about words, and it lies at the heart of human thinking. Man encounters this thankfulness as a response to the silent voice of Beyng.

---

98 Martin Heidegger, "Postscript to 'What is Metaphysics'" in idem, *Pathmarks*, ed. William McNeill (Cambridge: Cambridge University Press, 1998), 236-237.
99 Ibid.

We can see how Heidegger's succinct sketches resonate with the poetic intention of Stefan George as well as the sacrificial motif of the Germanic myth of Odin's self-sacrifice.

***

Speech is one of the important existentials of Dasein. By way of speech, Dasein projects and constitutes the beingful world in which it discovers itself. At the same time, Dasein comes to know itself, learns information about itself, and interprets the surrounding world through a multiplicity of different speeches, or discourses, which is to say that here-being is first interpreted in terms of others. In the German language, the impersonal neuter pronoun "*das Man*," that is the "anyone," the "they," the everyday "whosoever," is used to denote a generalized and averaged subject of discourse. Dasein's existence in the world happens between two poles: its own, the authentic (*eigene*), and the inauthentic (*uneigene*), the alienated submersion in the vain commotion of everydayness, the whirlwind of philistine worries and leisure. The latter mode of being is the regime of *das Man*, in which "man" hides, dissipates, and forgets about himself and is inattentive to himself, for attentiveness boils down to being-towards-death, i.e., to recognizing the finitude of one's presence. This thinking is traumatic and disturbing, so Dasein turns away from it and invests itself in the commotion of everydayness, public opinion and recognition, and the idle chatter and rumors about it and about the beings all around it. Instead of existential speech (*Rede*) about itself, Dasein surrounds itself with, and itself produces, only the idle chatter (*Gerede*) of *das Man*.

Although the pole of everydayness is the unauthentic mode of Dasein's existing in the world, it still fulfills a "positive" function in safekeeping here-being from the anxiety and trauma of the finitude of its presence. In all likelihood, the mode of everydayness underpins the very possibility that the world and others can maintain themselves in their existence and diversity as projected by all the other existentials (*Sorge*, "care," *Mit-sein*, "being-with," *in-der-Welt-sein*, "being-in-the-world," *Neugier*, "curiosity," etc.). Heidegger remarks in passing that even in the inauthentic mode of attentiveness to everything outside of it, out in the world, Dasein still remains its own. It is always the very same presence that is either authentic or inauthentic. The chatter and various turns of everyday discourse figure as the starting point on Dasein's path to authentically interpreting itself. Present opinions, chatter, and rumors about beings and Being are in essence the beginning of the hermeneutic circle, the starting point for when our cognition sets off from the pre-understanding already given to us about what there is and how it is in the middle world (i.e., the "objective truths" that we have uncritically and naively assimilated about the world and ourselves from culture, education, politics, etc.). Going through the hermeneutic circles, exercising the exegesis of meanings, uncovering the discursive practices of the contemporary world and everyday life, and making our way to our selfhood, the starting positions of the opinions of the majority can and will be radically rethought and even discarded.

If Dasein stubbornly persists in refusing itself and turns away from the call of Beyng, which calls it to its selfhood amidst the indistinguishable mass of *das Man*, then Dasein plunges ever deeper into the extreme limits of its existentials. Curiosity and concern for beings turn into obsession with machinations upon them as if everything were ready-to-hand raw materials. Discourses turn into chatter about nothing, or speech disintegrates in such a way that the very prospect of inevitable death and the end of speaking can be chatted away.

Finally, of no small import is the change in Dasein's leading mood over the course of the unfolding of its history, which is the history of Western thinking. In German, "mood" is *Stimmung*, but Heidegger emphasizes the more musical meaning of this word as an "attunement," i.e., a "mood" that is tuned to a certain tone of perception and attitude. *Stimme* also means the sound of the voice, vocals. Mood or attunement is the according following of the totality of the leading voice. Western philosophy, that is the passageway from the poetic song of *mythos* to *logos*, was born amidst the mood of astonishment, when the first Presocratic philosophers wondered at the fact that there are beings and that there is presence amidst beings. This initial mood gave impetus to man's curiosity and concern for the world around him and led him to question its structure and his place within it. But Western philosophy (metaphysics), and consequently the history of the West itself, comes to a conclusion in the midst of the mood of Dasein's profound boredom among beings. Boredom, *Langweilig*, may be literally translated as "the long-lasting meanwhile." Heidegger devotes a detailed analysis to boredom and highlights three gradations of submersion into this state. The first type of boredom, which everyone encounters, is described by the philosopher as the situation when one arrives at the provincial train station too early. Waiting for his train at this unfamiliar stop, he paces back and forth, looks at his watch, repeatedly revisits the schedule and posters, etc.; in other words, he is simply bored because he has nothing to do here, and nothing draws his interest. He is fully aware of his bored mood and is simply waiting for the event of the train's arrival. Such boredom is understandable.

The second boredom is more complex, and Heidegger begins his description of it with the example of a pleasant evening at a party, where friends are drinking, chatting, smoking and flicking their cigarette butts, playing the guitar, singing, etc. The evening passes pleasantly and with ease, full of small, joyful events. But later, upon returning home, the partygoers find themselves overwhelmed by the revelation that the evening was quite frankly a waste of time. All the events of the party slip away into the void of the meaninglessness of everything with which one passed the time; the whole event was but a not too successful filling of the void which has now returned with a vengeance. This type of boredom catches up with the person who is bored after the fact, bringing them down and exposing the true mood underlying their previous actions and events.

The third type of boredom of our world is full of agitation and activity. Man is fascinated and engaged by a life full of events, leisure, hobbies, gadgets, scientific work, various machinations with beings, and engagement in Modern and Postmodern culture, politics, etc. The problem here is that this form of boredom is so deep that the bored subject forgets without a trace the very fact that the underlying core of all his engagements and activities is filling the void of boredom. In other words, this third type of boredom is so deep and deaf that the very problem of alienation is consigned to oblivion. Dasein has become so alien to something or someone that it has completely forgotten about this trauma. Unlike the second type, this attunement is not discovered after the fact, and it might even look like mankind is living a fully active life as "history and progress are bubbling and exciting." At the core of this life remains forgetfulness of the mood and alienation at hand. Close attention to culture and thinking shows that nothing fundamentally new or different is happening; there is no event, only the reworking and restocking of the same things in different configurations, colors, and attire. After Modernity, Nietzsche, and Heidegger, Western culture and thought linger in the third boredom of Dasein, which is left obsessed with kaleidoscopic machinations upon beings.

Despite the negative traits of boredom as a mode of oblivion and refusal, it is nevertheless the fundamental attunement of Dasein today, and as such it speaks to us of Dasein's state and relation to beings not only around it, and not only to the world as ready-to-hand raw material, but towards itself. After all, as a human, Dasein is also a being, one that is essentially present. Recognizing and honestly acknowledging boredom to be the mood of (Post-)Modernity and, more importantly, one's particular presence, is already something of much gravity for Dasein and our adequate understanding of ourselves in the whirlwind of history and culture.

To return to speech (*Rede*), the call of Beyng that calls Dasein back to its self out of the masses of *das Man* is a call to stop interpreting oneself through the chatter of others, and instead turn to oneself and self-interpretation. This call of Beyng resounds in silence, as Dasein's true speech is speaking to itself and no one else.[100]

Following the event of the "Turn" in his work, Heidegger rethought his early phenomenological interpretation of Dasein. The focus of attention shifted to the word and its relationship to a thing and to the beingful world as a whole. Speech is needed for questioning the truth of Beyng as the unconcealing relation of Earth, Heaven, Immortals, and Mortals. For Heidegger, poetry at large is existentially significant and responsible speech.

If poetry corresponds to the cyclical structure of time, then its disintegration correlates to the general innerworldly decomposition, and therefore is characteristic of the end. We already encountered the destruction of poetics, rhythm, and rhymes in the avant-garde and experimental poetry of Modernity.

Let us turn to the German Neoplatonist and Romanticist Hölderlin. Raised on Greek poetry and tragedy, Hölderlin devoted special attention to the poetic caesura. Translated from Latin, caesuras means a break, a disconnect, and is used in music and poetry as a pause or break in poetic line to impart an additional emphasis and diction to a verse. The poet Hölderlin saw in the caesura a special force that accentuates the spirit of tragedy, the strain and inner experience of the hero. Caesura emphasizes the hero's separation from his environment and his being placed face-to-face with fate.

A caesura is sometimes expressed in writing with a literal line break, a conscious break in the structure and rhythm that separates the final words with a phonetic and visual gap. But it also acts as a bridge and link; the pause is important as a silent accent that connects and raises the two sides of the verse. In a poem, this is expressed by the silence of the narrator or the protagonist himself — this is the turning point upon which he

---

100 See Egor Falyov, *Germenevtika Martina Heideggera* (Saint Petersburg: Aleteia, 2018).

either overcomes fate or is crushed by it. This is the time when "beginnings do not rhyme with ends." The latter apt definition offered by the poet also suits the eschatological moment when the caesura acts as a guillotine executing the tale: on the precipice of the culmination, the tale breaks off. The caesura goes on and on, whereby the pause becomes something unpleasant, something dragging on for entire epochs down to "infinity." The next line never begins, as the being of the tale hangs in the pause of the incompleteness or the absence of its beginning anew. It is a long, lingering *noch nicht*.

The caesura that lasts too long comes close to the meaning of the Greek term *epokhe* (ἐποχή), which means stopping, delaying, withholding, or standing in front of something at a short distance. The practice of *epokhe* means that the tale stops, and everything that has been said is "bracketed," or what was said is taken outside of the context of the pause itself. Here, various options appear. The first suggests a long era leading to madness. When the tale is cut short and the last echo of the last spoken line's meaning gradually fades out, and the telling as the sound ending the verse, teleologically and eschatologically concluding the tragedy, still never begins again, then the consciousness harkening and attuning itself to the voice ends up torn between the "no longer" and the "not yet." We can once again find an interesting correlate to this among patients with schizophrenia and psychosis who often hear auditory hallucinations (from simple to complex, including speech, commands, and dialogues). Expanding this metaphor in our direction, we can speak of spontaneously arising hallucinatory delusions as a traumatic reaction to the lack of completion of an authentic tale, or to the absence of any such tale whatsoever.

Being-in-*epokhe* is being in the gap, in standing-before-the-end, an end that is postponed. If the caesura is long enough, then the conclusion of the long since silent tale will be not so much an end as a pointless phrase dropped into a void, the meaning of which no one remembers. The listeners will have parted ways, forgotten the lack of end, and dwelled in the world in such a way that the absent conclusion replaces progressive expectations for a better future ensured by successful political and scientific-technological arrangements of the poverty of the present being endless.

But the long pause itself can be recognized as an already happening end. Instead of awaiting the end of a severed strophe, the silence itself is understood as the end-right-here, the already-end. The very refusal of the tale is the "missing line" itself in the form of its absence. The caesura places us not in front of expectation for when the still not said will be said, but before itself as the anguishing exposure of the tragic fate of Being.

Epokhe, as the practice of bracketing and removing from context the whole preceding exposition and evaluation, thus opens up the beginning of another tale. The silent void of the caesura gives open space for singing to the one who will be courageous enough — and their courage will not be the audacity of hubris (ὕβρις) against Tradition, but rather, on the contrary, their courage will be another beginning of Tradition's endless possibilities and forms for the manifestation of the sacred.

Caesura-*epokhe* thus reveals itself to be a possibility for turning (and curing) the situation of *noch nicht* into a firm refusal and a transgressive turn towards understanding the void in the spirit of a Zen koan.

Mathematics

Yet another approach to language is presented by the Anglo-American branch of philosophy better known under the name of logical positivism and analytical philosophy. The latter was one response to the linguistic turn in 20th-century continental philosophy.

The specific precursors of analytical philosophy that laid out its ensuing trajectory included Bertrand Russell's neo-realism and positivism, Charles Peirce's pragmatism and doctrine of common sense, and the empiricism, scientism, and logical positivism rooted in the Vienna Circle and Ludwig Wittgenstein's logic. On these grounds arose the fundamentally anti-metaphysical, atheistic, and pro-scientific orientation of analytical philosophy, which treats the corpus and methodology of the natural sciences with great reverence and relies entirely on logic, or even hyperlogicism, materialism, empiricism, physicalism, criteria of scienticity (verificationism), and mathematics. Language entered the center of the neo-positivists and analytical philosophers' attention later than logic, and their approach to and methods for working with language were inherited from the spheres of the natural sciences and logic, which they applied to everyday language as well as to the use, play, and variations (distortions) of language involved in formulating, expressing, and understanding philosophical judgements.

Most interesting to us here is the Austrian thinker Ludwig Wittgenstein and his key early work, *Tractatus Logico-Philosophicus*, some of whose theses became iconic for all of neo-positivism and the analytical trend. It bears noting that some of the singular, succinct formulations of the *Tractatus* can be read in an absolutely opposite vein to the one envisioned by their author and the ensuing school, i.e., they can be read in the direction of the metaphysics of language and sacred linguistic monism. This is despite the fact that the general context of the work and its ensuing train of thought ruled out such a possibility by proclaiming a lack of any alternative and asserting a predetermined philosophical starting point and trajectory.

For Wittgenstein, the main problem boils down to the pair of language and world: language completely reflects and accounts for the world, and the structure of language is the ontological structure of the world. There is nothing outside of language, for language contains all possible variations of facts and relations, i.e., everything that is possible in the world. The world consists of facts which correspond to simple propositions. For Wittgenstein, propositions are the minimal units of language. In point 5.526 of the *Tractatus*, he concludes: "We can describe the world completely by means of fully generalized propositions, i.e. without first correlating any name with a particular object."[101] Here, we encounter a fundamental disregard for what is of cornerstone importance to other philosophical and traditional schools of thought: the name (the word). Wittgenstein subtly proclaims that it is not necessary for a name to agree with an object, which is to say that the nomination of things is strictly arbitrary within his system. It is not necessary for a name or signification to essentially or teleologically agree with an object. Such are the requirements of the logical approach, whereby in the place of a special symbol in an equation, formula, and function one can substitute any arbitrary signifieds: objects, subjects, things, properties, actions, etc. this is consistent with the program proclaimed in the *Tractatus*:

> 4.112 Philosophy aims at the logical clarification of thoughts… Philosophy does not result in 'philosophical propositions,' but rather in the clarification of propositions…

> 4.116 Everything that can be thought at all can be thought clearly. Everything that can be put into words can be put clearly. [102]

Wittgenstein calls simple propositions, the minimal combinations of things and objects, "atomic facts." These facts

---

101 Ludwig Wittgenstein, *Tractatus Logico-Philosophicus*, trans. D.F. Pears and B.F. McGuinness (London: Routledge, 1974), 61.

102 Ibid., 30.

are independent of one another, hence the world and language are not one-in-many or a continuum, but a fragmented multiplicity. Cognition as the accounting for and analysis of facts thus comes to the fore. Language is to be purified of ambiguity and polysemy in general, and Wittgenstein believes that classical philosophical problems are based not on actual questions, but on misunderstandings of language and statements. Purging language is to automatically lead to solving such questions or removing false problems from thinking. We read further in the *Tractatus*:

> 6.234 Mathematics is a method of logic...
>
> 6.343 Mechanics is an attempt to construct according to a single plan all the true propositions that we need for the description of the world...
>
> 6.3431 The laws of physics, with all their logical apparatus, still speak, however indirectly, about the objects of the world.[103]

These theses are in agreement with neo-positivism and analytical philosophy's reliance on physicalism's total reduction of all beings and thinking to physical reality and cognitive processes in the brain. The consequence is a hypermaterialism which interprets man, his thinking, and his experiences in physiologico-biological and biochemical terms. Physics and physicalism are reducible to mathematics as the main apparatus, and mathematics, in turn, is completely reducible to logic as its operative base. Clarity of analysis and the manipulation of logical signs guarantee the correctness and verifiability of statement and theories, thus once and for all achieving the transparency of thought and coherence of thinking.

Wittgenstein believed that his *Tractatus* finally solved all philosophical problems, and he practically never entered into discussions on it. But the transparency of the language of mathematics and logic is fully analogous to a totalitarian dictatorship, in the likes of the prison architecture of the Panopticon, built inside thinking. It should come as no surprise that the the invention of the Panopticon model belongs to the

---

103 Ibid., 80.

thinking of the English utilitarianist Jeremy Bentham. Just as any prison implies walls, Wittgenstein formulates the boundaries of what is thinkable and sayable:

> 6.5 When the answer cannot be put into words, neither can the question be put into words. The riddle does not exist...
>
> 6.53 The correct method in philosophy would really be the following: to say nothing except what can be said, i.e. propositions of natural science — i.e. something that has nothing to do with philosophy — and then, whenever someone else wanted to say something metaphysical, to demonstrate to him that he had failed to give a meaning to certain signs in his propositions.
>
> 7. What we cannot speak about we must pass over in silence.[104]

Thus Wittgenstein concludes his *Tractatus Logico-Philosophicus*. The final points openly contradict the language of metaphysical traditions, theology, and poetry, which do nothing other than speak and hint with decorations, frames, and metaphors at the central diamond of the ineffable, the darkness of the Divine and the void of the Nothing.

Rejecting the polysemy and metaphoricity of language means rejecting human language as such, whereby the high abstractions of natural languages that require complex and multilayered metaphors (cf. Lakoff) are reduced to the sterile and atomic abstractions of logical equations and formulas, i.e., to synthetic languages oriented towards calculability. Such an approach to language and philosophy makes impossible not only metaphors but also genuine stories and tales about something, narratives and myths, given that they inevitably contradict the dry formalism of the logico-mathematical apparatus.

Mathematics takes on special significance in the philosophical current of speculative realism, which is centered around the task of overcoming the situation of correlationism and privileged access, as the French philosopher Quentin Meillassoux put it.[105] The principle of correlationism lies in

---

104 Ibid., 89.

105 See Quentin Meillassoux, *After Finitude: An Essay on the Necessity of Contingency*, trans. Ray Brassier (London: Continuum, 2008).

the correlation between being and human thinking, whereby any knowledge in essence does not have anything to do with an objective and independent (external) world, but always operates with a system of relations. Accordingly, philosophies of privileged access are all those schools which proclaim that the human being and human ways of thinking de facto have direct access to things, while other objects have no such privilege.

The human being is the subject, bearer, and witness of correlations, hence the world is understood strictly anthropocentrically: the word in all the diversity of beings is given to man, for man and for his thinking. The understanding of any object is always compensated by our notions about it, by how we use it or how we might use it. In the end, even our innate sense organs, from which we move on to develop judgements and thoughts, distort access to objects. In speculative realism, we are dealing with the problem articulated by Immanual Kant, and more specifically with a new posing of the problem of thinking/accessing the *Ding-an-sich*, the "thing-in-itself." Kant closed this possibility by arguing that man is in principle not capable of cognizing any thing within its own being-for-itself and outside of any correlations and relations involving man. In question here is the ultimate objectivity and independence of objects from the subject, even on the level of the subject's thinking about objects. The latter is taken to be obviously impossible.

All the philosophical projects of object-oriented ontology are built on this assumption of the autonomous, non-human "in-itself-being" of any (*ergo* totally all) objects.[106] Object-oriented ontologies postulate an ontological egalitarianism of objects, wherein the human is only one among others and is not superiorly distinguished on any plane from nuts, planets, beer molecules, tires, grains of sand in the Sahara, webpages, etc. Every object is an object-in-itself, and the sum of all objects does not constitute anything bigger; hence, for example, any living organism or composite mechanism is nothing "whole"

---

106 See Ian Bogost, *Alien Phenomenology, Or, What It's Like to be a Thing* (Minneapolis: University of Minnesota Press, 2012); Levi R. Bryant, *The Democracy of Objects* (Ann Arbor: Open Humanities Press, 2011).

with some inherent, classic dialectic between its parts and its whole, but is merely a constellation of autonomous objects in the darkness of their own "self-orientation." Interaction between objects is described in the likeness of a cartoon or Pidgin, i.e., whenever one object "knows" or interacts with another, there is only a situational, accidental interrelation between the traits and qualities of one object that might be recognizable or disturbed by the capacities of another object. In other words, we can speak of the color and extension of an object because we have such corresponding sense organs, and we can recognize density and hardness because we have hands, but these qualities and capacities for use are nothing more than correlates that are intrinsic to our biological constitution. Therefore, speculative realists and flat ontologists argue that we actually know nothing about objects as such; instead, we are always merely perceiving their cartoonish caricature drawn by an artist who hypertrophies some traits while diminishing others which are not as important or unique to us.

Hence begins speculative realism's programmatic declaration: let us leave behind the privilege of anthropological access and correlationism in thought, let us put aside the compromising affects intrinsic to human thinking, and let us seek to gain non-anthropological access to objects. This subtly levels not only the ontological status of the human being, but any subject capable of constructing an ontological hierarchy and affirming the power of some objects over others.

This project once again leads speculative realism and object-oriented ontology to mathematics. The point is that mathematics and the physical constants and laws it describes existed before the appearance of any human or life in general, which means that this "language" is objectively non-human and pure from any correlations. Mathematics is the only instrument for describing beings that is autonomous from human thinking. Mathematics de-subjectivizes our consciousness and thinking because it immerses us into the spheres of unstable, non-human laws. The world of mathematics is a world without a subject —

a subject can engage or ignore mathematics, but for mathematical relations and laws themselves this is irrelevant, for it is a world of the purest and absolute logic. Mathematics, therefore, is not a product or invention of human culture — mathematics was discovered when humans stumbled upon something that had always existed before man and and will continue to operate after man disappears.

The cognition of objects by mathematical instruments means mathematizing (describing in formulas and functions) all mathematizable qualities. These qualities will be genuine for the thing-in-itself, with means that mathematization leaves the bare "truth" for the thing-in-itself after discarding the non-mathematizable qualities that are the distortions and importations of human presence. What is measurable — a number, a function — is objective and independent, whereas everything else is an anthropological correlation and a repressive projection of the anthropological factor/access onto other equal objects.

This type of thinking about objects is what interests those engaged in apologetics for flat ontologies. Insofar as mathematics exists and its provisions are correct without, before, and after man, it can be deemed not only non-human, but something altogether "beyond" — even "beyond the grave." Numbers and functions merge with the element of death as understood by modern, post-sacred culture, i.e., as absolute withdrawal, exclusion, inaccessibility, the impossibility of the subject returning to presence in the world of the living. Death is simply an end, a forever extinguished screen behind the surface of which there is nothing whatsoever. This is in accord with the purely physicalist approach that treats consciousness as a product of the cognitive work of the brain. Speculative realism and object-oriented ontology call on us to think as if humanity has gone completely extinct. On interesting example on this note has been presented by Eugene Thacker, who speaks of the logical subtraction of the human being from the world. Thacker proposes three images:

1. The world-for-us — this is the world that man and society see, the ordinary "world" as it is known and understood by the ordinary human being and the scientific worldview of Modernity. This is the world of correlation and privileged access to things.
2. The world-in-itself — the planet Earth as the Kantian "thing-in-itself," indifferent to mankind and turned unto itself, the material presence of nature without the gaze of the human observer.
3. The world-without-us — the planet after the extinction event of mankind. This is how "we" would need to think of the world-for-us — not only as separate nature, but as encompassing all the artefacts and constellations of objects created by people and machines — from the standpoint of logically excluding man as an observer, actor, and central subject by default.

Hereupon arise images of humanless, distant, cold, outer-space or hypochthonic landscapes, tectonic layers of archaeological fossils, colonies of mucus and fungi spreading in the darkness of the world's axils, fields of computers, cyber-cities, fiber optic pipes *à la* cyberpunk, etc. The human is absent, but numbers and relations remain. Their laws are eternal, sterile, and indifferent in the absence of any soul, like endless black space in which thought was never born.

In our middle world, this scenario is fully complementary to the conscious and galloping process of digitizing beings and the introduction of digital, AI, and machine technologies and solutions in all spheres of life. Mankind is consciously migrating into a virtual environment. With the digitalization of consciousness as part of the transhumanist project, the literal extinction of mankind won't even be necessary. We will disappear, and all that will be left of us will be a digitized binary mathematical surrogate, the purest nihilism of matter imitating absent presence, all the way down to filigree speech synthesis using neural networks. Thus, it turns out that mathematics and logic take on the traits and qualities of language only upon being given their subjective use by man in his activities and thinking, and the latter set the boundaries and distances in relation to the nihilistic element concealed within numbers.

But in the body and the non-human subjectivity of the *Gestell*, mathematics is striving towards full liberation, domination, and the annihilation of existential presence in the world.[107]

In their very essence, speculative realism and object-oriented ontology are a conscious turning upside-down of Martin Heidegger's ideas and the world-forming (*Weltbildend*) role of the human that he saw in the world. In their most radical versions, the human as Dasein who projects the world is excluded altogether. Heidegger saw the final oblivion of Beyng in the triumph of the Gestell, whose thinking is exhausted by machinations and calculations of beings. For Heidegger, such is the utter end of thinking in the final phase of the dementia of Western thinking. Calculation and computation instead of thinking and poetry, absence instead of presence, "pure" beings instead of Beyng — all of this is identical to the pure presence of a body without Dasein, i.e., a corpse, a decaying and decomposing piece of matter.

We have arrived at the formulation of extreme antitheses: on the one hand, we have human thinking and presence, whose roots go back into the most ancient *mytho-poiesis* that expresses the world through language and tale about it and itself; on the other hand, we have neo-positivism, analytical and object-oriented philosophy, and the anti-human uninhibitedness of digitalization and mathematics.

Moving on from language in its verbal and textual forms, we can cast our glance at representational art as the graphic dimension and expression of poetics. We are talking about the natural ornamentations that are typical of Europeans and Indo-Europeans — like ancient meander designs, floristic designs (medieval *Laubwerk*, *Rankenwerk*, etc.), and animal ones (Scandinavian *Borre*, *Urness*, etc.). The close interweaving of branches, roots, leaves, trunks, paws, the tails and necks of snakes, dragons, horse, bears, and people, is a graphic correlate

---

[107] We have expounded a detailed study of the Gestell, transhumanism, and digitalization in Askr Svarte, *Tradition and Future Shock: Visions of a Future that Isn't Ours*.

of poetic tropes, diction, structure, and metaphor. Animal and plant ornamentations are another dimension of mythopoetics in stone, wood, and bone carvings or in embroidery and frescos. These images act as a completely intelligible language expressing mythological plots and scenes and reflecting the surrounding world. On the ontotheological level, natural ornamentation postulates the immanence of the manifestation of the Divine and a single continuum of nodes, links, and interweavings between the world and language in visual art.

On the other end of this spectrum are extremely acute and abstract geometric ornamentations. Overall, geometry is reducible to mathematics, and this means that it is analyzable, calculable, reasonable, and constructible by way of functions. The theological correlate of this is the aniconism of the creationist religions and prohibitions on depicting God or other living beings. If in the domain of aesthetics European Christianity fully inherited the canons of Greece and Rome, and thereby had a significantly diminished and corrected pathos with respect to the transcendence of God *vis-à-vis* the world, then this pathos found full realization in the geometric ornamentations of Islam, such as in *khatam* and especially *girih*. Such patterns have no proto-image or correlate in the middle world, which is to say that they are abstract and point only to an even greater separation from the world, referring us to the Abrahamic "God" separated from the world and man. Here, we are dealing with an ontologically "dissected" metaphysics: God is fundamentally separate and different from the world. Thus, we see that the aesthetics of creationism are directed not only away from the world, but even against the world, for the world is "created," and worshipping creatures instead of the Creator is a great sin awaiting harsh punishment by a jealous figure. The mathematical foundation of purely geometric ornamentation points us to the chthonic rather than uranic roots of this aesthetic. This raises the question of whether with the "God" of creationism we are actually dealing with an opposite, Titanic figure as understood by the Greeks in their story of the Titanomachy.

As a form of mythopoetics and the manifestation of the Divine-in-the-world in graphic depiction and art, ornamentation contrasts the cold, analytical calculation of aniconic geometry. The latter's correlate is the non-human instance of number and relation. Hence is exposed the erroneousness of postulating mathematics as the "language of the Divinities and theology" as if by virtue of its extreme abstractness, strictness, and ideal quality. The history of the oblivion of Being over the course of the metaphysics of the West in its unfolding into Gestell shows us an altogether different role for numbers and mathematics in the construction of an ideal, logical, and unambiguous language — from Plato to Leibniz[108] to Wittgenstein and the popular neuronetwork linguistic models and graphic design assistants. All of this goes against the flexibility of poetics and the vine that is the symbol of the middle world and the human being. Therefore, Pythagoras and his "ecstatic theology of number" seem to us to be a path that is dubious to the greatest extent.

The human being is now colliding with the truly non-human, the inhuman. This situation bears likeness to the tragic hero's standing before his fate and the inevitability of the caesura-era. In a number of its intentions, the humane and existential position of Martin Heidegger's philosophy is consonant with traditional notions of the leading role of language in theo-ontology and culture. Meanwhile, the language of analytical philosophy makes it easier to enter into relationships with technology, gadgets, software, or assemblages of material objects rather than with people. The language of analytical philosophy is fundamentally oriented in the opposite direction from the human being; it is the hubris of number and digit, the crowning completion of nihilism and the "language" of sterile death.

---

108 See Gadamer, *Truth and Method*.

Towards Another Myth

Mythos itself tells us of its own — and our own — aging, dilapidation, and gradual depletion of grace and initiatic power along the path of decline into the end times of the Iron Age or Kali-Yuga. Etymologically, "tradition" comes from the Latin *tradere* and literally means to hand down, to pass along, to transmit. At this point, we have the right to pose the question: What exactly is transmitted in tradition? One could classically and fairly distinguish the customs, external forms, and historically conditioned rituals as well as everyday practices that settle down into folkloric-ethnographic heritage. Without a doubt, such things are instruments and developments rooted in the principles of sacred doctrines and applied to actual life in all its diversity. But they are profusely mutable and secondary, and custom should not be substituted for tradition in the high sense of the word. This is partly why accepting the eschatological and existential drama leads one to a rapid devaluation of all kinds of archaeological and ethnographic heritage from the past, while others are drive to merely reassemble and reverify the worship of forms without content.

The latter treatment of tradition resembles a situation in which a grandfather teaches a father how to build a good log house, starting with laying a strong foundation on solid soil. The father teaches the same to his sons, and they, in turn, teach their descendants. After a few generations have passed, the soil becomes muddy and unfit, but the sons and grandsons continue to lay the foundation in the same way over and over again. The foundation begins to shift and requires reinforcement, the house starts to warp, the logs slide in different directions, the crowns rot from dampness, and healthy life is no longer possible inside. On the one hand, the situation demands taking a step back and radically rethinking the behests of the fathers, maybe driving piles and raising the house above the ground, or leaving the land and moving deeper into the forest. On the other hand, even if one changes the exterior customs around raising the house, such as the rituals and blood sacrifices performed in antiquity, then any new approach still retains the intention of building a house and dwelling in it on the earth and under the heavens. That is, even given a significant or complete change in paradigm, the orientation remains unchanged, but continuing to "do it the old way" despite the obvious, total deterioration of the environment and conditions would be foolish. Thus, in merely exterior reproduction, tradition is turned into an ossified relic, a simulation of authenticity amidst clearly manifest inadequacy. The task is to pass between the Scylla of the suggestiveness of the bygone past and the Charybdis of the enveloping present without losing oneself.

What should remain unchanged is the immovable center, the ultimate concentration of the Divine and sacred oneness in cult. But even here, we know of frequent shifts in the heads of pantheons or the variability of leading cult figures and their myths. One classic example is the dominant Deity changing from Creator to Destroyer when the world's lot falls to the latter and the time comes to die.

What is necessary is that tradition transmit the apophatic core that by its very nature as such cannot be held in one's hands. *Mythos* thus comes to the fore with all its poetic and prosaic ways and tropes, metaphors, suggestive and ecstatic rhymes, deictic symbols and hints. That which points to the apophatic source and Beyng at one time as a cataphatic manifestation, in a beautiful pattern and literal weaving out of all our myths, (hi) stories, and forms of everyday being, can radically change.

Innerworldly authenticity, that is making the surrounding world one's own, is directly tied to dwelling in a particular locus and within the lifeworld as a whole. This means becoming local, one's own, for these lands. Heidegger associated this with the feeling of Homeland, *Heimat*, whence *heimisch* ("of the home," "native," "local"). In the German language, the state of rootlessness, homelessness, and foreignness is expressed as *unheimisch*, which barely differs from the word *unheimlich* — "uncanny," "terrifying." Through the *heim* and the *un-* resounding in these two words, Heidegger draws the connection between the state of rootlessness and submersion in an uncanny, frightening alienation from the world.

Myth is the space of thrownness in which we find ourselves and in which we need to dwell as if at home. Once dwelling within it authentically, with the course of historical time and metaphysical fall we find ourselves among the ruins of our well-furnished Being. The uncanniness of the world and the problem of dwelling within it, amidst conditions that are already radically different and fatally worse, unsettles us. Rising up before us is an aporia and a koan: dwelling in the absent myth of Being-as-Nothing.

The search for ultimately credible grounds of truth, like searching for radical, unimaginable, and impossible otherness, are the essentially cursed and ancestral questions of the West. Therefore, any rational, linear solution of any koan as if "head-on" is erroneous and comparable to man's incapacity to decode and understand idiomatic expressions in speech that sometimes contradict their direct lexical meaning.

The beginning of Another Tale is bound up with the problem of the "new." Heidegger left us with a two-pronged passage on this note: "Belonging to the genuine transition are, above all, courage for the old and freedom for the new."[109] But the old, Heidegger says, is nothing "antiquarian" or something from historiographical tradition. It cannot be surpassed by anything younger, and it reveals itself historically (*geschichtliche*). Rather, what is at stake is something primary, a matter of principles and beginnings. In turn, the new is not equal to Modernity or any illusory novelty that tries to substitute itself for an event (*Ereignis*). Rather, the new is "the freshness of the originariness of re-beginning, that which ventures out into the concealed

---

109 Heidegger, *Contributions to Philosophy (Of the Event)*, 343.

future of the first beginning and thus cannot at all be 'new' but must be even *older* than the old."[110] For calculative Modernity, the syzygy of the old and the new, like the thinking of those whom Heidegger calls the "transitional ones," is fundamentally unintelligible. Counting the old as only the archeological and the temporally prehistoric ("the more ancient, the more reliable"), we remain within the framework of the calculable, the quantitative approach, and error. Understanding the new in the spirit of fleeting, momentary pseudo-events of marketing and media, or as necessarily contrasting and overturning what just preceded, we equally remain within the framework of false temporality and historiography.

The problem of the radically new in the philosophy of the eternal return has been examined by Sergei Zhigalkin.[111] At the core of his thoughts and constructions lies the idea that any and every instant belongs to eternity. The world and all of history are not so much the unfolding of eternity in time, moving away and coming back around in a circle, as much as they are the pulsation of eternity-time and the always-belonging of the moment to eternity itself. Intrinsic to Zhigalkin's metaphysics is a special understanding of cyclicality and the eternal return obviously inspired by Nietzsche. We are peculiarly accustomed to understanding time through the metaphor of a wheel, as turning and moving in a circle. That which was, can return again with insignificant details and changes that do not affect the "plot." It would be more correct to affirm that the past can return anew as literally the same, completely identical in all of its infinite details. A hair will lie in exactly the same way on every head, grains of sand will be blown by the wind on all the beaches of the world in exactly the same way. We can live through incarnations in the world, as can the world itself and all cosmoi, and return again and again.

---

110 Ibid.

111 Sergei Zhigalkin, *Metafizika vechnogo vozvrashcheniia*, 2nd ed. (Moscow: Kul'turnaia revoliutsiia, 2011).

Yet, Zhigalkin introduces an important detail to this picture of infinite turnings of the wheel. Everyday thinking takes into account the turns of the wheel and the returns of one and the same. It is as if the world will be reborn and grow again right after its destruction, whereby we are multiplying the count of the repetition of events by one: the second return of the same, the third, the fourth, infinitely many. In this lies a certain error and mix-up of register. Zhigalkin repeatedly emphasizes that the eternal return happens without any one-by-one multiplication of the turns of the wheel of time and the cosmos.[112] There is the flow of time and history, and there is return, but there is no increase in the number of (re)turns. It seems to us that the whole beingful world does not simply return again as absolutely the same, but as if "for a second time." Hence, in Zhigalkin's metaphysics of time, every moment of being is eternal and "returns" not simply "a second time," but returns to itself and its "singularity." Insofar as there is no counting of this pulsation of eternity, we can consider the return to be the "first" only by force of convention. Every moment is equally far away from the beginning, from the end, and from its "repetition." It is eternal in none other than its transient instant. Therefore, Zhigalkin's cosmos of time is pulsating eternity. Such a metaphysics is quite hermetically sealed, closed off, but it is not a world of ideas in the likes of a form of super-being(s), but the relation of time to eternity and to the return of "cycles" without quantitative multiplication. It is out of this exposition that Zhigalkin raises the problem of the new.

Firstly, we can understand the "new" within the framework of everyday thinking as that which is "had for the first time." This new is relative. It was already in the plan of possibility, in the sphere of potentiality. For example, any spontaneous number that a person utters first (i.e., no one ever uttered this number before) really sounds new. But, in essence, it was already given

---

112 Sergei Zhigalkin, *Ob inykh gorizontakh zdeshnego: apologiia vechnogo vozvrashcheniia* (Moscow: Iazyki slavianskikh kul'tur, 2019).

in potentiality, in the infinite range of numbers and methods of addition or some other calculation; our saying it aloud is only a translation or transmission of it into the state of actuality, into presence. The same is the case in the raising of a house: it is new and really never did exist in this given place, but on the whole it is similar to others and is merely another embodiment of the Platonic Idea of House.

Secondly, the new can be understood as that which is opening up, revealing itself. For example, a hitherto unseen landscape opens up before us, or we experience insight into understanding a philosophical idea. In this case, we imply that the landscape and the idea were there before and without us. They became new only in our consciousness upon first encountering them or catching (in)sight. Such examples of what already exists in the world of ideas in the state of potentiality (which can be derived through well-known procedures of combining and reasoning) are not "new" in the genuine, ontological sense of the word. For instance, if a wanderer arrives at the end of the earth and beings and thrusts a spear into the boundary, then it will not pierce the boundary through, but will only extend the sphere of the already extant to the depth of the spear's penetration. The new, thus, seems to be altogether impossible, a false end.

Immersion into the problem of the new is also inevitably bound up with thinking in terms of aporias and antinomies. Logical rationality will not help us here, and it should be discarded like ballasts or even shackles containing the mind. Zhigalkin writes:

> But let us return to the question: can we call something "new" that was already known, even if only potentially, or existed before? Neither the one nor nor the other can be called new in the full sense of the word. What, then, is new? The new is what there was not. It is something that wasn't at all — neither in the world of changes nor even in eternity — yet which has arisen right now before our very eyes. New is that which never existed anywhere. Neither in actuality nor in potentiality. In other words, what is new itself not only did not exist, but also no "seed" of it from which it might grow ever existed

either. The new is not a consequence of the old; behind it there is no chain of causes stretching back into the past. The new is new; it does not arise from anything. The new is what has arisen for the first time, that which is unexpected and unexplainable for all. [113]

Upon first approach, it seems that this determination is the very same "accursed questioning" and voluntarism. However, Zhigalkin proceeds, let us look at the origin of the universe in the broadest possible sense as everything that is and can be perceived in any form. Once upon a time, everything appeared and was new. What interests us here is the theological line: If the world was created by a creator, then did he know what he was going to create beforehand? Was there a form, idea, or design for all being(s) even before creation? If there were, then the universe is not new, or only relatively so, because here we once again confront the pre-existence of the world before its creation, which means that it is not new, but a translation of the potential into the actual. This applies, for example, to the Platonic Demiurge who contemplated the ideas and created the world: he is not a pantokrator, but a mediator.

Once again, everyday thinking pushes us to pose the question: How can something be created without being anticipated by feeling, reason, intuition? How can nothing lead to something? This is a purely logical problem and classic antinomy. In monistic doctrines, the Absolute Divinity (not the middle or "central" one) possesses pure spontaneity, and its emanations are not determined by anything. Its manifestation of itself as the world happens in an instant, i.e., in a single moment of time which might best be described by analogy with the infinity of a geometrical point represented as an object with a base and space value of zero. The whole beingful world arises as something genuinely new, something never here before, something spontaneous and impossible, immediately and for all. The new is the impossible that has happened. The very existence of the universe — not even only our particular cosmos, but all

---

113 Zhigalkin, *Metafizika vechnogo vozvrashcheniia*.

existence as such, everything of which it may be said "it is" in any way whatsoever — comprehensively confirms the possibility of the new. The correspondence between the world and the Divine is established ontologically-retrospectively. The manifestation of the world is a gesture of the Divine throwing itself "blindly," as it were, out of self-concealment into something that is not pre-established. The world is one possibility, not a necessity, of the Divine's ecstatic vision of itself in the act of its own sacrifice in which it might conceal itself in ontological pain.

But now the opposite problem stands before us: the path to the new from within the already present, from the beingful world in the noetic and metaphysical form in which it is, i.e., in deep decline and alienation. Zhigalkin cites the quite relevant argument that all of "our" thinking naturally resists the idea of the new. "We" simply want for the impossible to have been and remain impossible. This actually simple, understandable, irrefutable desire is a refuge from facing the metaphysical problem. Denying the new is an escape from selfhood into deep "slumber," which corresponds to Dasein's dissolution amidst the structures of everydayness and rejecting freedom in favor of usurpation by the Gestell. Zhigalkin proposes to make a move, a gesture, in the opposite intellectual direction: let us consider the new to be possible. Firstly, what will we find ourselves facing, i.e., what should the new look like? Must the new necessarily be unconditionally other, radically different and unimaginably extravagant in comparison to the already present and known? Insofar as the new is what is fundamentally not grounded in anything, then attributing to it any necessary otherness means bringing it down to some ground and annulling its newness. In attributing to the new any otherness, we dictate limitations to it, we make the new derivative from the old, which means that it is no longer what we have been speaking of. For example, the new, as something radically different to the already present-in-here-being, would be the very same One (ἕν) of Neoplatonism that encompasses the many without cancelling the ensuing stages of emanation into the many. An analogous structure can be found in Kashmir Shaivism, in the relation between the fourth type of speech, Paravac, and the three preceding ones in the ontology of the world's unfolding.

Paradoxically, thus, nothing prevents the new from being both radically different from all present being and similar to it, or even the very same. Zhigalkin concludes that the matter is not in appearance, phenomenal forms, analogies, colors and contours. The new is distinguished from the old in essence. Even if they are identical, the old is still wholly derived from preceding preconditions and being(s), whereas the new is "the irruption of the metaphysical."[114] The irruption of the new is the experience of the world and the self within it as special, hitherto unknown, yet still irrupting in the midst of this particular (or any other) beingful world. The votive voice of this special feeling is categorical. For Zhigalkin, this boils down to a state of "extreme awakenedness" and "power over one's essence."

This situation can be summed up metaphorically as turning away from the world and towards the world of false dreams and altogether concrete virtuality, inside which the exterior, genuine world seems to be something false. After all, all the structures of the nightmare work to strengthen the subject's bond to his illusions. These illusions are our world, the empirical reality of the author and readers of these lines. But this metaphor of "wakefulness vs. slumber" does not unfold within a completely intelligible distinction between being awake "in the real world" and a state of dreaming and deep slumber or delirium. Both modes are mixed together and collide with one another in the single space of our being-here-in-the-world. They are described through cultural and philosophical dynamics by the historiography of Traditionalism or by Martin Heidegger's History of Being. Here, we already catch a sense of the tune of

---

114 The qualification should be made that Zhigalkin's use of the terms "metaphysical" and "being" does not coincide with the broader definition of these terms in Heidegger. The resonance between these ideas is in the spirit, not the letter.

the history of the paradoxical identity and difference between the Nothing and present being(s), between *Sein* and *Seiende*. We also sense that the re-founding of present being(s) proceeds by way of entering into the unprecedented and "uncanniest" that does not belong to present being. The world, as a flash of something in the midst of nothing, is an Event.

In our case, we can speak of how, looking from the (opened-up) One, we see no difference between apophatic Nothing-selfhood and cataphatic being, because being is the when-where-how of the is-not of Nothing.

Zhigalkin's notion of the new is fully analogous to the Other. Despite the problematic nature and difficulty of thinking through this topic and its spaces, nevertheless, the very word "Other" is an aspiration. It is an unsettling deictic sign that calls everything into questionable relativity and impossibility. Other is a synonym for Nothing.

Another Myth needs its midwifery art, its other tale and teller. Yet, it seems absurd to pose the question of the right to tell forth a myth. Vladimir Toporov has emphasized that the Latin word *auctor*, whence "author," comes from *augeo*, that is to "cultivate," "expand," "multiply," "strengthen." Treating it as a verb of creation, he puts it on par with the Indian *vāc* (speech, word) and German *wachen* ("to be awake," "to keep watch").[115] We have already seen that all three of these semantic lines are tightly intertwined, especially in European philosophy.

The autonomous author dies in Postmodern culture following the Divine, the author *par excellence*. The traditional notion holds man to be co-teller, i.e., it is not man alone, but the Divine and the sacred that express themselves through man's (our) mouth, eyes, and hands. Herder's apt aphorism that "peoples are thoughts of God" can be developed in this direction

---

115 See V. Toporov, "Ob odnom spetsificheskom povorote problemy avtorstva" in *Scribantur haec. Problema avtora i avtorstva v istorii kul'tury* (Moscow: Russian State University for the Humanities, 1993), 48-58.

to say that those among the peoples in the world who think the Divine in its extreme dimensions and atheophanies are Tradition itself in essence.

But all of these are forest paths and poetic tropes of the tale itself. Who the author of the tale is, and who its listener is, the tale itself will tell. A tale that sounds like impossible concealment of silence. Especially in its caesura, where the voice is no longer here, but its sound is still fading.

It should be declared outright that the absolute arbitrariness of Another Myth does not need sufficient external grounds.

What kind of myth corresponds to our position? What is our position, what are its prospects? The eschatological motif determines everything that we have repeatedly said. It is quite logical to imagine that the worst state of the cosmos, the worst conditions for a breakthrough to authenticity, for a sacrocentric awakening, will come at the point closest to the end of the old cycle and the beginning of the new cycle: at the moment of the universal winter solstice, when the disintegration and degradation of the world, the alienation of man, and the diminishment of light, sacred, and memory of them will reach their lowest depths, when their meaning will be the lowest. Indeed, everything seems to suggest that the worst will be the very last moment in the extreme darkness just before the very first, timid flashes of lightning.

In this metaphysical picture, the darkness is not absolute but relative. There is always some echo and flash of light, no matter how unimaginably small. The last scattered drops are the souls who remember, who are looking for their own kind and seeking the traces of the departed Divinities in old tomes. This is the Platonic movement of emanation (πρόοδος) towards the lowest possible limit in order to push away from it and begin the reverse ascent (ἐπιστροφή). For this sake, the emanation, the light, needs to preserve and distinguish itself amidst the darkness at the lowest levels of the cosmos. Even if it will be indiscernible to the eye, this emanation will be an unimaginably small fraction lighter than the surrounding darkness. A very similar motif is present in the monistic *imaginaire* of Shiva, where all the worlds and atmans are essentially the space in which the Deity hides from himself in order to rediscover and return to himself. The Deity enjoys the theatrical game of concealment and revelation. Everything that ever happens always has some kind of caveat.

But the votive voice of the poet calls for risking one more breath, and we see no hindrance to finally tell of the future that is obviously awaiting the world.

Classical theo-ontology associates the factual presence of the world with the existence of the Divine as its ground, its principle, upon which rests the cosmos and from which it flows forth. Even the darkest, ignorant eras belong to this order. Insofar as the world still exists, albeit in its most perverted and inferior, materialist forms, then the Divinity is still somewhat, in some minimal forms, maintaining its existence. But we allow for the historical possibility that the world exists in a situation in which its sacred or theological principle (the Absolute and the principle of the Perennialists, Traditionalists, and believers) literally disappears from the world and is no longer even mentioned. Even the very fact of its oblivion will be forgotten — no one will ever say: "It seems that we lost something at one point." This is obviously the concrete historical future stemming from the deep foundations of the dominant futurological projects of the global, Western-centric culture.

The radical limit is not the minimal share of light amidst the pitch-black darkness, but the darkness in which there is no light at all, in which the very appearance of light is impossible. It is not difficult to imagine a situation in which it will be impossible to pose the question "Who is God?" due to the utter oblivion of this topic and the erasure of such words from history. The world will no longer be fundamentally theomachic, but merely, extremely, unqualifiedly stone-cold and sterile. Such a literalist, radical leap into the distant but still quite possible future brings the current preconditions for the loss and dispersion of the sacred to their end. This metaphor relies on the dichotomy of light and darkness, whereby the former is testing itself against and amidst the latter. The dynamic and tragedy are quite clear. But there is another approach, one which can be considered a different dimension or scene of the very same act.

This approach says that the sacred, traditions, religions, and the Divine will still be present in the future in approximately the same way as they are now, only with a great contrast and variation, namely, that the paths of the oblivion of the sacred and the alienation of the world and man from their deep selfhood will be paved through the structures of irony, play, copies, and imitations. Aspirations and talk about the Divine will continue, but as absolutely superficial, empty, synthetic, and profane discourse. We already hear an abundance of various rumors and misinterpretations about the Deities and traditions, but they are empty and uninviting chatter and idle talk. When questions about the Deities will be answered with hundreds of links to TV series, churches, groupings, neural network chat bots for direct messaging, etc., the situation will be all the more paradoxical because, amidst so many discussions and cults, the Divine will be nowhere and in no way present. This metaphor is one of the testing of false light that disperses the original light in the midst of the same dark backdrop.

We have preliminarily determined that the darkest, most alienated, and metaphysically and existentially unbearable eschatological point will be the final, dark instance before the shift in the course of the cycle. But in the "point on the eve," there is still hope that these are already the final moments, and that the new flashes of the lightning of dawn will manifest themselves right around the corner.

A much more radical initiatic test rises with awakening to and genuinely understanding the whole preceding path of history, as well as everything that is to come, not at the end of the eschatological period, but already at the beginning, i.e., when man recognizes his ontological and existential situation by already here and now looking at the closing sunset and the last burgundy-violet shades of the sky melting away before our very eyes. When all ensuing prospects and perspectives are already clear, and the resolution and reaffirmation of the dignity of the holy light of the Divine are put off into the infinite (surely it is such for life on earth) ages ahead of us. The hardest and rawest lot falls not to those who awaken and know themselves at the very end of the cycle, but to those who awaken and become witnesses to the sunset, to the decline of the sun that is predetermined by the due and whose trajectory was already outlined back in the era when the sun was still at its zenith of glory and might, when, so it seemed, tradition appeared to be undeniably eternal in its triumph and nothing suggested the contrary. In this lies the bitter knowledge of allotted fate.

In this point lies the fundamental fork in the road of assessing the contemporary moment in terms of Modernity and Postmodernity, as well as in terms of Tradition and Traditionalism. Should we try to catch up with the already setting sun, redraw the shades of the sky from memory, and imitate its light with lamps and gadget screens? Or should we accept the primacy of the night and its own rays along the path of transgressive (post-)Traditionalism? Following through the night, which is the apophatic sun, does not mean being in solidarity with the contemporary era in all of its aspects, but rather finding another dimension of tradition in the landscapes of the future that isn't ours.

For the world, that is for the de facto unfolded and present Divine that has essentially turned away from itself, not many prospects and perspectives remain.

The One can so intensely conceal and disperse itself in the many that it might no longer find itself and simply disappear forever, leaving a hermetically sealed world of people one-on-one with themselves and the cold matter of mathematics.

The One can revise the structure of its *imaginaire* in favor of unfolding the Other Beginning, the telling of Another Myth, and inevitably reestablish the whole beingful world anew out of Beyng.

Finally, through a sharp and impossible awakening, the One will arrive at the decision to totally reject any forms of the many and even the one-many. This would mark the final winding down of all ensuing cycles and rebirths. The play in the universal theater will become boring and evaporate like a mirage — and take us with it.

IV
HEIDEGGER
AND TRADITIONALISM

Heidegger and Traditionalism

The fundamental philosophy of Martin Heidegger has for a rather long time already been at the center of attention of representatives of another grand and influential school of thought, Traditionalism. In the very least, we can name Julius Evola, Alain de Benoist, Collin Cleary, Alexander Dugin, and the author of these lines. Both of these philosophies developed in parallel in the 20th century, and both of them claim to radically pose the question of the current state of human being, thinking, and the historical paths of development. This opens up a two-pronged position for mutual critique as well as for seeking out common grounds and consonant intentions. In a number of Traditionalist works, Heidegger's critique and his philosophical accomplishment have been taken into account and woven into the general narrative as an opinion, as methods, and as the pathways of thought of one of the foremost thinkers of our era who has influenced all of Western thinking — and not only Western thinking. Both currents are also united by the fact that they were precursors of the paradigm of Postmodernity. Although Postmodernists refer to Heidegger to a greater extent, albeit at times aggressively and at times frivolously, Traditionalism sets its task as constructing a completely alternative paradigm, a specific life activity, and an historical project against the ideas of the Enlightenment, Modernity, and Postmodernity.

Nevertheless, although the fusion of the ideas, ways, and discourses of Heidegger and Tradition in Traditionalist works already appears to be natural, the key moments and core ideas of these two philosophies are still in need of clarification and correlation with due rigor. This is an extremely voluminous task that requires a broad range of knowledge and deep immersion in understanding both philosophies. Therefore, in this section, we will not dwell on the arrangement of details and historical excursions, for which it is enough to refer the interested reader to the impressive oeuvres of the Traditionalists and the German philosopher.

This task is complicated by the problematic and at times fundamentally impossible difficulty of translating the thought of the German "prince of philosophers" into Russian and English, or into any other languages for that matter. Any translation already unavoidably means an alternative interpretation of the original thought by virtue of lexico-semantic shifts and cultural referents within language. Translating Heidegger is its own philosophic-linguistic problem, one which we are compelled to bracket on our journey, but which we nevertheless recognize to be important and worth mentioning. In particular places, we will present the necessary etymological and contextual clarifications, but our approach prioritizes striving to think together with the philosopher and in the directions he indicated rather than creating a line-by-line, expert commentary on each of his words and terms.

We place at the center of our attention the key themes and "philosophical programs" of these two schools of thought, and we will show the possible variations of their mutual cross-questioning, at the same time problematizing a converging comparison of them. We have already partly expressed a number of theses and illustrated the possibilities of a mutual upholding of Heidegger and Traditionalism's discourses in the preceding chapters and in our previous works.[116]

We hereby join in the labor of raising a bridge between these two philosophies, but the unsettling question remains open: Will this bridge unite Traditionalism and Heidegger's philosophy, or will it irrevocably transport us from one bank of the river to the other?

---

116 See Askr Svarte, *Gods in the Abyss*; idem, *Tradition and Future Shock*.

A Preliminary Exposition

The ideational core of Traditionalism as principally formulated in the works of René Guénon and Julius Evola is structured around the assertion that there has been a disruption and falling away from a certain (Primordial) Tradition, the world of which was the classical Golden Age of spiritually realized mankind. According to the doctrine of cyclical decline and degradation, the world descends from its ideal state to utter disintegration, destruction, and then rebirth.

According to Guénon, the Primordial Tradition is a particular, ancient ur-religion of mankind that historically branched out into many different traditions and religions which, in turn, harbor traces and the initiatic message of their source. Every people's tradition is a reflection of the original light. Therefore, the methods of comparison, intellectual intuition, and metaphysics are called to aid Traditionalists in ascending back to the source.

A later linguistic pivot in Traditionalism adjusted this notion: Tradition is to be understood not so much as a concrete ur-religion that once existed in the past and which can be restored in one way or another, but rather as a meta-language and system of grammatical rules, structures, and distinctions which uphold a plurality of forms of the sacred throughout the cultures of the peoples of this world.[117] We consider this to be the truest correction of Guénon's original ideas.

As an extremely critical position towards the world of the ideas of the Enlightenment, and later as a current of thought and fully-fledged philosophy, Traditionalism took shape in our

---

[117] See Alexander Dugin, *Filosofiia traditsionalizma* (Moscow: Arktogeia, 2002); idem, "René Guénon: Traditionalism as a Language" in Jafe Arnold, Evgeny Nechkasov, Lucas Griffin, and Luca Siniscalco (eds.), *Passages: Studies in Traditionalism and Traditions* 1 (2023), 17-56.

modern era as a deep reflection on, and complete rejection of, the structures of Modernity. Hence the second most important postulate: We live outside of the world of Tradition, in a world which does not simply reject this Tradition out of indifference, but which is systematically and on all fronts annihilating it.

Traditionalism frontally rejects Modernity and dethrones its pathos and pretenses to being the only correct, scientific, progressive interpretation and instrumentalization of the world and society. Traditionalism speaks from the position of radical sacrocentrism and puts forth its project for the total ontological, gnoseological, and socio-political restoration of Europe in the light of the values of Tradition. Guénon spoke of the need to raise a new spiritual elite that will rescue Europe out of its modern state and bring it back to its premodern ideals. He deemed the Middle Ages, or even earlier eras, to be model examples. This position is wholly continued by Alexander Dugin. Julius Evola insisted on the Roman ideal and nurtured the hope — which turned out fruitless, as he later admitted — that the fascist regime in Italy could be reoriented in a Traditionalist vein and that Traditionalism could influence the spiritual seeking then ongoing in the Third Reich. Such an approach largely prefigured the now current reduction of Traditionalism to political conservatism and activism, with secondary roles left to dry academic scholasticism.

Of interest to us are Evola's later intentions once he thought through the failure of the restorationist project of Traditionalism and acknowledged the impossibility of such ever being implemented. Evola posed the question of possible alternative paths for maintaining an inner vertical orientation towards the world of Tradition in the midst of conditions in which Tradition is already de facto a thing of the past with no possibility for return in the present or future. This led Evola to a transgressive understanding of Traditionalism and to formulate the metaphors of the "man among the ruins" and "riding the tiger."[118] The metaphysical situation of the man of Tradition in the midst of the anti-traditional world becomes a paradoxical aporia (or even caesura) in the spirit of Zen, a passing through the darkness of dissolution. Evola also hoped that insofar as Europe was condemned to be the first to fall into the darkness of Modernity, it was likewise fated to be the first to come out on the other side, having passed through the greatest trial and tribulation. As long as our task is to preserve ourselves, our light and our will, we must keep a firm hold on the tiger. The book *Ride the Tiger* is also the site of the first — and unsuccessful — Traditionalist approach to understanding Heidegger's ideas, to which we will return later.

Martin Heidegger's philosophical program developed along a quite different trajectory. Having become disillusioned with Catholicism and theology in his education at the University of Freiburg in his early years, Heidegger completely switched to philosophical positions under the influence of Edmund Husserl's phenomenology. At the heart of Heidegger's philosophy is the return to the question of Being (*Sein*) and the problem of Being's complete oblivion over the course of Western thinking from the ancient Greeks to his day. In the main work of his first period, *Being and Time*, Heidegger tried to approach a phenomenological interpretation of Being through the temporality of here-being (*Da-sein*) and analyzing its existentials that project the structures of the lifeworld in which the human being finds himself in different modes of authenticity. The leading role here is played by the ontological difference (*ontologische Differenz*) between beings (*Seiende*) and Being itself (*Sein*). The "ontic," which refers simply to present beings, is different from the ontological. In the German language, the first word is formed from the latter, but Heidegger insists that over the history of thought Being (*Sein*) has been

---

118 Close in spirit to Evola's *Ride the Tiger* is Ernst Jünger's *The Forest Passage*. Taken together, these works can be seen as a diptych of reflection on the possibility of existing in a totally estranged world.

substituted by and forgotten amidst beings (*Seiende*). Being as such is not a being (that which is given in present experience), but it grants beings the possibility to be as they are. Being must be strictly delineated from beings, which in turn promises to bring clarity to the existential analysis of Dasein, thinking, and philosophy. The German masters says that we can go through all beings, but we still won't find a trace of Being.

Later, following the so-called event of the "Turn" (*Kehre*), Heidegger acknowledged the undertaking of *Being and Time* to have been unsuccessful, overly burdened by phenomenology and the Dasein analytic, and he thus began his program anew by paying close attention to language. The linguistic turn in ontology brought him to the hermeneutics of here-being, the problem of the Event (*Ereignis*), and to arguing for the necessity of Another Beginning of Western philosophy. To this end, he needed another way of philosophizing and style of speaking, a non-conceptual language that would include Swabian dialectisms and archaisms.

According to Heidegger, the oblivion of Being inlaid in the very beginning of Western thinking led to the triumph of nihilism and a calculative, utilitarian relation to the whole beingful world: to nature, society, and man himself. All beings are turned into alienated objects and raw materials for machinations (*Machenschaft*). European thinking is built on this error in its foundation, and historically this has led to the extinguishing of this thinking at its own impasse.

Here comes the first convergence and partial coincidence between Traditionalism and Heidegger's fundamental-ontological project: a radical critique of the modern era, its intellectual foundations, and the current state of decline with an eye to the bleak prospects of its further history. Both Heidegger and Traditionalism converge on this point, even though their programs developed from different starting positions of thought. A rigorous awareness of alienation from an ancient source or deep existential homeland (a state of unsettled homelessness — cf. *unheimisch*), as well as a search for a way out of the situation through an alternative to Modernity — these two intentions are common to both philosophies.

And yet, Traditionalism's position of critiquing Modernity and Heidegger's might exclude each other on the grounds of deeming each other to be varied manifestations of the very same Modernity.

Metaphysics and Being

Martin Heidegger's philosophy is a philosophy of the eschatology of Beyng (*Seyn*) and the decline (*Untergang*) of thinking and Dasein's existing in the world. The only important history is the History of Beyng (*Seynsgeschichte*) and the events of thinking within it which echo in philosophy, politics, and society, and constitute the whole historiography of Western civilization to which we're accustomed.

Translated from the ancient Greek, ἔσχατος means "the end," "the final." Eschatology is the final, definitive, closing word. In Heidegger's philosophy, the eschatology of Beyng begins with the word ἰδέα in Plato, i.e., it is in Platonism that the understanding of truth as unconcealment, ἀλήθεια, was ultimately and decisively replaced: the space of the non-being of the clearing for the *physis* of the beingful world was closed off by the wooden shield of the world of ideas and the supreme Idea of the Good as the spilling out of the cornucopia of all beings. Heidegger writes that the ἰδέα ruins the structure of ἀλήθεια, and that this is noticeable already in the shift of emphasis in metaphors: the clearing space of unconcealment → the idea as that which is visible and intelligible. The primordial openness in the groundlessness of the being of beings, which can be understood as a void or as the Nothing, is replaced by a two-floor topography of ontic beings (the whole diversity of things) and ontological beings, the ideal world of ideas which reflect and, by dint of the distortions of matter, form the diversity of things in the middle world. A supreme being becomes the source and measure of other, lower beings belonging to the register of "is." We thus end up in a world of beings that is closed on all sides, and henceforth Being refers to different variations of the supreme being that is posited to be the source, matrix, or model for a present-at-hand world. This is the classical metaphysics of Plato and Aristotle, the event of the eschatology of Beyng that took place in ancient Greece and predetermined the whole intellectual, and therefore factual, life of Europe for thousands of years down to everyday and sociological nuances.

Philosophy began among the Presocratics with their divine wonder and astonishment at the fact that the world is and that they are in the world. This enigma and thought of the being of beings was an event of insight. But for Plato, Aristotle, and their followers — and according to Whitehead, all of Western philosophy consists of footnotes to Plato — "everything was clear" with beings and their logic. Thus, the ancient Greek philosophers could be called the first modern men, whose thinking we have inherited down to this day. Thus began the long end of Western thinking.

A significant contribution to this structure was later brought by the creationism of the Abrahamic religions in the form of Christianity, with its principle of *ens creatum*, which holds that things, man, and the world are created. This principle of creation, of the crafting of all beings "by the hands" of a being, God, laid all the grounds for what would later in history, freed from the shackles of church dogma, turn into the unbridled triumph of technology, *Machenschaft*, and the Gestell, that is a relation towards beings as mere raw material subject to various kinds of machination, exploitation, and instrumentalization.

The wooden shield of the Platonic ideas turned into the concrete Platonic-Christian wall that firmly closed off the truth of Beyng and even the very question of Beyng for thousands of years. The whole ensuing history is similar to when a powerful river gradually flows out of a small source, reaching its apogee and then inevitably beginning to shrink, breaking up into separate streams and drying up, leaving only a muddy riverbed.

What interests Heidegger in the History of Beyng are the fundamental milestones of thought, their echoes and iterations of the initially inherent error: Descartes and his subject-object topography inlaid at the foundation of Modernity; Hegel and his dialectic of the Absolute Spirit; Nietzsche and his attempt to overturn and overcome the Platonic-Christian metaphysics with his doctrine of the will to power, etc. In the natural-scientific picture of the world, the metaphysical structure was transformed into epistemological rules and procedures for producing scientific knowledge, into methodology, into the correspondence theory of truth, and into the principles of verificationism proper to the Vienna Circle or Karl Popper's falsifiability. Truth was replaced with ordinary correctness and accuracy.

What, then, are Traditionalism and the Traditionalist program in the light of Heidegger's philosophy? Traditionalism is largely based on Indian (Advaita-Vedanta and Advaita-Tantra) and (Neo-)Platonic philosophies (including the Abrahamic religions and Western traditions), the mutual translatability of which was accepted by default. All beings are a manifestation of holy Divinehood (the Absolute, the Intellect) or the creation of God in the Abrahamic religions. This is what Heidegger calls ontotheology, or the reduction of the source of all beings to a singular (monism) or one and only (monotheism) Divine instance. Moreover, Traditionalism is primarily concerned with cataphatic theology and even hierohistory, or the history of the concealment and secret inheritance of the primordial fullness of Tradition in the era of decline.

In the European case, Traditionalism defends this Platonic-Christian metaphysics, or what Heidegger calls metaphysics as such. For Heidegger, this is not a matter of defending specific ideological derivations and political arguments, but rather the deepest structures and procedures of thinking that belong to the erroneous decision on the question of the status of beings and their relation to Beyng in the First Beginning of Western philosophy. These decisions led to Modernity, which can be defined as the logical negation of Tradition combined with a mirror-like, inverse reproduction of its structures in the secular and science-centric paradigm (in Hegel or Marx, for example). In the optic of Heidegger's philosophy, it can be said that the desired world of Traditionalism and the world of Modernity, despite their qualitative and total differences, are both nevertheless founded on the same noetic, intellectual platform established in ancient Greece and Christianity. Traditionalists do not raise the question of overcoming metaphysics, but instead struggle to change the configuration of metaphysics in favor of sacrocentrism and the restoration of ontotheology on the level of socio-political and natural reality. But this path is doomed, because sooner or later it would lead to repeating the whole situation of the fall: after heading up a river, you will inevitably over time be carried back down into the valley by its flow. In general, this is even quite consistent with the traditional doctrine of cycles and the inevitability of the eschatological, catastrophic resolution of the history of the sublunar world.

Inability to pose the question of Being, or even fear of doing so, leads some to, as Heidegger remarked, simply "bury their heads in the sand of metaphysics," or to fall into banal mysticism (irrationalism) and thereby refrain from serious thinking. Metaphysics was the relevant fate of the whole West as the realization of the First Beginning of philosophy, but it has fully exhausted itself in both forms that concern us: in the form of Tradition and in the form of the project of Modernity. Every ensuing iteration or reassembly of one or another metaphysical project will be increasingly scholastic, hollow and shallow, and gradually lead to the processes and cascades of Postmodern simulacra of quasi-"grand" narratives. From the Greeks through the Christian theologians to modern philosophers of science, what is at stake in metaphysics for Heidegger is the history of a fundamental and fatal error, one which humanity could only commit in its existence on earth. This error must be studied in order to be qualitatively overcome in the Event of grounding Another Beginning and awakening bored Dasein out from under the veil of the disintegrating structures of thinking whose functions are increasingly taken over by the procedures of the Gestell.

Dasein

The key notion of Heidegger's early works, one which retained its significance in his subsequent unfolding of the question of Being, is the practically untranslatable term *Dasein*. This term, which is often encountered throughout German philosophy, literally consists of "*da*," that is a situative indication of place, "here" or "there," and *sein*, that is "being." Dasein can therefore conditionally be translated as "here-being," as individual and particular presence, as existing in the world. Although it is conventionally maintained that Dasein refers to the human being, it is rather the case that the human is one possibility of Dasein, and not vice versa.

It is important to take into consideration Heidegger's later qualification that the form of writing "Being" as *Sein* emphasizes the aspect of Being that is commonly understood as being present, i.e., in connection with "beings," *Seiende*. To distinguish Being as such from the being of beings, Heidegger reintroduces the old form *Seyn*, or Beyng. After all, Being as such "is not" any one being, and therefore "is" Nothing.[119] Dasein is the "embassy" of Being in the phenomenal world of beings and is a special form of present being which on the one hand belongs to beings (the human is, and is a part of all present being) and on the other hand (through thinking and poetry) can apprehend all existing, all Be-*ing*, among beings as distinct from beings as a whole (*Seiende-im-Ganze*). To underscore this distinction, Heidegger on more than one occasion uses the construction *Da-seyn*, or "here-beyng," which can be interpreted as the "presencing" of the Nothing immersed among beings, the bearer and *topos* (*da*) of which is the human. *Da-seyn ist Da-Nichts*.

---

119 Heidegger introduces a distinction in verbs for existing, because Being cannot be articulated through "is" or "exists," hence Heidegger retrieves the old form *wesen*, which in Russian and English is translated as "essencing." *Das Seiende ist, aber das Seyn west.*

The starting point of the unfolding of this German philosopher's thought is Dasein and its being in the world in which it discovers itself. This is akin to how the author of a text discovers one of his personas and has the possibility of writing and describing the world around him and himself in it, or, by way of alienation, adopting the faceless position of an object (*das Man*, the inauthentic mode of existing). In this lies the dual nature of Dasein as a being and as something greater at the same time.

The anthropocentric world and its cultural-philosophical foundations are the result of Dasein's projections through the realization of its existentials of thrownness (*Geworfenheit*), understanding (*Verstehen*), attunement or disposedness (*Befindlichkeit*), language (*Sprache*), etc. As follows, the content of the world is the sum of Dasein's decisions and concern (*Sorge*) over what there is or is not. Dasein should be strictly delineated from the Cartesian subject or the psychological ego, for Dasein is here-*being* amidst the world that is projected by itself ahead of itself. Dasein is non-metaphysical, it has no model outside of it; moreover, everything that there is does not appear as if before Dasein, but along with Dasein as its projections. Dasein's existentials are given in pure form: *Sorge* is care as such, and what and how (i.e., in which mode) Dasein will care about things is realized in its projected culture. Analogously, being-in-the-world (*in-der-Welt-sein*) does not predetermine a template given in advance for what the qualitative content of the world will be, what the structure of this *being-in*-the-world and *being-with-others* is, what such otherness will be, etc.

Heidegger's philosophy is anthropocentric and of the middle world: the human being is *Weltbildend*, "world-forming," unlike animals, which are "world-poor" (*Weltarm*), the difference between which is manifest in the human's "eating" and "dying" and the animal's "devouring" and "croaking." Finally, inanimate natural objects, such as a stone or a fallen tree trunk, are entirely "worldless" (*Weltlos*), closed, and inaccessible. They are simply materially present objects of nature whose meaning and use are granted by man.[120]

The world in which Dasein discovers itself and which it projects and changes, is made not out of or by virtue of what Dasein chooses, but by virtue of that which Dasein refuses, that which Dasein denies coming into being. Dasein is constantly moving and evading, because it chooses between and in favor of one or another being and decision. At the same time, Dasein is constantly exhausting possibilities and pushing itself into the remaining projections of what it has decided upon, what it considers of interest to itself, what it cares for, and later, what fills up its boredom. Therefore, Dasein is not static, does not lie in some concrete place, but rather must constantly be apprehended, returned to itself. This is suggested by language itself, where the particular "here" in German is *Hier*, the particular "there" is *Dort*, while the *Da* in Dasein is the in-between, "neither here nor there."

We can already map out an essential divergence between this starting point of Heidegger's and Traditionalism. For the Traditionalist, the starting point is the Divine Absolute, the supreme source of the sacred, of which the world and man are manifestations. This world is fundamentally predetermined to decline, to become involuted, and to degrade — and it is in this disenchanted world that we discover ourselves and with which we disagree. Moreover, whereas Heidegger says that animals are world-poor and not subjects, but rather like fixed automata, and that stones and other objects are simply silently present, the Traditionalist will respond by citing numerous examples from traditional mythological plots about the realms of animals, plants, stones, wise wolves, snakes, and boulders which teach a person, or running trees, speaking winds, etc. Traditionalism

---

120 See Martin Heidegger, *The Fundamental Concepts of Metaphysics: World, Finitude, Solitude*, trans. William McNeill and Nicholas Walker (Bloomington: Indiana University Press, 1995).

affirms the truth and normativity of such a world, one which has been tragically lost, but to which it is necessary to return by re-enchanting the world.

Heidegger proceeds from a different normativity: he takes the world around him in the early 20th century as given, ignoring altogether the remarks and demands that Traditionalists would put forth. He develops his philosophy out of the world that already is as it is, out of the middle slice of the being of beings in the era of Modernity. Phenomenologically at first and heremeneutically second. His analysis of the world-poverty of animals and the wordlessness of stones is needed in order to sharpen the existential problem and role of Dasein/man as that instance which still undoubtedly is, which bears responsibility for the world and thinking, and which takes fundamental decisions on the Beyng of the human and the grounds of the holy and the Divine. Roughly speaking, Heidegger considers everything else to not be his problem. That the world was traditional may as well mean that there was such a form of care and projection of beings by Dasein at one stage of its unfolding and existing amidst beings, but man later gave into the attraction of machinations upon the ready-to-hand world of beings and increasingly exchanged the qualitative content of the world for the Cartesian, Modern, and then Postmodern world. We have here a coincidence of intentions: the shifting course of history is a history of alienation and oblivion, which corresponds to the Traditionalists' doctrine of cycles of degradation. But, roughly speaking, the scale of the brackets with which Heidegger frames the being-historical process of eschatology is broader than in Traditionalism.

Ultimately, we find ourselves in a world constituted by many decisions taken by Dasein, all of them in the shade of one fundamental error in the First Beginning of philosophy, one that laid out the whole trajectory of alienation which has led our here-being to the fundamental boredom of our current era.

Returning to the preceding stages of alienation fundamentally changes nothing and would take place against the backdrop of the very same foremost mood (*Stimmung*) of Dasein. Therefore, we must unfold the program of fundamental ontology and the decision on the key problem of Beyng starting from the world as it is around us and us ourselves as we are in the current point of the History of Beyng, and not from what we and the world would be "if only…"

The Holy

At the beginning of his path, Heidegger studied at the Faculty of Theology at the University of Freiburg, where he would later start teaching philosophy. The development of Heidegger's thought soon led him to diverge from Catholic theology, which he left and turned to current Protestant theologians, only to leave them as well and ultimately break with Christian theology as a direction of thought altogether. Much later, in his *Black Notebooks* from the 1930s-40s, Heidegger repeatedly summated that Christian thought is completely incapable of solving philosophical questions.

Nevertheless, the question of the holy (*das Heilige*) appears in Heidegger's works as one of the most important matters in connection with the origin of creativity and, more broadly, the origination of beings out of Beyng; moreover, the holy directly affects human presence in the world and the possibility of Dasein turning its attention to itself.

A key influence on Heidegger's notion of the holy was exerted by the outstanding German theologian and scholar of religion Rudolf Otto, the author of the work *Das Heilige*. In the latter, Otto calls the experience of the holy "numinous" (from the Latin *numen*, or Divinity) and draws out the linguistic connection of these two instances. The holy is the special, fundamental experience of *Mysterium tremendum*, which is characterized by several inseparable elements, namely:

- Awfulness or trepidation (*Tremendum*)
- Fascination, rapture, astonishment (*Fascinans*)
- Elation in the face of greatness (*Majestas*)
- The sense of secret mystery (*Mysterium*)
- Partaking in the energy of the Divine (*Energicum*)

The experience of the holy is one of being seized out of the world in a moment of the highest tension and syzygy of horror and delight, of individual or collective immersion into the revealed mystery in an instant in which it is as if the presence of the surrounding world is removed or recedes into the background. The holy is the primary phenomenon of any tradition, and the experience of the sacred precedes any conceptualization and rationalization. Vesting the experience in poetic tale comes close, but still only trails behind the experience itself, its source, its compelling premise.

Despite the fact that Rudolf Otto was an evangelical theologian, his notion of the holy is fully derived from pre-Christian traditions and metaphysics. In particular, Otto was the German translator of the *Bhagavad Gita*, in the eleventh chapter of which we encounter a dialogue between the charioteer Krishna and Prince Arjuna. Arjuna asks the *deva* to reveal his true face, to which Krishna responds that man cannot bear the pure face of the Divine. Nevertheless, by virtue of his power, Krishna grants such vision to the prince. To Arjuna is revealed the infinity of the cosmic and powerful faces of Krishna, all the devas, spirits, ancestors, living beings, and worlds; thousands and thousands of eyes peer into Arjuna out of the cascades of infinity, and he sees countless mouths, jewelry, crowns, and weapons. Feelings of jubilation and awe give way to horrifying pictures that overwhelm Arjuna, who describes terrifying faces, flaming eyes, thousands of hands, as well as a horrifying mouth with fangs into which all the lives of people are heading — here, Krishna reveals himself to Arjuna in his most wrathful hypostasis, Bhairava. Unable to bear such a spectacle, Arjuna bows and praises the genuine Purusha-Krishna, and asks for mercy so that Krishna might reappear before him as his friend and charioteer. We might also recall the bitter fate of Semele, who asks Zeus to reveal himself in his true form so as to assure her that the Deity standing by her bed is really him. Consequently, she was incinerated or, according to another version, died from the horror of beholding the radiance and barrage of lightning bolts unleashed by the Thunderer. Rudolf Otto's merit was that he translated such mythological plots, which are on the whole normative for the traditions of the old world, onto the plane of phenomenology.

We also encounter the notion of fear in Heidegger already in *Being and Time*, where *Angst* plays one of the most important existential roles. For Heidegger, the distinction between fear (*Furcht*) and angst is fundamental. Fear is what pushes Dasein into dissipation, to hide from itself in other people, the world, things, idle chatter (*Gerede*), everyday commotion, and in psychological introspections, excavations, and analytics. Fear is altogether understandable, and it can be objectified: we can say what it is that we fear, or what or who fills us with fear. But angst seizes us from out of nowhere, opens up the phenomenological presence of Dasein in the world, and turns Dasein towards itself. When we analyze angst, we come to the conclusion that nothing is really threatening us, yet the horror remains, and, as Heidegger notes, fear is only a secondary experience that is founded on angst. What so horrifies Dasein? The Black Forest shaman concludes: *Das Wovor der Angst ist das In-der-welt-sein als solches* — "That about which one has anxiety is being-in-the-world as such."[121] The horror that seizes Dasein does not come from the world of being(s), because it is in being(s) (in all multiplicity, diversity, situations, etc.) that Dasein still manages to hide. Therefore, if we seek the "object" that horrifies us in beings, then we will find it neither "here" nor "there," but "nowhere." What terrifies us is but our own being-in-the-world and presence as such. These notions flow into one another throughout the lines of *Being and Time*. It is not something concrete in the world but the world overall that frightens us, because if it is, then this means that we, as Dasein, are already in it, and this plunges us into an abyss of angst.

This state of existential angst returns and puts Dasein before its own finitude on the one hand, and in front of the freedom of its possibilities on the other. In one of Heidegger's most important books, *Contributions to Philosophy (Of the*

---

121 Heidegger, *Being and Time*, trans. Joan Stambaugh (Albany: State University of New York Press, 2010), 180.

Event), he succinctly remarks that existential angst "opens up the nothing," when all beings slip out from under our feet and, as it were, are annulled.

The later Heidegger speaks of Dasein having a threefold mood of being "startled" or "alarmed" (*Erschrecken*), restraint (*Verhaltenheit*), and timid or shy fear (*Scheu*). The latter kind of fear does not repulse and make one run away; on the contrary, it is a reverent fear which gives rise to an ambivalent mood of fear-and-attraction. This is Dasein's mood of questioning, as it at once fears and yet respond to the call of Beyng to become itself.

If we were to voluntaristically compare the description of Dasein's seizure by angst with Arjuna's coming face-to-face with the true, boundless face of Krishna, then we can note two interesting parallels. Firstly, Krishna reveals himself to the prince as the total Absolute, that is literally everything, "beings-as-a-whole," whereby even Arjuna the viewer is Krishina himself. Powerfully seized out of all beings and closed unto himself in horror-and-astonishment, he is compelled to behold "everything there is" in an instant right before the fulfillment of due dharma. Secondly, the cascades of poetic descriptions of the Deity's guises that we find in the *Bhagavad Gita* balance on the border of apophaticism and ineffability, as they constantly break up into "countless" determinations and yield the impossibility of beholding any one form. In other words, even while being totally all beings in all worlds (*Saguna*), the deva's true nature is obviously irreducible to any being, and instead ascends to the apophatic Nothing (*Nirguna*). But the language of poetry in its maximal tension is capable only of balancing on this edge between nothing and something. The limitation of telling predetermines the belonging of the tale to the order of beings.

In the ensuing unfolding of Heidegger's thought, the notion of the holy is directly and fully connected first and foremost with poetry and art. The key moments here concern interpreting the poetry of Hölderlin and other German authors. Now it is the poet and poetry who name and say what is called the holy, *das*

Heilige, and Heidegger elevates the poet to being a semi-divine mediator between immortals and mortals, between Being and beings.

Yet the situation is even subtler: Heidegger, following Hölderlin and Otto, posits the holy to be the primordial given in relation to which the Divine is secondary and derivative. *Poiesis*, therefore, speaks to both sides: to the Divine and to the human. The philosopher writes: "The holy is not holy because it is divine; rather the divine is divine because in its way it is 'holy.'"[122] One important feature of the holy is its openness, the revelation of the sacred, and this disclosure is the space wherein different things come to presence — or, we might say, come into presence in the shade of that which is holy by and large, that is in the form of poetry and the craft arts.

Heidegger writes:

> Thought in terms of nature (φύσις); chaos remains that gaping out of which the open opens itself, so that it may grant its bounded presence to all differentiations. Hölderlin therefore calls "Chaos" and "confusion" "holy." Chaos is the holy itself. Nothing that is real precedes this opening, but rather always only enters into it.[123]

Chaos should be distinguished from the later meanings of "disorder" or political anarchy. The ancient Greek works χάος comes from the verb χαίνω, "to open up [the mouth]," "to yawn." In Greek mythology, χάος is he primordial "instance" from which, as out of the nothing, all beings emerge forth (φύσις). In Germanic mythology, chaos has a full analogue in the dark *gap*, which etymologically also means an empty space, a kind of clearing, a free space in which the first cosmogonic acts of the manifestation of beings (ice and fire) take place. In the Russian language, the equivalent of chaos would be *zev*, which at once means a gully, a break or hole in the ground, and in the later verb *zevat'* means to open one's mouth wide. These primordial cosmogonic principles are always described apophatically, and

---

122 Heidegger, *Elucidations of Hölderlin's Poetry*, 82.
123 Ibid., 85.

after showing themselves in a flash at the very beginning of myths, they then usually disappear into the backdrop of all other events and stories. Almost no attention is paid to them thereafter, as they are overtaken by the plot of the history of the beingful world.

Chaos is disclosedness and clearing. Heidegger take this to obviously refer to the notion of ἀλήθεια, that is truth as unconcealment and the clearing for the occurrence of beings and thinking. Thus, the notion of the holy merges with truth and Beyng. In *On Inception*, Heidegger writes that, although being two different words, the holy and Beyng name one and the same:[124]

Das Heilige und das Sein sind — erfahren und vorgedacht — die Namen des anderen Anfangs. Sie lassen sich nicht zurückverlegen in die Geschichte der Metaphsik, auch nicht in den *ersten* Anfang (φύσις), der aller Philosophie voraufgeht. Das Heilige und das Seyn nennen die eigenste Geschichte des anderen Anfangs.	The holy and beyng are, experienced and thought-ahead, names for the other inception. They cannot be displaced back into the history of metaphysics or into the *first* inception (φύσις) that precedes all philosophy. The holy and beyng name the most proper history of the other inception.

Here we might also draw a parallel with mythologies in which the whole focus of attention is closed onto beings, onto something, onto events, characters, etc. Such myths deal with what arose (φύσις) out of the open expanse (χάος) and became the center of the questioning of the First Beginning, when the source and beingness of beings was named and designated in terms of another super-being (the cataphatic Divine, the world of Ideas, λόγος, etc.). In this instance, Heidegger says that it really is the case that Beyng as unconcealment and as Nothing evaded or, more precisely, were discarded by thinking and attention as inessential or even impossible to comprehend and instrumentalize. Therefore, the truth of Beyng as

---

124 Martin Heidegger, *On Inception*, trans. Peter Hanly (Bloomington: Indiana University Press, 2023), 130.

unconcealment and Nothing, the correct relation to Beyng, is the problem, task, and fate of the Other Beginning of Western philosophy. The holy is another name for this "instance," which in the history of traditional and then post-sacral metaphysics has had a different fate and employment. It has survived as a fundamental experience. Through the existential fascination of horror, the holy has retained its basic possibility of returning our presence to its sources.

Also of interest is Heidegger's approach to *mythos*.[125] In his first years of teaching, Heidegger did not devote any special attention to myth, which he instead only situationally referenced in passing in various lectures. For Heidegger back then, myth is either the genealogy of steps along which the cosmos unfolded, the model of which is Hesiod's *Theogony*, or an auxiliary explanatory element, such as in the case of Plato's myth of the cave. Similar to *physis*, myth was thought to be like the path of the concealment of the truth of Being. In *Being and Time*, Heidegger referenced the works of Ernst Cassirer on mythical thinking in the light of his polemic with Kantianism, and in one passage he suggested that Dasein can interpret, albeit primitively, the reality of its being-in-the-world in mythical and magical terms. Later, over the course of pondering Cassirer's ideas, Heidegger came altogether close to posing the question of "our own approach to the philosophy of myth," in which special importance is attached to the question of the "constitutive function of myth in human Dasein and in the all of beings as such."[126] Myth is revealed to be a primordial possibility of Dasein (mythical Dasein), wherein Dasein's myth contains its own truth and laws, i.e., is genuine within its own narrative. Heidegger unexpectedly draws on something that was then widely discussed in academic literature, namely, the Melanesian notion of *mana*, that is a magical force that

---

125 Jafe Arnold, "The Eternal (Re)Turn: Heidegger and the '*Absolutes Getragensein*' of Myth", *Phainomena: Journal of Phenomenology and Hermeneutics* 31:120-121 (2022): 93-119.

126 Heidegger, *Kant and the Problem of Metaphysics*, 186.

permeates all beings, things, and the world, analogues of which can be found if not among all, then among the overwhelming majority of traditional peoples. Myth and all-pervading *mana* thus become one particular, altogether concrete configuration of Dasein's being-in-the-world and understanding of Being.

Here, nevertheless, there is still a particular relation of "mythical Dasein" to beings. Heidegger suggests that in the structure of mythological being-in-the-world Dasein remains beholden to, carried by, and directed towards other beings. Dasein's existential care is "suspended" (as if "care-less," *Sorglosigkeit*), because "primitive Dasein" is supposedly beholden to and carried by nature itself or other beings, for example Deities. Such an approach leads us to the modern notion of naturalism, according to which ancient peoples were completely ruled by the natural elements and worshiped merely the forces and phenomena of nature, which they personified as Deities and spirits. As if they were weak in strength and will, ancient people's decisions were made for them by "older" beings or by nature and its laws. Heidegger rejects such an approach, and the "carriedness" of here-being and the weakness of care are, in the spirit of the standard practice of his philosophy, taken to exhibit ways of disclosing Being as such. In the end, however, Heidegger abandoned this approach to myth.

Following the event of the turn (*Kehre*) in his philosophy, as he turned his attention to language and poetry, Heidegger's thinking on myth beings to unfold almost as if from a blank slate. Hölderlin's verse, "we are a conversation, and we can listen to one another," and the phenomenon of poetry in general transparently relate to *mythos* and to tale, to telling tales and to discovering oneself in language, dialogue, and listening. Key to all of Heidegger's thought is a passage in his work *Contribution to Philosophy (Of the Event)* in which he reproduces the essence of Hölderlin's poetic line in maximally ontological and ontolinguistic terms:[127]

---

[127] Heidegger, *Contributions to Philosophy (Of the Event)*, 401.

Wenn die Götter die Erde rufen und im Ruf eine Welt widerhallt und so der Ruf anklingt als Da-sein des Menschen, dann ist Sprache als geschichtliches, Geschichte gründendes Wort.	When the gods call the earth, and when in the call a world echoes and thus the call resonates as the Da-sein of the human being, then language exists as historical, as the word that grounds history.

We can see here the very same "we are a conversation." More precisely, the concrete here-being of the human is a response to the questioning call of the Divinities of the earth and the world, and in this existential and anthropological response in language is born the innerworldly word that rules history.

Heidegger once again turns to *mythos*, but now as "primordial saying." *Mythos* is the (hi)story that goes on through us. Hence, "authentic understanding of the μῦθος means experiencing its speaking, its resonance as 'something unavoidable.'"[128] If previously one of the main points of Heidegger's philosophy concerned the paths of the oblivion of the truth of Being along the axis of φύσις—λόγος, then now Heidegger turns to the pair of μῦθος—λόγος, for man lives by and large in language and speaking.

Logos, according to Heidegger, is the asserting law of the gathering-together of beings that openly gives them their structure. In a determinate relation, *logos* stands against beings like a scythe at harvest cuts crops (cf. the original meaning of the verb *legein*). Dasein has power over beings by way of the *logos*-word, by way of naming (onomastics), speaking, and affirming that and how things are in a rather rational form. But reducing *logos* to pure, cold, dry rationality, to un-human "logic," is the result of the autonomous development of the sciences and their procedures of thinking being spread onto the spheres of thought (which is ὕβρις). *Logos* was originally connected to *mythos* and

---

[128] Arnold, "The Eternal (Re)Turn), 109; Martin Heidegger, *Being and Truth*, trans. Gregory Fried and Richard Polt (Bloomington/Indianapolis: Indiana University Press, 2010), 98. It is noteworthy that the English word "understanding" has the subtle signification of "standing under," i.e., entering into understanding something means entering its zone, standing within and under it, which means that understanding is a strong form of belonging to something.

grew out of it, and etymologically both are interchangeable synonyms. Mythos is more primordial, and its telling does not stand against beings. The language of mythos is the language of indicating, hinting, deixis, and describing.

In this light, the ontotheology of traditional high metaphysics is the development of *logos* as a rationalistic setting-forth-against *mythos*, whereby the very clearing of *aletheia*-truth is covered up. Myth, however, even though it can be read metaphysically, is not yet defined out of itself, and it can be read "flatly" or "immanently" to itself as a self-telling in the constantly present play of concealing-and-unconcealing what is not subject to being said and told directly. We can therefore correct Jacques Derrida's maxim to say: the whole world is not a text, but a self-telling.

Finally, in his lectures on Parmenides from 1942-1943, Heidegger says what is for us the most important about myth. Μῦθος is a telling, a tale, which the philosopher takes to be the primordial essence of speech:

> Μῦθος is the Greek for the word that expresses what is to be said before all else. The essence of μῦθος is thus determined on the basis of ἀλήθεια. It is μῦθος that reveals, discloses, and lets be seen; specifically, it lets be seen what shows itself in advance and in everything as that which presences in all "presence." Only where the essence of the word is grounded in ἀλήθεια, hence among the Greeks, only where the word so grounded as pre-eminent legend [Sage] pervades all poetry and thinking, hence among the Greeks, and only where poetry and thinking are the ground of the primordial relation to the concealed, hence among the Greeks, only there do we find what bears the Greek name μῦθος, "myth."[129]

Thus, Heidegger directly links the authentic telling of *mythos* with the occurrence of truth as the clearing of unconcealment. Literally, the tale of the Divinities and of the whole beingful world "grows" out of the void, out of silence, out of the Nothing. The mythical and myth are thus the word that seizes at once upon the concealment of the truth-clearing and the

---

129 Martin Heidegger, *Parmenides*, trans. André Schuwer and Richard Rojcewicz (Bloomington/Indianapolis: Indiana University Press, 1992), 60.

unconcealment of Being (*Sein/Seyn*) as such. The primordial telling of myth, although it conventionally unfolds forward like ordinary practices of speech, always has its other ending in the deictic dark. The German master also emphasizes that myths are always about the Divinities, and if myth is the wording and naming of Being, then it names Being with other, primordial, radiant names, namely those of the θεῖον, the Deities.

We can presume that Heidegger would agree with Walter Otto that myth is not a concept, phantasy, or mode of thinking, but the self-opening and self-revelation of Being. Heidegger's later approach to myth becomes more detailed and more complex; the original approach to Dasein and Being changes in favor of a "mytho-philosophy" and speaking in and of the concealment-and-unconcealment of Beyng. It is obvious that the classical contrast of "μῦθος vs. λόγος" is left far behind in practicing the method of the hermeneutic circle of questioning and exegesis.

Moreover, if *mythos* as the telling of Being is more primordial than *logos* (whose role in the erroneous formulation of the First Beginning and the ensuing ossification and collapse of Western philosophy and history is obvious), then the potential and possibility of myth can be directly connected with the posing of the question of the Other Beginning of Western philosophy and the other resolution of how and why there is something rather than nothing.

Traditionalism treats mythology and *mythos* as a component part of the "Primordial Tradition." *Mythos* is the transmission of the sacred and a special means of expressing the sacred (in an interconnection of form and content). Therefore, Traditionalist re-sacralization within metaphysics implies the rehabilitation and return of myth and mythological thinking, such as in the slogan "Myth is our Homeland." However, as we already concluded above, Traditionalism harbors a reactive and retrospective element, i.e., it turns to what already was with the aspiration of preserving the last flame and heat.

Proceeding from the classic definition of Modernity offered by Max Weber, that is the "disenchantment of the world," the old *mythos* has been weakened and lost its positions, which for Traditionalism is the manifestation and realization of the eschatological motif of which myth itself sings. Thus is the due fulfilled. But Traditionalists would like to see the world re-enchanted. In the operative language here is manifest an essential nuance between the phrase "re-enchant the world" in the sense of enchanting it back as it was, and enchanting the world anew.

In the fourth volume of his *Black Notebooks*, Heidegger discusses a number of "loopholes" to which people resort in striving to turn away from or, as they imagine, overcome the globally extended power of the technological world that is the culmination of the oblivion of Being and the collapse of metaphysics. Among them he names "flight in to the Christian faith" and "experiencing nature, exalting simple life, pitiful prayers to Pan, historiographical renewals of ancient myths, digging up archetypes and delving into the irrational."[130]

When it comes to speaking of the faithful followers of various traditions and Traditionalists, we can confidently assert that what passes for their "sacred experience" can really be explained in terms of different forms of emotional agitation, excitement, corporeal reactions, effects, intoxications, and impressions. In saying so, we do not have in mind situations in which people really experience genuine sacred experience only to denigrate it, disenchant it, or describe it in the profane categories of modern psychology. Instead, our sober statement is intended to underscore the extreme exclusivity and difficulty of ever achieving a genuine *mysterium tremendum*. The fact that many faithful people and religious institutions, communities, and churches pretend to be such is only an exhibit of the very same emotional-psychological agitations and periodic seances of strong sensations. It is precisely such falling into the vanity and pleasure of all kinds of impressions that Heidegger repeatedly

---

130 Heidegger, *Zametki I-V (Chernyie tetradi 1942-1948)*, 294.

warns against. Replacing the sacred with surrogates is possible precisely because of man's loss of and rift with the deep source of the holy. This verdict is quite harsh, but on the whole fair and right, because between modern man and old tradition lies not one but several chasms of alienation. *Ergo*, appealing to what already once was, exposes a gesture of helplessness, a hope for pain relief rather than a cure. This is radically different from consciously passing through the forest of the most bitter vale of tears, from going through the absence of tradition as an initiatic concealing-dying without any guarantees, descriptions, or contours from the other side.

Enchanting the world anew, as opposed to "re-enchanting," means turning to the deepest source of *mythos* and undertaking to tell it forth anew, reinterpreting and re-telling the whole (hi) story, the present moment, and the future. Such an approach affirms that what once was has finished and irrevocably departed, and that Traditionalists must rethink and overcome this caesura of nihilism. Like when a new tree breaks up through the earth and offers the possibility for the whole tree to live on after the old trunk dries out and disintegrates.

Amidst his general empathy and sympathy for *mythos* as an ontological principle of extreme importance in culture and thinking, Heidegger's program nevertheless does not propose returning to one or another mythology, even the Greek, as a form of identity, state religion, or system of values.[131] Instead, he speaks of the non-metaphysical, groundless (*Ab-Grund*) and poetic refounding of the whole of *mythos* and the holy on the horizon of Another Beginning. For Traditionalism, this means being compelled to seek out and tell forth Another Myth.

---

131 For Heidegger, the notion of "values" is one of the last, faded forms of the degeneration of metaphysical truth, even lower than the concept of truth as correctness.

Theology

Martin Heidegger's theological project is a question of special interest. Despite the philosopher's early phenomenological and essentially secular approach, in the second phase of his thinking the topic of theology becomes one of the most important, and at that one to which he turned in his key work *Contributions to Philosophy (Of the Event)*, in his series of *Black Notebooks*, as well as in the volumes *Mindfulness, The Event*, etc.

As we noted earlier, despite his early involvement in Catholic and Protestant theology, Heidegger decisively and unconditionally denied that Christian religion and theology are capable of addressing the question of Being. In the *Black Notebooks*, Heidegger directly contrasts the Christian faith and philosophical thinking, deeming them to be mutually exclusive. Here, Heidegger is not acting as a mere anti-Christian, and he is not disputing the ethical or moral aspects of Christianity and its different churches; instead, the rejection he postulates is not only of Christianity as the Abrahamic religion dominating Europe, but of the very basic ontological principle underlying Christianity. In polemicizing with Christian theology, Heidegger is polemicizing with the Platonic-Roman-Christian principle of *ens creatum*, which holds that all beings are created by God and therefore all of nature is taken to be something created. This createdness, widely known by the metaphor of the craftsman and the pot, is the doctrine of creationism, at the core of which lies a fundamental and insurmountable difference in ontological natures between the Creator God and the world and man created by him. For Heidegger, this is an archetypal manifestation of the purely metaphysical vertical of thinking, and consequently of man's relation to the world, to the earth, to other people, and to the Divine. "Biblical-Christian" being, Heidegger concludes, can be perceived either through the prism of faith, which completely blocks philosophical thinking, or through secular knowledge.

The structure of truth as *aletheia* is collapsed, and in come the rules of various machinations (*Machenschaft*). Everything that is accessible to man in the world is created and given to him as ready-to-hand, which predetermines his relation to beings as beneath him and as raw material given unto his disposal. The focus of existential attention thus falls onto beings alone, on to what is already here and the operations that can be done with such. It is therefore fully logical that in the Enlightenment era the new European subject rejected any God and Divine and instead posited himself (with his ideological, economic, political, and other interests) as the center and measure of things. In the two-floor metaphysical topography, the upper pole of the supernatural, the superrational, the sacred ideal, eternity, and truth can be discarded as naive delusions from the childhood of mankind. Everything can then be reduced to what is empirically observable and accessible for analysis, exploitation, and commerce.

Within the First Beginning of philosophy, Heidegger speaks of the emerging forth (*physis*) of beings out of unconcealment (*aletheia*, chaos), sung by maieutic myth and cut into bundles by the *logos*-word (theo-ontology).[132] Traceable here is the idea of organic nature in the form of the famous agrarian metaphor, as well as the clear influence of the Presocratic thinkers, especially Heraclitus. But the First Beginning comes to an end already in Socrates and Plato, and Christian theology simply finishes it off. Heidegger unambiguously disavows his relationship to the latter, hence there are no grounds whatsoever to regard him as a follower of one or another Christian theology.

Heidegger's understanding of the Divinities was largely influenced by the ancient Greeks and their mythology. Even later, when the philosopher expressed original provisions about the Deities, which can hardly be attributed to any pantheon, the

---

132 On this point, we can take note of something interesting: all beings, including Deities, arise and are facilitated through the telling of the word, through *poiesis*. At the same time, they are also cut into bundles by words and speech. Thus, speech finds its power to be everything and, once again, to tell itself outside of the familiar logic of linear and determined sequence.

Greek tinge of his descriptions is palpable. In his *Parmenides*, Heidegger summarized the maxim of his approach to the Greek Deities thusly:

> As long as we make no attempt to think the Greek gods in the Greek way, i.e., on the basis of the essence of the Greek experience of Being, i.e., on the basis of ἀλήθεια, we have no right to say a word about these gods, whether in favor of them or against them.[133]

In his deliberations on the question of ἀλήθεια, Heidegger concludes that *mythos* is the primordial form of the telling and self-revelation of Being in the special form of concealment, yet this concealment does not imply deceit or the obscuration of truth in the likes of a "wall on which the truth is reflected" that would replace the truth as such. Heidegger says that there are possible forms of concealment which "in a unique way impart and bestow what is essential."[134] He calls "secret" or "mystery" (*Geheimnis*) one such form, but such more fully corresponds to *mythos* as the space of telling (language and speech) in which the Divine manifests itself in concealment. Finally, Heidegger insists that myths are primarily about the Deities. Hence, the Deity in a myth can be understood as one name, possibility, or way of the self-concealing and self-revealing of Being.

Another important feature of the Divinities is their subtle nature, even their "meekness" or "timidness" in relation to the world of people and to our thinking. The Divinities cannot stand pressure, crude self-confidence, compulsion, or the sudden intrusion of human presence. They are easily frightened, like gentle nymphs and muses, and they always manage to slip away. A person must show delicacy, careful questioning, and tact in order to approach the Divinities and enter into dialogue with them. A sharp contrast to the Greek Deities is presented by Friedrich Georg Jünger, who described the industrial landscapes of the modern era and concluded that the Deities could not possibly live and exist in the midst of such commotion and alienation. The noise of machines is the clothing of titanic,

---

133 Heidegger, *Parmenides*, 61.

134 Ibid., 62.

anti-divine powers, and "wherever there are no Gods, there are the Titans."[135] Of course, this subtleness does not exhaust the nature of the Olympians, and we can see an even grander contrast in comparing them to the Germanic Aesir and Vanir, who are figures of a rougher, forested, mountainous landscape. The evident difference in these styles (*logoi*) can even be observed between the luminous and carefully accounted antique Roman colonnades and the thoroughly Germanic, Gothic architecture of the Middle Ages.

When it comes to the end of the First Beginning of philosophy, it could be said that the Divinities gathered themselves to set off far away from the Greek *polis*, where at the symposiums of Plato and his students "everything became clear" about the higher world of ideas and the classical structure of metaphysics took on its traits and was erected in thinking.

Another important characteristic of the Divinities which the German master often treats as a synonym for them is that they are immortal. This distinction is significant in light of the earlier interpretation of Dasein out of the temporality of being present in the world, which is to say Dasein's inevitable finitude, *ergo* human mortality. People are mortal, their life is short and bitter, and mortality is what makes the human a human. Only the human dies and can be dying, whereas animals simply croak or perish. The opposite of the human is the Divine, the immortal Deities for whom the life of a people is a mere instant, while they for us are eternal. For us, time and the horizon of its finitude are important, whereas for them the problem of death and time is unimportant. If we try to pose the question of interpreting "divine Dasein," then there is no way for us to build such out of the structures of the phenomenology of time. The divine relation to Being and to the *da* that they by their very structures provide for Being will be radically distinct from human presence in the middle world. We can only point out that temporality applies to the various theophanies and metamorphoses of the Divinities,

---

135 See Friedrich Georg Jünger, *Grecheskie mify* (Moscow: Vladimir Dal', 2006).

that is the guises and masks which they are compelled to put on for human gaze to bear their presence.

The Greek theo-personification of eternity is Αἰών, a word which we encounter in one of Heraclitus' enigmatic fragments: αἰὼν παῖς ἐστι παίζων πεσσεύων·παιδὸς ἡ βασιληίη, that is "eternity is a child playing with dice on the throne." Another fragment has an even more interesting thought to say: ἀθάνατοι θνητοί, θνητοὶ ἀθάνατοι. ζῶντες τὸν ἐκείνων θάνατον, τὸν δὲ ἐκείνων βίον τεθνεῶτες — "immortals are mortals, mortals are immortal; living the other's death, being dead in the other's life."[136] Pondering this phrase leads us to one of the acutest problems that was radically formulated by Nietzsche, the "death of God":

> God is dead; but given the way people are, there may still for millennia be caves in which they show his shadow... Do we still smell nothing of the divine decomposition?—Gods, too, decompose! God is dead! God remains dead! And we have killed him! How can we console ourselves, the murderers of all murderers![137]

Among traditional myths we know of plots about the death and even murder of Deities. The Titans attack Dionysus while he is playing on the throne and, upon catching him, tear him apart, boil him, and devour him. Only Athena saves his essence — his immortal heart. The blind Höðr, initiated and led by the hand of Loki, kills the young Baldr, and no one is capable of bringing him back from the kingdom of Helheim until the cosmos begins its cycle again. According to legend, all the old Aesir and Vanir will die in the fire of Ragnarök. In the wrathful form of Bhairava, Shiva cuts off Brahma's head. Somewhat indirectly, we could also mention the image of Shiva pretending to be dead in order to bring the mad Kali to reason. Isis mourns her murdered and dismembered husband, Osiris. The ancient Greek historian Plutarch tells the story of a helmsman steering his ship past the

---

136 Dennis Sweet, *Heraclitus: Translation and Analysis* (Lanham: University Press of America, 1995), fragment 62.

137 Friedrich Nietzsche, *The Gay Science*, trans. Josefine Nacukhoff and Adrian del Caro, ed. Bernard Williams (Cambridge: Cambridge University Press, 2001), 109, 120

island of Paxi, where he hears a bitter cry from the shore: "The great Pan is dead!" The latter message is regarded as the end of the whole cosmos of classical antiquity.

We have other plots and events bearing numerous interpretations, ranging from agrarian and seasonal motifs (in the spirit of the dying and resurrecting sun) to eschatological signs of the change of epochs and cosmic decline. Perhaps what is common to them all is the motif of the relative death of Deities, as they always return in a new cycle, and their deep nature is either saved or the very event of their "murder" is simply ignored, the Deity reappearing with the same name or a new epithet. This corresponds to the fact that traditional man did not have the death that is intrinsic to us modern people, that is the absolute, irreversible, irrevocable absence or withdrawal that leaves a purely present body as an entity without the presence of Being. For the traditional world, death has a larger circle of correspondences, including metaphors, initiations, wanderings, and departing far away from the middle world, but all with the open possibility of returning.

Insofar as we posit theistic Advaita-monism to be the highest and crowning form of traditional ontotheology, we can interpret the "death of God" in the following variations. Theistic Advaita-monistic metaphysics postulates the doctrine of the manifestation of the world as the self-revelation of the Divine, and therefore the world and man are essentially one with their Divine source. Here, we immediately see a divergence with the creationist principle of *ens creatum*, which postulates an ontological rift between God and his creation. The world is manifested by the Divine in its singing, telling, unfolding, self-concealing, imagining, etc. If the Divine were to be represented as a higher being, as a figure, then we would be dealing with its cataphatic hypostases and emanations which in the myths often undergo various concealments and "deaths." In its ontological aspect, the literal death of such a Divinity would mean the literal disappearance of the world as such. But here we come to a contradiction with the fact that the world, no matter its characteristics and the cultural languages describing it, still exists factically. Advaita-monism allows for the possibility of the Divinity "existing" in a conventionally designated "time" even when there is no manifested world whatsoever. It is not beyond time and space, as if at an extreme distance from the world (for time and space are the manifestation of the Divine in fundamental and factical categories), but as if "before" all of this. Brahma closes his eyes and the world is folded back up along with his gaze, or he inhales, which is the eschatological return of the exhaled manifestation of the world in the tale.

But the "death of God" tells us of the opposite situation: the world exists, but the Divine is absent. In Advaita, this situation could be interpreted as a radical degree of *avidya*, that is ignorance, delusion, or man's alienation from his source, when it only seems to him that there is no one else, only he himself alone as the autonomous subject. But what could be the meaning of such a situation of alienation and oblivion? It could be, for example, a test.

The death of which Nietzsche spoke will be better understood if we turn to the Abrahamic doctrine that played such a key role in the development of European Modernity. Traditional societies do not know absolute death. Radically irrevocable death is owed to the Christian pathos of death and the resurrection of Christ. For mythological being-in-the-world, there is nothing unique in the latter event, as myths know of numerous plots about dying and resurrecting Deities, special cases of returning, and ransoming or saving souls from the netherworlds. In order for Jesus Christ's victory over death and his resurrection on the third day to become a genuine and exceptional miracle, it was necessary for it to take place in a fully material, historical world. Such is the nature of the miracles, epiphanies, angelic messengers, and other preconditions for the hierohistory of the Abrahamic religions — they are "not of this world," i.e., they happen against the backdrop of an already virtually disenchanted world of *ens creatum*. There are no Deities overflowing with the sacred in the world; the sacred is concentrated in one God who is far away, and the world is presented as put at the disposal of man, as something that ultimately exists simply on its own in accordance with its own laws. The world of Modernity is already implicitly given in this picture of the world, only its traits and reality are colored by Judeo-Christian hierohistory and messianism. The Enlightenment era's deists and apologists for the natural sciences simply took these intentions inlaid in the Platonic-Christian paradigm to their logical end, first by taking God out of the equation as a "resting watchmaker" and then by abolishing him altogether as a superficial, unnecessary variable that does not affect measuring instruments and the accuracy of formulas. It is in such a world that death is an event of insurmountable power for man, as death is subject to one God and his will. This death is fully, strictly natural-scientific and biological. For *mythos*, such a notion of death is insulting, impudent (ὕβρις), and extreme. If this kind of death is interesting at all, then it could, of course, be regarded as a force signaling withdrawal into the metaphysically unfavorable conditions of the eschatological times, or as yet another manifestation of *avidya*-ignorance. But, on the other hand, we could pose the question: What does such a death mean for *mythos* in its phenomenological originality, what does this fundamental change point to, and why does everything now boil down to *zum-Tode-sein*?

Nietzsche's proclamation that "God is dead! We have killed him!" was sounded in the era of already galloping Modernity, and at first glance it appears to address the Christian faith that had outlived its own. But this is not entirely correct, because Nietzsche's verdict was addressed to the whole structure of the West's Platonic-Christian metaphysics and its degeneration into nihilism, which Nietzsche tried in vain to overcome through the will to power and the transvaluation of all values from new standpoints. The "death of God" becomes one of the foundations of the philosophy of Modernity, and its echo is reflected in Postmodernity in Barthes' "death of the author," Foucault's "death of man," and Lyotard's "collapse of grand narratives," etc.

It is also no coincidence that Nietzsche says that "we killed him," for this is essentially one of the decisions taken by Dasein as it is increasingly and evermore deeply alienated from itself and its source. This is the Being-Historical (*seinsgeschichtliche*) milestone in the oblivion of the question of Beyng even in the form of ontotheology and the passage to the positions of beings — present beings alone — on the lower material level, starting from Plato's idealism (which in one way or another remained the dominant line in Western European philosophy), running into the Enlightenment and to materialistic, scientific metaphysics. The "murder of God" was not an event of overcoming metaphysics, an exodus from its closed, two-level structure, but the final fixation on the level of the ruins of its lower level. The setting sun of metaphysics is prolonged in its decline and pause, the *logos* degenerates into logistics and the jostling and shuffling of values, and modernist rationality slips into irrationalism, into simulacra of mysticism, phantasms of corporeality, and the commotion of Deleuze and Guattari's "desire machines."

This deed was done by human hands. The death or murder of God is addressed not only and not so much to Christianity in particular, as it is a de facto summary sentence passed on the sacred as a whole, as the exterior source of Being, truth, and morality. For Traditionalism, overall, this means finally removing the pole of the sacred and breaking with Tradition itself, albeit in its ossified Abrahamic forms. It is quite right that Nietzsche refers to Plato's cave as if the many shadows still show the Divine even when it has died — Nietzsche thus anticipated the presence of diverse simulacra of traditions and spiritualities. But this image might also be recognized as signifying Dasein's flight into what is already extinct and gone in the History of Being, what Heidegger called "hiding in metaphysics" and fruitless pleas to Pan. It does not matter from which tradition or how detailed these shadows are, nor does it matter how fully their heritage, mythology, etc., have been preserved.

The "death of God" is the sharpest cry of man in a world in which he has genuinely found himself thrown and abandoned, alone and without any universal law or guarantees. With reference to classical mythologemes, we might say that man has been left without his Heavenly Father and Mother Earth, and therefore without a family and homeless. Heidegger associated the latter theme of being homeless (*unheimisch*) with feelings of anxiety, uncanniness (*unheimlich*), and detachment both within and from the world.

Nietzsche's words are a hyperbolic trope, but they should be perceived as an extremely serious and adequate expression, a speaking forth of how things are. Without Nietzsche, for example, existentialism and the problem of human freedom in the face of the Nothing would be impossible. Yet, despite the hyperbolism and metaphor, for us the absence of the holy and the Divine in immediate presence here is a fact.

But Heidegger understands the Divinities in the Greek, Presocratic way. Acknowledging the crisis of metaphysics, a certain correctness on Nietzsche's part, and seeing his philosophy as the final accord of metaphysics in its own self-exposing and attempt at self-overcoming, Heidegger understands the "death of God" in a different way. For Heidegger, the following formulation is key: "the old gods have left, but the new ones haven't yet arrived." A significant part of what could be called Heideggerian theology is structured around this idea. Let us hear Hölderlin's lines once again:

> But friend, we have come too late. It is true the gods live
> But over our heads, above in another world.
> Work without end there and seem to care very little
> Whether we live, so much and so well do they spare us
> The vessel is weak and cannot always contain them,
> Only at times can humanity bear the gods' fullness.
> Life is a dream of them, after.

In destitute times, the poets are those who follow the tracks, the footsteps, of the departed Divinities. The philosopher, and man in general, lives in the gap of the interregnum, in a sleepy daydream about the Divinities — but those which have already left, or those which are only about to come? The "tracks" are a symbol, a testimony that the Divinities were still here. A romantic can read the tracks of the Divinities as a sign that they are just up ahead, and rush into an endless pursuit of them. Others might elevate the footprint itself onto the altar and built a cult around it as having its own value, like the shadows of the "killed God" in the caves of *das Man*. But the foremost significance of the tracks is that they testify to the fact that the Divinities can be anywhere, but they are concretely no longer here.

Only lone, singular ones, Heidegger says, find the barely noticeable, dust-covered paths along which the Divinities fled, but they have no traces to find of them returning to the already shifting sands of a world of beings that has been handed over to exploitation, desolation, and the masses. For modern man, the absence of the Divine is indeed identical to the death of the Deity, for its presence is in no way registered by instruments and does not affect the unquestionable physical laws at work in any moment and in any place. The Divinities have left us in a hermetically sealed sphere of being one-on-one with our "clear" picture of the world. Therefore, we are most likely likely living in a tabooed part of the cosmos which the immortals won't visit.

Metaphors of paths and forest trails are very important for Heidegger. One of them leads us to the Black Forest master's frequent evocation, recurring in some of his most enigmatic passages, of whether there are many "gods" or one "God." In *Contributions to Philosophy (Of the Event)*, Heidegger writes:[138]

| Das Seyn gelangt erst in seine Größe, wenn es als Jenes erkannt ist, was der Gott der Götter und alle Götterung *brauchen*. | Beyng attains its greatness only if it is recognized as that which both the god of gods and all divinization need. |

At first glance, the words "god of gods" prompt us towards the simple assumption that the Divinities, as it were, have their

---
138 Heidegger, *Contributions to Philosophy (Of the Event)*, 192.

own cult around one supreme Deity. Such a structure seems to unnecessarily multiply beings and relativizes Divinehood as such, thus opening up the way for hypotheses about cavalcades of "gods of gods" stretching into infinity. This solution is not relevant for Heidegger either; for him, there is no fundamental question between monotheism or polytheism: the Divinities themselves decide among themselves how many of them there are, one or many. In essence, this is the Divine's decision as to its own selfhood. Heidegger writes that the very plurality of Deities is not subject to any number, but rather relates to the inner abundance of grounds and abysses.

Here it is important to recall the German theologian, heir to Neoplatonism, and founder of the current of "Rhineland mysticism," Meister Eckhart, whom Heidegger cites. To Eckhart's thought belongs one of the most important distinctions in the deep structure of the Divine, namely between the specific Deity (*Gott*) and the apophatic Divinehood (*Gottheit*). If a Deity is the cause and ground (*Grund*) of the world (like the Abrahamic demiurge or the monistic Absolute), then the Divinehood is the deep, primordial ground (*Urgrund*) of the Deity. This *Urgrund* is at the same time the *Abgrund*, the abyss, which is apophatic, unknowable, and indefinable in terms of being, like a precipice into the dark of the Nothing that is the ultimate and most "solid" foundation that does not multiply profane infinity. From here we can draw the line that the Deity as *Gott* is the basis and manifestation of Being as *Sein* in its cataphatic aspects, i.e., the Deity as the world and manifestation in being(s) (*Seiende*). At the same time, the Divinehood, *Gottheit*, leads us to the apophatic understanding of Beyng as *Seyn*. Heidegger devotes great attention to interpreting the abyss, connecting it with various elements of his philosophy of the Event (*Ereignis*) and the Other Beginning. The abyss is the ur-ground as the clearing of the openness and "emptiness," like χάος. The abyss, the *Ab-Grund*, has a certain inevitable fate: to be concealed, to be consigned to oblivion, to be covered up by something that is not fundamental (*Un-Grund*) and which pretends to be the ground.

Heidegger does not name the Deities. The German word *Gott* is originally neuter, not masculine, and it goes back to the Proto-Germanic *gudą* and the Proto-Indo-European **ģhutós*, which has two possible meanings: "the called, the invoked" or "the one to whom a libation is made." These etymological roots connect the semantics of *Gott/Gottheit* to the power of vocal invocation, to speech, and to sacrifice using the classical and ancient ritual drinks of wine or beer.

Elsewhere, Heidegger points out that within ontotheology, where the Being (*Sein*) of all beings is identified with a Deity (*Gott*), the verbal connective "is" remains the only name commensurate with the Divine. This strictly philosophical approach really tells us a lot. If in classical mythopoetics we are most often dealing with the names of Deities in the form of epithets or kennings (metaphors, tropes, riddles, etc.), then Heidegger indicates that the fundamentally innerworldly name of the Divine is the "is" that permeates all of language. Nevertheless, in this unfolding of the Divine as the "is" of all beings, that is the world, we move away from and forget Beyng (*Seyn*) itself. This clarifies Heidegger's statement that the Divine is at once neither "existent" nor "non-existent." The Divine as *Gott* cannot be equated with Seyn-Beyng, so we are required to draw the cataphatic and apophatic distinction within it. Within the world, Beyng "is" ("essences") to man (Dasein → *Daseyn*) the possibility of being engaged as the "preserver of the site of the moment for the absconding and advent of the gods."[139]

This bears a direct relation to Heidegger's theological and ontological project. In *Contributions to Philosophy (Of the Event)*, he poses the question of "whether something like [B]eing can be attributed to gods at all without destroying everything divine."[140] For Heidegger, speaking of "the Gods" acts a synonym for the fundamental "undecidability" as to their number, about which it is worthy for a person to question. The Divinities, alas, are

---

139 Heidegger, *Contributions to Philosophy (Of the Event)*, 207.
140 Ibid., 345.

in need of Beyng, in need of the expressing word (*Spruch*) by which they are thought. Heidegger clarifies that the Divinities do not need Beyng like property in which they might find their place. His thought is more complex: The Divinities are in need of Beyng in order to be themselves, in their selfhood (*Selbst*), to belong to themselves through that which does not belong to them. This need of Beyng casts them into the abyss, which the master calls freedom, and expresses their refusal of any justification and proof. This formulation of the question leads the Divinities to the necessity of philosophy, not in the sense that they themselves should philosophize, but that man might be their ally on this path. "The Divinehood of the Gods is said in thinking," Heidegger writes in his *Black Notebooks*.[141] This, of course, is on the condition that the thinking of Beyng should not seek the essence of Beyng in the supreme Divine as if in a highest being, *ergo* in the cataphatic aspect of belonging to the register of "is." Beyng is neither beings nor Deities. Beyng is the interspace, the fissure between beings and the Divinities that is incommensurable with either of them. The philosopher's task is to think through this fissure out of the essence of Beyng itself, and this thinking is a place of struggle and deciding on the arrival or flight of the Divinities and bringing the Divinity itself to decision. Heidegger concludes: "Beyng is the trembling of divinization (the trembling of the resonance that announces the decision of the gods about their god)."[142] This trembling opens up space and time for further concealment.

This long and dense expositions brings us to the problematic situation of our interregnum: the oblivion and flight of the old Divinities, the understanding of man as the rational animal in the First Beginning of philosophy, and the history of the West as decline (*Untergang*). Heidegger connects the problem of the Divinities with Beyng, with the word, and thus turns its decisive solution into the future, into the horizon of the Other Beginning. Other solutions centered around refreshing

---

141 Heidegger, *Zametki I-V (Chernyie tetradi 1942-1948)*, 573.
142 Heidegger, *Contributions to Philosophy (Of the Event)*, 189.

or restoring the old metaphysics that has already degenerated into nihilism are labeled a flight into various theisms, whether monotheism, polytheism, pantheism, deism, atheism, etc.

At the same time, Heidegger brushes aside all accusations that he is atheist. He is no apologist for any special or pretentiously sophisticated form of atheism:[143]

Die Gott-losigkeit besteht nicht in der Verleugnung und im Verlust eines Gottes, sondern in der Grundlosigkeit für die Gottschaft der Götter; deshalb kann die Betreibung e es gewohnten Gottesdienstes und seiner Tröstungen und Erhebungen immerfort doch Gottlosigkeit sein, insgleichen der Ersatz solchen Dienstes durch Anstachelung von "Erlebnissen" und Gefühlswallungen.	Godlessness does not consist in the denial and loss of a god, but in the groundlessness of the godhood of gods. Therefore, the pursuit of customary worship and its consolations and uplifting can all the time be godlessness; equally godless is the replacement of such worship by enticing "lived-experiences" or paroxysms of emotion.

Furthermore, this also pertains to openly artificial attempts to invent or somehow weave together "new" Deities in the spirit of many currents of esotericism, mysticism, or social constructivism, as well as attempts to arrange a "God" out of mundane values. In the midst of this commotion, only the few are able to hear the song accompanying the flight of the Divinities.

What, then, is there left for us to do in this situation of radical forsakenness, in the current state of the world's impoverished lack of the holy and the high, against which Traditionalism also revolts?

"Not knowing the eschatology of Being, we cannot even think of the idea of one or another theology," Heidegger writes in his *Black Notebooks*.[144] The eschatology of Beyng is its oblivion,

---

143 Heidegger, *Mindfulness*, 210.

144 Heidegger, *Zametki I-V (Chernyie tetradi 1942-1948)*, 304. In this passage, the word Being is crossed out with the so-called "St. Andrew's Cross," which suggests understanding Being through the above-discussed Fourfold.

its turn and passage into the excommunication and refusal that constitutes our history. Therefore, the philosopher calls on us to realize, it is necessary to re-pose and re-decide upon the question of the truth of Beyng in the Other Beginning, and on this will depend the Being of the Divine ones in the world. In theology, this means a profound re-founding of the groundless ground of Divinehood out of the darkness of Beyng-Nothing. The task of man, the philosopher, and the poet is to prepare within his sacrifice of thinking and word the time and space for the coming of the new Divinities. Hence, any naming of Deities and any silence over the Deities becomes a question of mindfully apprehending the meaning of the History of Beyng.

When human thinking — the "embassy" of Beyng in the phenomenal world as here-being — decides that the cause and source of all beings is another extant something, even the highest, then the Divinities, turned into "only beings," albeit a special kind of beings, are, as it were, cut off from their non-extant source, their "ground" in the abyss. This would be like cutting off a river from its upstream source — without this connection with the deep waters, it is no longer nourished and inevitably becomes shallow until it dries up. The Divinities begin to be understood in one way or another, proof of their existence is demanded, this existence is taken to be forces of nature, prime movers, or even intrapsychic archetypes or cultural personages. All of these are stages in the oblivion and the emasculation of metaphysics, within which the Divinities no longer find expression in language.

The immortals are in need of Beyng, in which the gain the freedom to be who they essentially are without proof and justification. A Divinity is not a cause of Being; rather, Beyng is the ground of Divinities. The Divinities are in need of Beyng so as to comprehend their "is." From heaven they gaze and ask about Beyng, and on earth they are echoed from the horizon of the temporality of here-being by the human being who, like a shepherd, thinks attentively and delicately asks about Beyng. Once again, Heidegger points to astonishment and angst or horror as the primary and fundamental attunements connected to the groundlessness of the truth of Beyng.

How we refer and appeal to the Divinities belongs to their distant oblivion and absence here. We think of them in the old way, while Heidegger calls on us to think the Divinities not as the highest beings, but as those who belong to the needfulness of Beyng (*Seyn*) and are capable of enduring the Nothing as a moment of primordial origin. It is not that the Divinities create man, nor that man invents the Divinities, but that both decide on the truth of Beyng which essences between them. The way in which Beyng-as-Nothing is decided and passes into the being of beings correspondingly comes about with knowing and naming the Divinities. As in the case of his early passages on *Sein*, when he comes to the Divinities Heidegger emphatically calls on us to think of them not as beings which can be counted and calculated by man, but as manifestations of the truth of *Seyn*. After all, the Divinities are "great insofar as their divinehood comes from the primordial inceptuality of Beyng."[145]

But whither, to what *topos*, do the Divinities flee from unbearable and unbearing people? The Divinities flee into their Divinehood in self-refusal, which is the announcement of themselves in absence.

And what about man? Man remains alone with the world, but as *Da-sein* only he can ground in thinking and language the space and time for the coming and interplay (*Spiel*) of the new Divinities instead of the return of the old ones. Man is valuable for the astonishing and awaiting Divinities in that he is factical here-being, the one who in his authentic existing kindles the fire of the hearth to which the Divinities might descend with their song. In Beyng man acquires humanity, just as the Divinities acquire the space for manifesting here their Divinehood. In his guardianship of Dasein, man manifests himself as the one needed by the Divinities as their own guardian.

---

145 Heidegger, *Mindfulness*, 223, translation modified.

But still, the German thinker repeatedly emphasizes that oblivion and refusal are the fate or inevitable consequence of any decision which regards Beyng as some kind of "outside" source of all beings, including the world, man, and the Divinities. Beyng-as-Nothing cannot be permanently upheld in a state of openness, and in one way or another the focus shifts to what enters the clearing of unconcealment and its fate. The question of the paths, structure, and configuration of this conscious self-refusal and self-concealment is the most important decision upon the truth of Beyng and the further path of the thinking and Being of the Divinities. Heidegger once again insists: "To bring God into the vicinity of Being means losing God under the condition that Being is worthy of thinking. To bring Being into the vicinity of God means parting ways with thinking under the condition that God is the Worthy of Worship in the actions of the believer."[146] We can leave the interpretation of this passage within the scope of this philosopher's intrinsic counterposing of simple faith and philosophical thinking, between which he calls on us to choose "either-or." But it bears going even further and paying attention to the extreme apophaticism that crown non-dual monistic theologies and philosophies.

The essence of the apophatic method lies in "defining" or "delimiting" Divinehood, which means that we are speaking strictly about the ascent from *Gott* to *Gottheit* by way of cutting off any properties, i.e., terms, that limit it. Despite the fact that the innerworldly Divinity can truly be anything, the ascent occurs through litanies of discarding all of its properties, which ultimately always leads us into the apophatic dimension of the pure Nothing. Here we are faced with a paradox: in ascending to the innermost heart of Divinehood, we are overcoming its limits, because in the apophatic Nothing there is no "Divinehood" or "theology." Otherwise it would turn out that, having separated all definitions and epithets from the Divinehood and coming close to the darkness of its *Nichts-Selbst*, we would still be holding

---

146 Heidegger, *Zametki I-V (Chernyie tetradi 1942-1948)*, 437. "Being" here should be read as "Beyng," which is reflected in the Russian translation by the capitalization.

somewhere to the side a final definition that would indicate that this "Nothing" is nevertheless the Divine, which means that we have traversed a path that is still theological. Then our apophaticism would remain incomplete, not carried out to the end. We would be limiting the Divine, denying it the freedom in our thinking to groundlessly be anyone or anything whatsoever, even something radically different in relation to itself or being its not-self, *ergo* "being" Nothing. To this sphere pertains the classic problem of the difference between theistic monism, which most often boils down to a cataphatic, supreme being, One Divinity, or Being (*Sein*), and non-theistic monism, the path to which runs through an extreme apophatic theology that overcomes — but does not deny or abolish! — the very boundaries of the Divinehood. Recalling Eckhart's Neoplatonism, we know that one is based on, or rather even grows out of, the other.

Heidegger takes the Greek Ἕν to refer to a supreme being, the *logos* and demiurge through Θεός, whereas we know of a purely apophatic reading of the One that is open on top. Thus, the Neoplatonic structure is more flexible and allows for the thinking that we need. However, it bears acknowledging that this line was never dominant in the vein of Platonic-Christian theology, but rather always remained in the periphery, left to mysticism or heretics. The Abrahamic God is still a being and the *logos* still "is" as a being. Accordingly, if we bring the Divinity to Beyng-as-Nothing, then we are actually stepping beyond the "divine" definition in apophaticism. And vice versa, by putting extreme emphasis on the cataphatic, innerworldly manifestations of the Divinehood as a multitude of Gods, and by raising such into a cult, we lose sight of Beyng as the groundless ground.

As we have already said, monism holds that the world is the manifestation of the Divine, in which the Divine unconceals itself in concealment. Within the world, the Divinity should be totally everything. The myth and cult of any Deity can be theologically elevated to the monistic dimension, that is, any Deity can be revealed and read as a path of the expression and ascent to the One. Therefore, when man as *Da-Sein* prepares and carries forth in silence the place and time for the coming of the new Divinities, he is partaking in the decision-making at the hearth of Beyng on the re-founding of the whole grounding of the Divinehood out of its flame. The Divinities should be in all the power and freedom of their Divinehood. This means that, with the joint decision on the Being of the Divine ones and beings, man steps aside in order to let the Divine reveal itself ontotheologically as the cataphatic One. Then the Nothing remains concealed as the heart and self of the Divine, as the innermost, the sacred, and the horrifying.

Furthermore, the non-dual structure of ontotheology posits the oneness of the Divine and the word and of the Divine and man. This is expressed in the classical formula "atman is Brahman," wherein the individual person's soul is literally identical to the Absolute of Brahman, and their difference is conditioned by the play of illusions or the intent of the Divine. Closely related to this is the notion that the mind and thinking of man are essentially a literal reflection belonging to the Nous (νοῦς), to the Demiurge-Intellect. If man is a direct, intrawordly manifestation of the Divine, which, according to the latter's intention, is separate from it, then it follows that the Divine and man's common need and guardianship in relation to Beyng can be recognized to be the Divine approach to Beyng from two differential ontological horizons, both of which are essentially the one Divine. This explains man's inheritance of the nature of the Nothing: Man is the bearer of the Nothing which might disclose itself as the nihilism of God-forsakenness in history. This forms a recursive loop that cannot be unraveled logically, as introducing any linear determinism would only shift the emphasis onto one of the two poles and predetermine the point of view and unfolding of all ensuing conclusions and discourse. For the mythopoetic approach, however, the entirety of the described structure of "reflections" is harmonious, beautiful, transparent, and graspable as a whole despite all of its complexity.

But everything that has been said above still necessitates resolution, decision, and the overcoming of metaphysics in order to break through to the very space of unconcealment in which the shepherds of Beyng can light the fire of the hearth and, with their sacrificial diligence in the word, perhaps invite the Divinities to come down and dwell with us. To this end, man must overcome the decline of the West, the decline and collapse of metaphysics, the "death of God," and nihilism. Man must shift into the authentic mode of existence and enter into the leading mood of angst.

> *Along with losing the gods, we have lost the world*; the world must first be [*seyn*] erected in order to create space for the gods in this work; yet such an opening of the world cannot proceed from, or be carried out by, the currently extant humanity—instead, it can be accomplished only if what basically grounds and disposes the opening of the world is itself acquired—for *Da-sein* and for the restoration of humanity to Da-sein.[147]

---

147 Martin Heidegger, *Ponderings II-VI: Black Notebooks 1931-1938*, trans. Richard Rojcewicz (Bloomington/Indianapolis: Indiana University Press, 2016), 154.

The Fourfold

The complex relations between the Divinities, people, the world, and Beyng can be clarified in terms of the structure of the Fourfold (*das Geviert*), which Heidegger proposed as an alternative to the classical, two-level metaphysics in all of its variations.

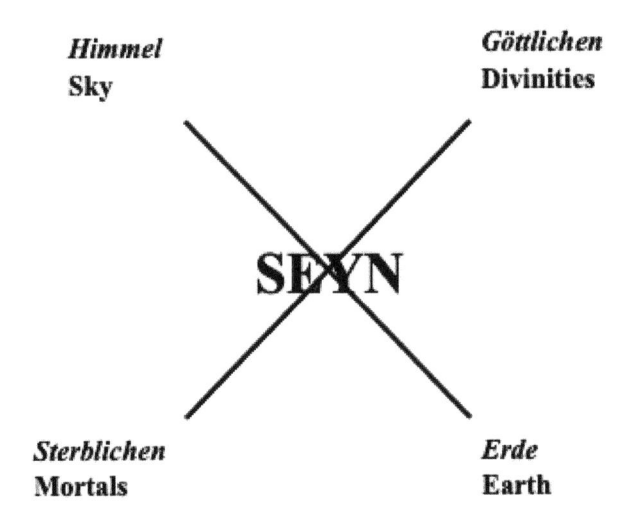

```
  Himmel                    Göttlichen
  Sky                       Divinities
         \              /
          \            /
           \          /
            SE⧲N
           /          \
          /            \
         /              \
  Sterblichen              Erde
  Mortals                  Earth
```

At the core of the Fourfold is an oblique cross, but this cross should not be identified or interpreted through any symbol known to us from traditions, such as the solar wheel or "St. Andrew's cross."

Das Geviert is not a mapping of space by cardinal directions, a symbol, or any numerological reference. The Fourfold shows us the structure, or more precisely the "fittingness" (*Gefüge*), and method of Heidegger's philosophizing, the path of his thinking, and the relationship between the key nodes in the final period of his work. The Fourfold is given to us as a whole — we cannot add anything to it nor take anything away from it; moreover, it is always necessary to think of all four elements at once. If we mention one, then we must mention the other three. At the ends of the two axes are the primary and fundamental manifestations of Beyng in the center. In his writings, Heidegger started writing the word Being crossed out.

Heidegger characterizes the relations along the axis of Sky-Earth as dispute or strife, πόλεμος. Sky and Earth are constantly arguing with each other, yet this *polemos* should be understood not merely as strife, but as the leading principle of the distinguishing of beings, of multiplying the many (πολλα). Relations along the axis of Divinities-Mortals are characterized as confrontation. This is a subtler nuance, because confrontation can also be understood as strife, as struggle, as "going against one another," but in its literal meaning, it is a standing opposite to one another, and this might not imply enmity. The main point is that they are separated from each other on the same axis, i.e., positioned at different levels of the cosmos from which they look at and respond to each other and make their decisions.[148] It is also obvious that this arrangement has the Sky and Divinities at what would be the "upper" pole of the Fourfold, while the Mortals and Earth are at the "bottom." This gradation most likely speaks to the metaphysical reflex that is inherent in us, but it is secondary when it comes to the Fourfold.

The Sky (*der Himmel*) is what gives openness (*Offene*), spaciousness, and illumination fro all beings. Heidegger sometimes identifies this Sky with the notion of World (*die Welt*). The Sky or World offers endless space for things to be, to rise up into being(s) (φύσις). Living under the open Sky and in its openness, a people decides on the fate of Beyng.

The Earth (*die Erde*) is what bears, grows, nourishes beings, and lets them presence. Unlike the Sky, the Earth is closed-off; covering and guarding are its foremost quality. Therefore, Sky and Earth are in dispute; they are essentially polarities. In their dispute, together with the confronting and appropriating between the Divinities and people, opens up the clearing of the "space-dispute-time" (*Zeit-Spiel-Raum*) in which beings

---

148 See Heidegger, *Mindfulness*.

arise. This arising is owed to the openness of the Sky and is simultaneously, by virtue of the principle of Earth, the loss in concealment of this clearing.

The Divinities, "God," the Deities, or simply the immortal ones, are special beings which Heidegger understands in the distinctively Greek way as the subtle, delicate, sad ones who are of great importance over the course of the unfolding of Beyng. These are the Deities who easily tend to flee from the slightest self-confident assertion by mortals, but at the same time they are in dire need of *Seyn*-Beyng and are ready to take part in the decision, if people prepare this possibility. Heidegger's Divinities are essentially the Divinities of Beginnings. In the words of the master already cited above, "Beyng is the trembling of divinization (the trembling of the resonance that announces the decision of the gods about their god)."[149]

Despite the innerworldly anthropocentrism intrinsic to Heidegger's philosophy, we find that people are not in the center in relation to the truth of Being, but at one of the poles. They are essentially those whom Beyng itself needs for its guardianship in being decided upon. Heidegger writes:[150]

| Das Seyn braucht den Menschen, damit es wese, und der Mensch gehört dem Seyn, auf daß er seine äußerste Bestimmung als Da-sein vollbringe. | Beyng needs humans in order to occur essentially, and humans belong to beyng so that they might fulfil their ultimate destiny as Da-sein. |

In one passage in the *Black Notebooks*, Heidegger calls man the shepherd of Beyng and the regent of the Nothing.[151]

People are completely opposite to the Divinities, and this creates a space for different variations of their relations, from cult to war. One of them lives by the death of the others, and if for the "victory" over the Divine, man sets off on gigantic adventures and

---

149 Heidegger, *Contributions to Philosophy (Of the Event)*, 189.

150 Ibid., 198. In this passage, we hear a faint reference to the mood or attunement (*Stimme, Stimmung*) of man as Dasein.

151 Heidegger, *Zametki I-V (Chernyie tetradi 1942-1948)*, 387.

undertakes machinations upon beings (*Machenschaft, Gestell*), then the Divinities overcome people through playful and easy movement. However, the "victory" of the Divine over man does not mean that the latter is crushed and dies, but rather means elevation, awakening of the inner holy, being inspired by horror and astonishment, catharsis, enthusiasm, and even liberation from the alienating structures of the everyday life of *das Man*. Through the belonging together of people and the Divinities to one and the same axis, we can interpret the possibility of their non-duality ("thou art that") within the scope of what would resemble an innerworldly, monistic, immanent "metaphysics."

What is foremost is that people are mortal, they are the Mortals, and Beyng is thought by them to be the horizon of being-towards-death. Only people die. Dedicating oneself to Beyng means sacrifice and sensitivity to conserving and guarding. Heidegger speaks of a special "exposure" among beings of those people who open themselves up to understanding Beyng. This understanding is neither objective nor subject — Cartesianism has no relevance here. The philosopher speaks of throwing oneself "into" here-being, grounding oneself in a leap, and the very place from which this leap is made is itself grounded through the leap. Heidegger uses the verb form *erspringen*, where the prefix *er-* means the accomplishment of a result, i.e., something is achieved, reached, done. We understand this leap as a pushing away from something, a leaping from somewhere to somewhere. This meaning shifts in Heidegger's usage, hence *erspringt*, "leaps," is to be understood as closer to "experiencing," "exploring," "discovering," by way of the leap itself or in the fulfillment of the leap. That is, we don't see and we don't know where we are jumping, as such is a gesture of sacrificing oneself. Let us recall Heidegger's words from above: "When the gods call the earth, and when in the call a world echoes and thus the call resonates as the Da-sein of the human being, then language exists as historical, as the word that grounds history."

The word of Beyng resounds in the voices of poets and philosophers, who are essentially the voices of their people and in themselves are the people of Beyng. *Das Seyn ist ihre Heimat* — Beyng is their Homeland. They are in essence those of whom the Divinites are needful in their need for Beyng, and those whom Beyng itself needs for its disclosure and essencing. Everyone needs each other. And then people kindle the fire to which, like neighbors, the Divinities come down to join the Thing to decide upon and tell of Beyng, grounding, history, the holy, the thing, and their Divinehood. Heidegger writes: "Beyng: the hearth-fire in the midst of the lodging of the gods, a lodging which at the same time is the estrangement of the human being," and this "estrangement" is "the 'between' in which the human being remains a [the] stranger, precisely when the human being becomes at home with beings."[152]

Taken together, the four of the Fourfold form a fitting order with each other (*Fügen*). At the intersection of their axes is *Seyn*-Beyng which unfolds (*aletheia, physis, logos*) along the axes into the world, into beings, and along these axes people and the Divinities return to the Thing that gives space to the Earth under the open vastness of the nighttime Sky. Heidegger proposes to think of Being not as a cause, and not as an answer to the question "from where?", but as the grounding in which everything is grounded. Grounding is essentially the Abyss (*Ab-grund*): need as the openness of self-concealment. This is how space-time is born as a place for the instant of the dispute between Earth and World over Beyng or Non-Being. All beings are ways and means of the concealing of the primordial decision of the ones who are in dispute and confrontation over their groundless ground.

Besides Beyng, at the center of the Fourfold we might also place the thing, *Ding*, which Heidegger also draws back to the event of the Thing (from the Proto-Germanic **þingą*, whence Icelandic *þing*). Like the Thing, a thing is an affair, a matter, a decision, a resolution, and even a handcrafted thing is a combination of Earth as matter, Sky as the space to be, man as the creator, and the Divinities as the inspirers and sanctifiers.

---

152 Heidegger, *Contributions to Philosophy (Of the Event)*, 383.

To continue this synonymous series, the center of the Fourfold might also host *mythos*, the form of of the primal saying and self-revelation of Beyng that tells all beings through telling of itself. Then *das Heilige* would also figure here as what is most primordial, that which goes both ahead of people and Divinities, the poetic holding of the clearing of the between, from which people emerge as human, Deities as Divine, and Earth and World as extant.

And, of course, at the heart of the Fourfold could also be the Nothing, which Heidegger repeatedly either identifies with Beyng or treats as a complete synonym. The Nothing is neither privation nor negation of beings or *Sein*-Being (the being of beings, or beings as a whole, *Seiende-im-Ganze*). Heidegger writes:[153]

Das Nichts ist das erste und höchste Geschenk des Seyns, das dieses als Ereignis mit sich selbst verschenkt in die Lichtung des Ur-sprungs als Ab-grund.	The Nothing is the foremost and highest gift of Beyng, which along with itself and as itself gifts Beyng as the Event unto the clearing of the prime-leap as ab-ground.

This "ab-ground," or "groundlessness," should not be understood as lack or poverty, but as the need for the grounding of Being-as-beings, for there to be (some-)thing at all.

Elsewhere in his treatment of Beyng, the master poses one of the most important questions affecting us as existing Dasein:

> Is death the deep shadow that Being [crossed out] as Event casts off into its positioning? Does the light of Being flood into the human essence to the extent to which this essence belongs to differentiation? Is this light not the radiance of the sound of silence that takes over the world so that death not only does not appear in the world as if from somewhere unknown, but is the world itself?[154]

The human is the one who differentiates between beings and Beyng, and in this distinction the light of Beyng carries him like a flood in the world or — and here Heidegger draws an

---

153 Heidegger, *Mindfulness*, 263, translation modified.

154 Heidegger, *Zametki I-V (Chernyie tetradi 1942-1948)*, 395.

intersection between the metaphor of light-visibility and the metaphor of sound-audibility — envelops him in silence. Light and sound are the essence of the being of the world as beings, the intrawordly unfolding of beings from the ground that is the abyss. Then the very existence of the world is the death of Beyng, and in human existence the Beyng-Fourfold figures as the shadow cast by mortality. Within the world, however, this shadow also falls on the Divinities.

The eschatological unfolding of the History of Beyng (*Seynsgeschichte*) implies an inevitably disintegration of the structure of the Fourfold that can be traced over the course of history (*Historie*). Heidegger speaks of many centuries, acts, and scenes in this decline, sometimes directly and frankly, sometimes in passing and in hints, and at other times they can be deduced from his philosophy. Much of what he says, as well as what can be derived from the structure and trajectory of his thought, coincides with Traditionalist assessments and the Traditionalist historiography of the fall and decline of human culture into modern civilization.

The pole of people, cut off from the truth of *Seyn als Nichts*, as difficult as it is to bear in thinking and metaphysics, is reduced to mere beings, even if they have a "spiritual," or more precisely, cultural dimension. In Abrahamism, this is translated through the dogma of the created nature of man. Later, in the Enlightenment era, Descartes proclaimed man the subject, which was picked up in humanism. The next iteration reduces man to a convention at the intersection of evolutionism, biologism, and physicalism, which completely exhausts itself in the resulting strategies of transhumanism. The human being, once understood as merely a being, having become bored *das Man*, begins to subject himself to machinations and reassemblies.[155]

The Divinities are reduced to the ἰδέα and λόγος within the already sealed-off Platonic cave. From the Abrahamic Creator-God who is separated from the world and people runs

---

[155] See Askr Svarte, *Tradition and Future Shock*.

a direct road to the Watchmaker-God and the *deus otiosus* of deism. This, in turn, is easily inverted into phenomena of intrapsychic experiences in psychoanalysis (C.G. Jung) or is altogether discarded as fiction in atheism. Finally, "Deities" settle down into mass pop-culture like all other characters. All of these iterations are essentially metamorphoses on the wall of shadows — shadows of Divinities who long ago fled or even died.

The openness of the Sky is first replaced by the extant firmament and later is simulated as a gaseous atmosphere and the dumb infinity of space. The Sky is turned into a place for aviation echelons and satellite orbits.

Since "Biblical times," the Earth has been taken to be entrusted like a blind and inert creature to the complete dominion and disposal of people, which in the secular era is easily converted into treating the Earth as a ready-to-hand storehouse of free resources and treating nature as a task for excavation, exploitation, terraforming, etc.

All of this comes about as a form of the oblivion of the question of the truth of Beyng and, moreover, oblivion of the very fact that we have forgotten anything at all in the kaleidoscope of different theories, ideas, and flat ontologies. All the elements of the Fourfold are scattered, torn away from each other, ripped out of their fittingness (*Gefüge*), put out of tune (*Stimmung*), and removed from the hearth of Beyng.

The Last God

Heidegger begins the chapter of *Contributions to Philosophy (Of the Event)* on the Last God by radically demarcating this figure from all known pantheons and theologies: The Last God (*der letzte Gott*) is "the god wholly other than past ones and especially other than the Christian one."[156] This Last God is the most enigmatic and yet the most important figure in the sphere of the theology and the Divine of which Heidegger writes. The thinker draws a direct connection between the Last God and the Event (*Ereignis*) of the inception of the Other Beginning. The Last God is the one who passes people by on the distant horizon, giving but a subtle hint (*Wink*), like a nod or a wink, before passing into concealment and departing forever. Heidegger writes:[157]

Der letzte Gott ist der Anfang der längsten Geschichte in ihrer kürzesten Bahn. Langer Vorbereitung bedarf es für den großen Augenblick seines Vorbeigangs. Und zu seiner Bereitung sind Völker und Staaten zu klein, d. h. zu sehr schon alle Wachstum entrissen und nur noch der Machenschaft ausgeliefert. Nur die großen und verborgenen Einzelnen werden de Vorbeigang des Gottes die Stille schaffen und unter sich den verschwiegenen Einklang der Bereiten.	The last god is the beginning of the longest history on the shortest path of that history. A long preparation is required for the great moment of the passing by of the last god. Peoples and states are too small for the preparation of that moment, i.e., already torn away too much from all growth and delivered over only to machination. Only the great, hidden single ones will create the stillness for the passing by of the god and will produce among themselves the reticent unison of those who are prepared.

All the German philosopher's ontological, anthropological, and theological threads of thought converge on the figure of the Last God. Alexander Dugin provides a most rich passage: "It could be said that the theology of the Other Beginning is a movement

---
156 Heidegger, *Contributions to Philosophy (Of the Event)*, 319.
157 Ibid., 328.

towards the 'Last God,' who appears thereupon for those who have endured the 'death of God' without disappearing and steadfastly awaiting him (like a priest without a cult, or a priest dedicated to an unknown Deity)."[158]

In order to better understand the figure of the Last God, it bears examining his "existentials," that is the structural elements which are classically associated with Deities — but only inasmuch as they fit him and inasmuch as he stands out from them. To this end, we will ask about the Last God's language, name, theophany, cult, place, and people.

Everything that we know of the Last God was said and written by Heidegger in the second period of the development of his thought. All of this was said in the German language, which the philosopher enriched with Swabian dialectisms and archaisms as part of his undertaking to construct a special, non-metaphysical, non-conceptual style of speech, language, and philosophy, which he did with his typical teasing out of prefixes and roots, constant glosses between words with the same roots, all in the vein of the method of the hermeneutic circle of exploring and questioning an uneasy question. In this light, it bears taking the Last God's name as a whole in German, in the spirit of a classical heiti — *der letzte Gott*. Heidegger does not give a definite root or proper name to this Divinity, and only once does he name it in other terms: "the Concealed and Rarest."[159] As we have already clarified, the word *Gott* means "the invoked, the summoned, the called one." The Last God is therefore the "Last Invoked One." But this "lastness" is of a special kind. He is not the last in the sense of one who concludes something, after which there is no one else. Heidegger does not discount other, new Divinities coming after the Last God. The very multiplicity of Divinities, who are not subject to number and numerical order and who belong to the abundance of abysses, is relevant to the place and time in which the Last God gives his hint. It is quite likely that the Last God does not belong to that

---

158 Dugin, *Martin Heidegger. Poslednii Bog*.

159 See Heidegger, *Mindfulness*.

abundance of Divinities who might return to the world. Rather, he is the one who passes by, apart from all others, and simply makes a gesture.

Heidegger pays much attention to one — only one — theophany of this Last God: his passing by us on the horizon in the appropriating Event of Beyng in the Other Beginning. The passing-by of the Last God should be strictly delineated from any identification or comparison with the Second Coming of Christ, the figure of Odin the Wanderer (*Vegtamr, Gangraðr*), the Lord of the World of which the Völva speaks, or the sudden theophany of Dionysus. They have nothing in common. In this respect, the extreme "brevity" of his "appearance" and passing-by might be taken to be a reference to apophaticism, because statements about who or what he is are extremely sparse compared to the endless string of enumerations of who and what he is not.

Moreover, the Last God does not come into this world, he does not come to us, and we do not know at all where he comes from nor where he is headed. The Last God passes by us, at a distance from us, perhaps with some apprehension and disgust, as if "they are too rude to pass by too closely, to be noticed." Finally, he might not pass by us at all, instead remaining unnoticed as not-passing. Heidegger writes that the Last God is concealed in the Event and as the Event (*Ereignis*).

In his final interview to the magazine *Der Spiegel*, which was on his insistence published only after his death, Heidegger spoke of the Being-Historical (*seinsgeschichtliche*) abandonment of the world and thinking. He left us with the following enigmatic passage:

> Only a god can save us. The only possibility available to us is that by thinking and poetizing we prepare a readiness for the appearance of a god, or for the absence of a god in [our] decline, insofar as in view of the absent god we are in a state of decline.[160]

---

[160] Martin Heidegger, "'Only a God Can Save Us': The *Spiegel* Interview (1966)," trans. William J. Richardson, S.J. in Thomas Sheehan (ed.), *Heidegger: The Man and the Thinker* (Chicago: Precedent Publishing, 1981), 57.

Heidegger does not clarify what God he is speaking of, but the overall hints and context of this phrase, taken together with his philosophy as a whole, allow for us to follow the path to the Last God and to the need for man to become sensitive, gentle, and subtle in his thinking and aspiring towards the Divine. Then we will be able to see the only gesture that the Last God gives in our direction: his hint (*Wink*), his slight sign, his nod and wink, a gesture thrown in passing and confirming the event of decision. Here we might recall Hölderlin's words that "hints are, from time immemorial, the language of the gods."[161] Accordingly, Heidegger directly associates the passing of the Last God and his hinting gesture with the condition of lone humans who have prepared themselves with the primal element of language and speech. Heidegger insists on the need for the quietest silence in order for the Last God to be heard. Silence is the space through which the Last God passes. Man is the guardian of the silence of the passing of the Lats God, and silence is the source of the word. Man is called into silence by his Dasein, by its voice and conscience which calls us to ourselves.

Heidegger sometimes speaks of multiple hints that are intertwined as signs of ultimate need for the essencing of Beyng. For example, there is the rush and absence of the coming Divinities and the places of their dominion. "Why hasn't a single new God appeared in thousands of years?," Heidegger asks, obviously having in mind not the multitude of little gods invented on the pages of cheap esoteric books, but instead genuine and real theophanies clothed in all the power of *tremendum*. The flight of the old Divinities and the absence of the coming of the new Divinities is a special hint calling for the great differentiation of Dasein as we are left in the world alone in the loneliness of sacrifice and the choice of the shortest yet steepest path to the Event.

The passing-by of the Last God bears a markedly eschatological character, and Heidegger says on more than one occasion that the Last God will come at the moment of the most

---

161 Hölderlin, "Rousseau." Cf. Heidegger, *Elucidations of Hölderlin's Poetry*.

radical, utterly complete abandonment of Being, and the Last God's hint will reveal itself as the innermost finitude of Beyng. In the deepest downgoing (*Untergang*), the Last God arises as the suddenness of the nearness emerging out of the longest time of preparation.[162]

The word grows out of silence, and Heidegger speaks of blessed ones who, dangerously close to the fissure in Beyng, will become the ones who belong to the inceptual conversation of the single ones, in whose conversation the Last God will gives hint because it is thanks to them, thanks to the single ones conversing about Beyng, that he can pass by. We can once again recall Hölderlin's lines:

> Much has man experienced.
> Named many of the heavenly ones,
> Since we have been a conversation
> And able to hear from one another.

In the *Black Notebooks*, the thinker directly says that the poetic character of thinking could one day become the topology of Beyng. With the rigor and weight of poetry, thinking allows for the dwelling of the Last God in the place of Beyng to be expressed in language.

This wealth of hints from the Last God can, in a manner intrinsic to Heidegger's thinking, be seen not as a sequential chain of several gestures, but grasped as one telling, one tale, as the one-in-many that is told in the spirit of *mythos*. As Heidegger writes: "Follow in speaking the sign-hint of words. Avoid interpreting speechless words... Be silent in the word. And thus ground language."[163] The linguistic dimension of the Last God's hint is thus outlined by the Black Forest shaman himself: It is the word that is said in and out of silence, the word that will be the poetic and philosophical grounding of language and the truth of Beyng.

On the whole, we can trace the trajectory from metaphysical ontotheology (the completed form of the First Beginning

---

162 See Heidegger, *Mindfulness*.

163 Heidegger, *Zametki I-V (Chernyie tetradi 1942-1948)*, 48.

of Western philosophy still in its sacrocentric epoch) to the fundamental-ontology of the early Heidegger, and then, following the event of the Turn in his thinking, to the hermeneutics and philosophy of the Event. The Last God's hint has substantial (linguo-)ontological weight, it ensures the eventing of the Event, and, therefore, we can speculatively speak of the fundamental-ontological gesture-wink of the Last God.

Nevertheless, from the standpoint of the old metaphysics, and in the space of the interregnum between the old Divinities who have departed and the new ones who have not yet come, there are no grounds, and we have no right, to speak of any cult or idolatry of the Last God. His whole "structure" rebels against this, and the Swabian herald himself warns against such.

Besides the themes of silence, conversation, language, and word, Heidegger calls the place of the coming of the Last God the "difference" and "fissure" of Beyng, by which he has in mind its openness and the Fourfold. Heidegger writes: "The place of the Last God, if he is supposed to come to be and abide at all, is the difference as the overturning of Being."[164] In this difference, in the "place" of Beyng, Beyng is woven into poetic telling, into language as the placement of its truth. In the *Black Notebooks*, the master refers to his Contributions to Philosophy (*Of the Event*), where he wrote the following of the "fissure"[165]:

Wahrheit ist als das Ereignis des Wahren die abgründige Zerklüftung, in der das Seiende zur Entzweiung kommt und im Streit stehen muß…	Truth, as the event of what is true, is the abyssal fissure in which beings are divided and must stand in the strife…
Sie ist die abgründige Mitte, die erzittert im Vorbeigang des Gottes und so der ausgestandene Grund ist für die Gründung des schaffenden Da-seins.	Truth is the abyssal center which trembles in the passing by of the god and thus is the withstood ground for the grounding of creative Da-sein.

---

164 Heidegger, *Zametki I-V (Chernyie tetradi 1942-1948)*, 241.

165 Heidegger, *Contributions to Philosophy (Of the Event)*, 262.

Finally, in the unconcealment of the truth of Beyng out of the veil of time and space, the Last God essences. The flame of Beyng burns towards the Last God, sending him forth as the bottomless ground of the clearing between Earth and World.

Thus, the Last God harmoniously aligns with all the sides of the Fourfold: he is needful of people as the founders of the *Da* (*Dagründer*) as their own here-being (*Da-Sein*) and the world of his passing-by. The manifold Divinities, in their rush, flight, and return, are in reverent relation to the Last God's gesture and the fissure and openness of Beyng (*Seyn*).

All of this, however, requires something extraordinarily tense and difficult on the part of man, his thinking and existing (being-in-the-world). In essence, what is needed is a transition into a completely other way of thinking and language. In this way can the possibility of the Event be prepared. Heidegger writes:[166]

Wer dieser Vorbereitung sich opfert, steht im Übergang und muß weit vorausgegriffen haben und darf vom Heutigen, so unmittelbar dringlich dies sein mag, kein unmittelbares Verstehen, allenfalls nur Widerstand erwarten.	Those who sacrifice themselves to this preparation stand in the transition and must have reached far ahead; they also may expect from their contemporaries no ready understanding — as immediately pressing as that might be — but, if anything, only resistance.

---

166 Ibid., 42.

The Future Ones

At this point, it bears dwelling in detail on the special category of people who bear a direct relation to the Last God and the Other Beginning. Heidegger considers such outstanding (ex-isting) people to be poets, philosophers, and, obviously, himself. These people are the ones who, standing forth amidst all the alienation and eschatology of Beyng, persist in fostering the questioning thinking of Beyng and its truth. They are those who in their poetry (and poetry, let us recall from Golovin, "is not mere verses") and in their thinking prepare the space for the passing-by of the Last God and the Event (*Er-eignis*) of the Other Beginning.

Heidegger calls them "single ones," "strangers," "the few," "the transitional ones," and "the future ones," the ones to come: "Only the great, hidden single ones will create the stillness for the passing by of the god and will produce among themselves the reticent unison of those who are prepared."[167] Despite the differences between these names and the roles assigned to them, they often flow together in the master's passages and figure as synonyms. They are the ones who, behind the facades of religions and spectacles, hear the song accompanying the flight of the Divinities and find their tracks under the cover of dust. They are the ones who can return to the darkness of the abyssal ground to re-found the ground of the Divinehood of the Divinities instead of simply inventing some new religion or joining various theisms.

In his key work, *Contributions to Philosophy (Of the Event)*, Heidegger offers a lengthy description of the future ones, whom he also calls the "distinctive ones," the ones faced with the task of deciding on the "sheltering of the truth of the event into the great stillness of beyng out of the restraint of Dasein":

1. *Those few single ones* who, on the essential paths of grounding Dasein (poetry—thinking—deed—sacrifice), ground in advance the

---
167 Heidegger, *Contributions to Philosophy (Of the Event)*, 328.

sites and moments for the realms of beings. In this way they create the essentially occurring possibility for the various sheltering of truth in which Da-sein becomes historical.

2. *Those numerous affiliated ones* to whom it is given, in virtue of their understanding of the knowing will and of the groundings of the single ones, to surmise and to make visible, by carrying them out, the laws of the re-creation of beings as well as the laws of the preservation of the earth and of the projection of the world in the strife between earth and world.

3. *Those many who are referred to one another* according to their common historical (earthly-worldly) origin, through whom and for whom the re-creation of beings and thereby the grounding of the truth of the event acquire constancy.

4. The single ones, the few, and the many (not taken in terms of their numbers, but with respect to their distinctiveness) still partially stand in the old, common, and planned orders, which are either only a shell-like safeguard of the precarious continuance of the single ones, the few, and the many or the guiding power of their will.

The *agreement* among these single, few, and many ones is hidden, is not fabricated, and grows suddenly and for itself.

This agreement is pervaded by the essential occurrence (different in each case) of the event, wherein an original gathering is prepared. In this gathering and as this gathering, that which may be called a *people* becomes historical.

5. In its origin and destiny this people is unique, in accord with the uniqueness of beyng itself, whose truth this people must ground once and for all in a unique site and a unique moment.[168]

These single, future ones (*Zu-Künftigen*) are essentially the people of Beyng. After all, ordinary nations are insufficient, too "small" for such a decision, and they belong to the dying body of metaphysics (those peoples enslaved by the machinations of the Gestell). It immediately catches our attention that Heidegger thinks of their task in terms of the structure of the Fourfold, as in the strife of World and Earth. He calls them the "future ones of the Last God."[169]

---

168 Heidegger, *Contributions to Philosophy (Of the Event)*, 76-77.
169 Ibid., 316.

The single ones are those who prepare the most intimate and primary time and space for the concealment of Beyng. They lay down, ground, provide, and speak forth the very first, fundamental strokes of the project of Being and beings, which will later by picked up by the slightly more extensive (although the philosopher says that we are are not talking about quantity) stratum of those who will subsequently develop this project as philosophy.

The burden of the future ones is the heaviest and is directly associated with sacrifice. We have already repeatedly encountered this motif in Heidegger's philosophy, particularly when we spoke of the concept of sacrifice as a disinterested, uncalculating bestowing of oneself to Beyng, in response to which arises the foundational word (*das Wort*). Heidegger tells the reader that whoever sacrifices himself for this preparation — and therefore becomes a transitional one — should not expect any understanding from the current state of affairs, but on the contrary, should only except resistance. Out of the strife of Sky and Earth, the future ones reach the Event and a view of the whole history of Beyng as the greatest uniqueness. As for all the rest, Heidegger says that they will be plunged into a restless commotion of world-poor masses of creatures vainly hoping only for what was before, for returning to that which has passed. In this we can see a gloss of images with the Nietzschean "last people" and their blinking.

The sacrifice is to be offered up by those who measure and draw out the path from the very depths of the abandonment of Being, and thereby correctly describe fate of the West as decline (*Untergang*). By having this description, and through the awakening of their understanding of their existential situation as the abandonment of Being and God-forsakenness, the future ones become the ones who are prepared. Without sacrifice, there is no chance that the "twilight of the possibility of the Last God's hinting" will come.

The sacrifice is bound up with resolution towards the descent of the grounders of Beyng and and how they, as Dasein, endure standing in the deepest fissure of Beyng, defenseless and without support in the darkness of the abyss.[170] In so doing, Heidegger writes, clearly repeating after Hölderlin, humans "overreach" the Divinities: "This reaching *over* the gods is a going *under* as grounding the truth of beyng."[171] Thus, we have an interplay between "*over*-reaching" and "under-going." This "reaching over" is not titanic, theomachic hubris, but that which is open to the innerworldly being of man as the trial of grounding Being-as-beings, projecting its structures, and guarding the hearth of Beyng for the Being of the Divinities.

In this light resound Heidegger's most tense passages, which are about pain. "Pain is the pure form of the manifestation (*Austrag*) of the truth of Being," the master imperatively declares in the *Black Notebooks*. A little later, he uses the form *austragen* in the sense of "enduring," that is enduring or "bearing" the inception into pain: "In the ultra-nearness of its free silence in concealing the healing of unbearable pain, Being must be terrifyingly strange — no suffering in the fate of Being and no suffering [remaining] in the memory of man can change anything."[172] Heidegger draws a direct connection between pain and the Event (*Ereignis*), the appropriation of Beyng that makes Beyng one's own to dwell within. It is not man that has pain, but rather pain has man as the inception of the appropriation of the Event. Pain comes to figure as yet another synonym, albeit rare and lesser, for Beyng. We read in the *Black Notebooks*:[173]

---

170 Here it bears reemphasizing that Heidegger is not creating an esoteric teaching, but is pronouncing rather intelligible, non-metaphysical intentions when he speaks of simple grounding on the groundless, *Grund* and *Abgrund*. Therefore, we should be deliberate in cutting away any and all irrational-mystical impositions and connotations that surface in relation to the translations of his words.

171 Heidegger, *Contributions to Philosophy (Of the Event)*, 384.

172 Heidegger, *Zametki I-V (Chernyie tetradi 1942-1948)*, 138.

173 Heidegger, *Zametki I-V (Chernyie tetradi 1942-1948)*, 112.

Was kommt, aber in langer Zeit: der An-fang in die Enteignung zur Gelassenheit des be-freyten Erwohnens der Erde, daß erdend erst sie den Himmel die Bergnis dann öffne, aus wehender Welt Ding und Geschick die Weite der Weile erbauend der Gottheit, wartend des Gottes. All dies freyend ungesprochen im unscheinbaren Gedicht die Freyheit des Schmerzes: das Seyn.	What is to come, but in a long time: the inception into reclaiming for letting be freed dwelling upon the earth, so that the earth, in its earthing, opens up first the sky and then the mountains, building up out of the worlding world thing and fate, the breadth of the interim for the Divine awaiting the God. All of this freeing, unsaid in an inconspicuous poem, is the freedom of pain: Beyng.

Following the established rule of "when speaking of the Fourfold, we are to speak of all four at once," here we can note that Heidegger does not directly name people as mortals. Rather, he speaks of how Beyng is the freedom of pain in an "inconspicuous poem." What is this poem? The master immediately writes that "man is the incepted poem of the glimpsing of the passed truth of Being."

In essence, pain is Dasein, here-pain. The task of the future ones is to decide on the leap, the jump down to Beyng-as-Nothing, which is the source of the holy, the Divine, the thing, the world, the earth, and ourselves in authentic self-concealment. To endure the horror and pain of this sacrifice in existence, to clothe it in poetic telling, in *mythos*, which begins the run-up of its projection in silence.

Pain, in this case, whether physical or of the soul, is a direct, embodied experience of time as duration. Pain places us in withdrawal, marking out the boundaries of the corporeal and us ourselves within these boundaries. Pain closes us unto ourselves, leaving us alone with ourselves and our time, which we literally, empirically feel like the duration of pain or grief. Such an understanding of pain can be laid into the semantic chain of "Being—time—pain—Dasein."

This occurs against the backdrop, and against the grain, of the violent inertia and resistance of all the structures of *das*

Man and the machinations of the Gestell, which "compensate" misery with "lived experiences," "compromises," "success," and "exactitude" — "for the last god hates all those more than anything else."[174] In the midst of this world of beings and infinite reassemblies, commotion, false decisions and solutions, illusions, etc., the human being is "the *stranger* who undergoes the casting loose, who no longer returns from the abyssal ground, and who *retains* the remote proximity to beyng in this foreign realm."[175]

The transitional thinkers must clearly understand that their questioning and telling will be unintelligible to the present day, which is incalculable in its duration and its seemingly endless prolonging into tomorrow without history or event. Heidegger calls the aspiration for self-evident intelligibility the suicide of philosophy. Hence follows the implicit conclusion that the task of the transitional and future ones is not any simple, intelligible exposition or explanation of a philosophy of Beyng that is illustratable in schemes and formulas. The Black Forest shaman himself, of course, showed the path in his own style of writing and thinking.

In general, the "transitional one," or the "one belonging to the transition," is quite an interesting anthropological figure. In essence, the transitional ones are those who commit to the passage from one shore to another, and this means that in their very nature, history, and thinking they are alone and unique in belonging to both shores, to both ends of the bridge. Even if one shore is essentially their native one, and the other one is completely concealed, they are still the ones who decide to pass from one borderland of thinking to the other. It is quite likely that the fourth passage describing the future ones concerns them where it is said that they "still partially stand in the old, common, and planned orders."

---

174 Heidegger, *Contributions to Philosophy (Of the Event)*, 322.
175 Ibid., 387.

But if the future ones, concealed and solitary, those who remember Beyng against the grain of everything and dedicate themselves to its problematic truth and pain, are essentially the future ones of the Last God, i.e., the ones bound to the Other Beginning and the fundamental re-founding of the holy and the Divine, then who in this picture are Traditionalists? Traditionalism definitely has the possibility to become the space for the inception of the transition if its representatives recognize the deeper and non-metaphysical posing of the problem of Beyng and the oblivion and flight of the Divinities bound up with it. On this horizon, Traditionalism's problems and programs and Heidegger's fundamental re-founding of the holy and the Divine might coincide.

With their stoic principle of *semper fidelis*, Traditionalists might by analogy be called the remembering ones, those who remember and keep the memory of what was, what has gone into the past. They are the ones who cannot reconcile with this departure, in the spirit of the classical *Sehnsucht* of romanticism. The remembering ones aspire for the return of such, or for something similar. The past, or the preservation of the traditions that have collapsed, is like their painkiller. Traditionalism can cut off the pain as a symptom, but it cannot cure the very cause of this pain that is the metaphysically predetermined fate of decline, disorder, collapse, and end. In such a case, remembering, or returning the past by reminiscing and *imaginaire*, condemns us to emasculated repetition, to a lame return of one and the same with displacement and distortion — a distortion which, albeit barely noticeable, is such each time, like copies taken of other copies, reconstructions and restorations which inevitably drag everything into a growing procession of simulacra.

But Traditionalism has another side, and its most important one at that. If Traditionalism can take away Dasein's deep pain, then this means that its structures and intentions have a certain correlation with, or at leat some kind of relation to, the very source of the pain, and therefore Traditionalism points towards its cause. Heidegger often calls need and abandonment special ways of the manifestation and call of Beyng. Whenever Beyng is not here in a genuine way, its absence points us to its closest closeness. The strategies of *das Man* lead to forgetting this pain along with the very thought that "something is missing." In this case, any religious, mystical, and traditional intuitions and practices — themselves already overall alienated from their source, or already artificial — might facilitate Dasein's hiding from itself among beings. Traditionalism compensates for this vector with its radical rejection of Modernity and all of its structures; it takes one step away from the pain of Beyng at the point where *das Man* otherwise takes his happy gallop into Postmodern culture and web-surfing. Here we need the art of differentiating action, sacrifice, and being self-sacrificial. We are faced with two missions: on the one hand, we need to preserve memory in spite of everything, and to perform ritual even if the Divinities have left; on the other hand, we need to prepare the future coming of the Divinities out of the newly decided question over the abyssal ground of the holy telling of their Divinehood. In essence, we are dealing with the subtlest line of symmetry of a mirror reflection, where one side is "already past forever" and the other is the coming future, which is problematic and not guaranteed.

Can the remembering ones become the transitional ones? Without a doubt, yes. But this requires of them substantial and painful effort in fundamentally reassembling and transitioning to different structures of thinking and even deeper standpoints in philosophy and theology. It requires a more sober, painkiller-free recognition of the whole depth of the alienation and disenchantment of the modern world, without harboring any illusions.

Where might the meeting place of the remembering-transitional ones and the future ones be? This meeting place is a bridge. To the extent that it is possible to translate Heidegger's philosophical text and fundamental intention into other languages, including the languages of various traditional theologies (which, if mastered, will find their own thinkers who will follow Heidegger's thinking and proposed change in the *façon de parler*), a "people of future ones" might be gathered (*legein—logos*) out of the concealed single ones of all ethnicities and nationalities, those who emerge out of their womb and set off to blaze the trail and build a bridge towards other, endless possibilities of thinking and history.

Another Beginning

All of the above does not simply converge like threads woven into a knot, but is immediately offered up by Heidegger as a circle of interconnected and interflowing problems, paths, trajectories of thoughts, and questions whose posings lead to his main project: the Other Beginning, or Another Beginning, of Western philosophy, which he associated with the return of authentic history, the coming of the new Divinities, and a proper resolution and decision on the question of the truth of Beyng and human existence in the world. Over the course of our dialogue with you, dear reader, we have repeatedly spoken of Another Beginning, its principal conditions and project.

Unlike the First Beginning of Western philosophy, which Heidegger saw in the thinking of the Presocratics, when it comes to his own project he speaks precisely of an Other Beginning (*anderer Anfang*), not a Second Beginning. Continuing a numerical line of namings would not solve anything on the level of the attention to words and language that were of such great importance to this thinker. "First and Second Beginnings" would mean a potentially endless series of "one more beginning." For Heidegger, what is important is not an increase in number, nor a different reassembly of the same metaphysics that has already shown and exhausted its actual power and greatness, but none other than an Other Thinking, for which Heidegger created a different language and structure in his texts and the exposition of his thought. Here we can find one of the important precursors of future Postmodernity: the problematic instance of the "Other" and how (or whether) the Other can be understood.[176]

Heidegger's Other Beginning is directly connected with a different, more precise resolution to the question of the truth of Beyng, to man's existence as Da-Seyn within the world and

---

[176] Of course, Heidegger thought completely outside of the psychoanalytical and socio-political contexts that would dominate Postmodernity.

his relation to the apophatic source of Beyng. Insofar as the German philosopher considered Beyng's refusal, concealment, and abandonment of man to be inevitable and fundamentally "built into" the original structure of Beyng as the specific mode of "existing" through "revealing-itself-in-self-concealment," it is necessary to take this trait into consideration for the future philosophy. In essence, the concealment of the original truth of the First Beginning, *aletheia*-unconcealment, was the inevitable fate, outlined as it is in the agrarian metaphors of physis and logos. But the identification of Beyng with beings in the form of a highest, super-being, as in the spirit of Plato's proud delusion, was the decision and thought of man who has turned his gaze to beings alone.

The Other Beginning implies not only upholding unconcealment, but more so philosophers' and poets' principled guarding and preserving in silence of the refusal of Beyng. The direct "communion," connection, and flow of beings out of Beyng-as-Nothing must be preserved to nourish philosophy, myth, art, and history without severing this connection and replacing the source with a metaphysical instance (a cataphatic principle akin to a super-being, the being of God and the Church, fundamental physical laws, procedures of cognition, the autonomous subject, values, etc.).

Instead of the final oblivion and withdrawal of Beyng-as-Nothing as the source of all beings, and even the oblivion of the very fact that we have forgotten something, what is needed is the delicate concealment of Beyng in the groundlessness of the ground of beings. Beings and the "metaphysics" of the being of beings should be opened up towards their always own Nothing, just as Dasein is opened up by angst into its own finitude and the very same Nothing. Heidegger therefore speaks of the guardianship of truth (*Wahrheit*) by the single ones.

Heidegger writes in the prospect of *Contributions to Philosophy (Of the Event)* that "through a simple *thrust* of essential thought, the happening of the truth of beyng must be transposed from the first beginning to the other one, such that in the interplay the wholly other song of beyng resounds."[177] We can preliminary correlate this song of Beyng with a special myth whose diction does not conceal the open expanse of the clearing, but delicately yet confidently, deictically points to silence as the source of its telling. If classical myth and song always tell about something, i.e., a cataphatic something and its referential truth certified by the metaphor of visibility, then the other *mythos* must be entirely dedicated to itself as a tale that is immanent to Beyng-as-Nothing. In the First Beginning, the Nothing was disregarded and not thought, hence Parmenides' "Being is, Non-Being is not." The Other Beginning must solve this problem in a completely different way by acknowledging, including, thinking, and preserving the Nothing as the most intimate secret. Heidegger speaks of slipping into silence, wherein truth can once again decide to become a clearing for self-concealment.

The history of the First Beginning of Western philosophy, which unfolded as the particular history and culture of the West that has arrived at its total collapse, is for Heidegger a primordially predetermined fate of *Untergang*, descent, and decline. The thinkers of the Other Beginning must decide to go down to the lowest point of the dead and decaying metaphysics so as to recognize in it the final accord and no longer sounding final notes, so as to grab hold of and push off from them in beginning another melody, motif, and tale. To this descent pertains the interregnum between the departed, old Divinities and the new Divinities who have not yet appeared. This makes the descent to the decision upon Beyng an extremely tense sacrifice, one which must be endured without the gazing eyes of the Divinities and by preparing the space for the passing of the Last God.

At the same time, Heidegger most sternly warned of the risks of the Other Beginning becoming seized and substituted by a merely updated metaphysics that brings it back into its safe

---

177 Heidegger, *Contributions to Philosophy (Of the Event)*, 9.

circles. In the *Black Notebooks,* he warns that "common sense," "church faith," and "political enslavement" will combine forces to wean a people of thinkers and poets off of its thinking. Heidegger once again deemed Christianity and science to be counterfeit thinking.[178]

The decision and thinking of the single ones and future ones is not about somehow correcting the old metaphysics, as if by fitting another, apophatic dimension to it so that we might leave everything as it's been and rest content with an easy, cosmetic change of emphases. Transitioning to the Other Beginning and its truth implies, among other things, a specific, extremely clear, and direct change in man's attitude towards beings and nature, from treating them as ready-to-hand resources for machinations to treating them as the Earth and Sky in the structure of the Fourfold. This means not simply changing one's evaluative view, changing culture or the principles of art, but a total change in the whole modality, practices, and ways of man and his people's living, dwelling, and being in the world.[179] Heidegger devoted many tomes to thinking through and docking those trains of thought that lead to dead-ends or bring everything back to normal. Therefore, clear and specific programs, lists, manifestos, roadmaps, and algorithms cannot be given as guides to action for the Other Beginning in principle. The Other Beginning, like many of the most important elements of Heidegger's philosophy, takes on features which, if not outright apophatic, are definitely presented by way of contrast as "not as in the metaphysics of the First Beginning." The Event shall undermine the dominance of the old *Logos* and its machinations.

The Other Beginning is decided upon and flashes forth in the Event, the *Ereignis*. This term is difficult to translate, and Heidegger often emphasizes and plays with its various facets and synonyms. Ordinary thinking suggests understanding the Event as a certain moment in the arrow of time, as the instant

---
178 Heidegger, *Zametki I-V (Chernyie tetradi 1942-1948),* 107.
179 See Askr Svarte, *Tradition and Future Shock.*

when something happens, occurs, or "befalls," a moment which, as an event, divides the flow of time and history into "before" and "after." The Event is a change in the world, a fundamental one.

In his philosophy of the Other Beginning, Heidegger thematizes the Event as the essencing of Beyng itself in the appropriation of beings and here-being. This is, as we discussed earlier, the grounding moment of the truth of Beyng as concealment in descent. Here, Heidegger employs all of this word's facets. *Ereignis* does not only mean an event as some "happening," but has deeper roots which are more significant for us. This word combines two etymological lines which the thinker underscores. The first elevates the word to the meaning of "to make one's own," "to appropriate," hence the frequent motif of "appropriation" and rendering "authentic." This is akin to the important notion of dwelling in the world and one's home, becoming local, rooted, and native. This is analogous to Dasein's authentic (*eigene*) mode. Heidegger emphasizes this aspect with the prefix *er-*, as in *Ereignung*, "appropriating." The Russian translation of *Ereignis* as *sobytie* ("event"), which is literally "with-being" (*so-bytie*), accentuating jointness, togetherness, being side-by-side, brings more confusion rather than expanding and revealing the semantics intended by Heidegger's thinking. For Heidegger, the emphasis is not on becoming "joint" or "together," but on being one, one's own. This is traceable to the Proto-Germanic root **aiganaz*, whence German *eigen*, which also means to own, to possess, to hold in property, to take possession of. Semantically, this line comes close to the notion of "self," *Selbst*, which etymologically means "to be separate," "to become independent."

The second line is based on the dialectal *eräugen*, the root *augen* referring to eyes (*Auge*) and seeing. In this optic, an event is appearing to one's eyes, being visible. Here lies the nuance: what becomes visible in the Event is being(s), as the cataphatic manifestation of Being, while Beyng-as-Nothing itself is concealed in the silent groundlessness. If we see the world, this means that we as Dasein have already been appropriated in the Event of affirming the truth of Being and beings in their separation into apophatic and cataphatic poles, and we find ourselves within the world as already decided.

In the corresponding chapter of *Contributions to Philosophy (Of the Event)*, the master provides a whole series of indicative definitions of the Event which at once bring together the themes of the opposition between Sky and Earth, the dispute between Mortals and Immortals, the Divinities' needfulness of Beyng, the appropriating of here-being, the need and sacrifice of the single ones, the re-establishment of all grounds (Divinehood, the word, beings, man, etc.), the groundlessness of the simple, and the oneness-and-solitude of Beyng. On the latter, Heidegger says that, in the grounding of its solitude[180], Beyng only projects around itself the Nothing, which it most faithfully protects.

Besides its simplicity, the master calls Beyng the most uncanny, the most estranged. The extraordinariness of Beyng corresponds to the domain of the grounding of truth, that is the Nothing, and for here-being this is the uniqueness of death. Only man has this distinction, this differentiation, of standing in the face of death, and death is thus the highest testimony of Beyng. In this uncanniness of Beyng, which touches our phenomenal presence in the world with inevitable death — death which is always only our own and which is given to us in the solitude of being alone with ourselves — Beyng essences as the "event, the site of the decision on the nearness and distance of the Last God." Thus, the Event is sharpened into something unique and fateful that is not constantly present, but rather occurs as the ripened gift of Beyng itself. The Event is not to be thought of as something "planned for a period of time," but as that which most difficulty obtains as the rarest, most valuable, and fundamental

---

[180] We note that solitude is one of the modes of embodying selfhood (*Selbst*) as being separate.

turning point for all beings within the scope of philosophy and the innerworldly presence of Da-Seyn.

We now find ourselves at a fundamental philosophical and Beyng-historical pause. Heidegger anticipated the return of philosophy in Europe in 200-300 years, for now acknowledging that the disintegration of the *logos* of the First Beginning is still proceeding and has already given rise to the rhizome of the Postmodern paradigm. The iconic passage from the *Spiegel* interview in which Heidegger says that "only a God can save us" now sounds all the more intense as we know that we are living in a gap of desolation and interregnum. Heidegger writes:[181]

Das plötzliche Verlöschen des großen Feuers, das zurückläßt, was weder Tag noch Nacht, was keiner faßt und worin der zu Ende gegangene Mensch sich noch umtreibt, um nur noch am Gemächte seiner Machenschaften sich zu betäuben, vorgebend, es sei für die Ewigkeit gemacht, vielleicht für jenes Und-so-weiter, das weder Tag noch Nacht ist	The sudden extinguishing of the great fire — this leaves behind something which is neither day nor night, which no one grasps, and in which humans, having come to the end, still bustle about so as to benumb themselves with the products of their machinations, pretending such products are made for all eternity, perhaps for that "and so forth" which is neither day nor night.

This is how Heidegger summarizes the time to which he bore witness, the time in which we are still living, the larger-scale epoch of which will continue for many centuries to come. Of this pause and gap, Heidegger says "*noch nicht*" — "not yet." The run-up to the Other Beginning is not yet the beginning; the fading, oblivion, and blocking of thinking by the institutions and procedures of the Gestell continues. This is a long, long "still not yet." Heidegger writes:[182]

---

181 Heidegger, *Contributions to Philosophy (Of the Event)*, 207.
182 Ibid., 330.

…als müßteund würde der Mensch auf den Gott warten. Und vielleicht ist dieses die verfänglichste For der tiefsten Gottlosigkeit und die Betäubung der Ohnmacht zur Erleidung der Ereignung jener Dazwischenkunft des Seyns, das erst dem Hereinstand des Seienden in die Wahrheit eine Stätte bietet und ihm die Gerechtsame zuteilt, in der weitesten Ferne zum Vorbeigang des Gottes zu stehen, Gerechtsame, deren Zuteilung nur geschieht als Geschichte: in der Umschaffung des Seienden in die Wesentlichkeit seiner Bestimmung und in die Befreiung aus de Mißbrauch der Machenschaften, die, alles verkehrend, das Seiende in der Nutznießung erschöpfen.

It seems instead that the human being would, and would have to, await the god. Perhaps this is the most insidious form of the most profound godlessness. Perhaps it is also the stupor of the incapacity to undergo the appropriation of that intervention of the "there" of beyng which first offers a site for the standing of beings into the truth and grants them the privilege of standing in the furthest remoteness from the passing by of the god. The granting of this privilege happens only as history: in the transformation of beings into the essentiality of their determination and into their liberation from being misused by the machinations which pervert everything and exhaust beings for the sake of profits.

The Horizons of the Juncture

In the preceding chapters, we have provided significant comparisons between Martin Heidegger's fundamental-ontological project on the one hand, especially in the spheres of mythology, the sacred, and anthropology, and the Traditionalist ideational platform on the other. Now it bears turning to the specific attempts that have been undertaken in recent years to bring together and interpret the German thinker's philosophy and Traditionalism.

One significant attempt at understanding and evaluating Heidegger's thought belongs to the pen of one of the key "founding fathers" of Traditionalism, Julius Evola, in his book *Ride the Tiger*.[183] This work itself was a milestone and turning point for all of Traditionalism. Released in 1961, it contained a series of qualitative reflections on Evola's attempts at exerting a Traditionalist influence and implementing the Traditionalist project in the world by way of directly participating in Third Way politics in the period up to and during the Second World War. Evola acknowledged the impossibility of turning off the track of history, for the latter has been laid down as the due, that is to say as metaphysical and Dharmic predestination. Evola saw the Traditionalist's task as maintaining the inner vertical of the spirit and seeking out other ways and interpretations of the sacred in a dying world which awaits only further deterioration and decay.[184]

Thus, on the one hand, Evola's turn to deal with Heidegger's thought, which in those years had already been developing along the pathways of the "Turn" (*Kehre*), would be very logical and timely. On the other hand, however, it bears recognizing that

---

[183] Julius Evola, *Ride the Tiger: A Survival Manual for Aristocrats of the Soul*, trans. Joscelyn Godwin and Constance Fontana (Rochester: Inner Traditions, 2003).

[184] See Askr Svarte, *Tradition and Future Shock*.

Evola's attempt at understanding and interpreting the Black Forest master turned out to be extraneous and an utter failure.

Sixteen years after the end of the Second World War, Evola turned to the early, prewar Heidegger of the period of *Being and Time*. Evola's task was to put forth a critique of the "dead end of existentialism," and one can agree with a number of aspects of his harsh judgments. Evola taught the doctrine of the "differentiated man" who remains faithful to the ideals and spiritual vertical of Tradition in the era of maximal apostasy and nihilism, and he carved out this human type in polemic with the characteristic signs and teachings of modern nihilism. But, in the case of his references to Heidegger, we encounter a whole heap of problems pertaining to a lack of understanding of Heidegger's ideas and an ignorance of the broader contexts, details, and current state of development of these ideas outlined by Heidegger himself in the early 1960s. Evola blindly rushed into criticism, which *post-factum* renders his perspective weak and at a loss in a number of instances.

Evola noted that the roots of existentialism go back to the "lost generation" that was deeply traumatized by the most recent crisis of the modern world, i.e., the war. He imputed to armchair philosophers a petty-bourgeois way of life as well as, alongside the more active public non-conformists, an overall profanism and engagement to abstractions intrinsic to Western European thinking and cut off from their metaphysical roots. For Evola, existentialism is largely reducible to a form of nihilism, as it appeals to the theme of the "nothing" discovered after the death of the Christian God and the re-posed problem of existing in such a world. For Evola, existentialism in many respects continues the line of Friedrich Nietzsche and Søren Kierkegaard, that is to say a phenomenon of modernity cut off from the metaphysical spirit of Tradition. The ideologist of Traditionalism thus turned to attack what were, in his opinion, the key figures of existentialism: Jean-Paul Sartre, Karl Jaspers, and Martin Heidegger.

In the case of Sartre, Evola addressed the latter's classic theme, the "burden of freedom," that is the thrownness of the individual, lacking any roots in formerly traditional culture, into lonely confrontation with themselves, "sentenced to be free." Evola highlights the practically fatalistic and pessimistic tones of freedom in Sartre; for this left-wing French intellectual, freedom is what one is coerced to endure in a world without God. Our Italian thinker contrasts this to accepting freedom as a space of will, in which pain, tragedy, and death can be fully endured and transposed in terms of something greater.

Jaspers is the only one whom Evola mentions on a positive note as being "perhaps the only one among the existentialists to make a few superficial references to 'metaphysics,' confused by him with mysticism."[185] Throughout his numerous articles, Evola on more than one occasion harshly critiqued the relatively popular psychoanalysis and Freudianism of his time, which he called the "psychoanalytical infection" and deemed to be a force destroying European man and his connection with the sacred. Likewise, since his early years, Evola was critical of Christianity overall. Hence the inexplicable, self-contradictory nature of his minimal sympathy for Sartre's very same psychoanalytical existentialism and soft Christian theology

The problem with Evola's (mis)understanding of Martin Heidegger's ideas lies precisely in that he reads Heidegger's views from the period of *Being and Time* entirely through the prism of the extremely popular existentialism of Jean-Paul Sartre and Karl Jaspers. For Evola, Heidegger is of equal value to the latter two, and at times he appears to simply be their epigone. In other words, Evola refers to the Black Forest thinker as if to a "comma" appended to one of his German friends and one French intellectual, as if together they constituted some common field of ideas and were in solidarity with each other on the whole. In fact, however, the case is utterly the opposite.

---

185 Evola, *Ride the Tiger*, 79.

Back in 1946-47, Heidegger wrote and then published his iconic "Letter on Humanism" as a response to Sartre's theses. In this text, Heidegger radically demarcates his ideas from Sartre's and from the philosophy of existentialism as a whole. Without a doubt, Heidegger exerted a strong and even decisive influence on Sartre and Jaspers, but their ensuing, independent development of their own ideas led them in directions altogether opposite to the pursuits of Heidegger's project. Consequently, Heidegger considered it necessary to publicly, immediately after the war, distinguish how he did not belong to this fashionable philosophical current. For Heidegger, existentialism remains a kind of metaphysics, and, judging in line with his own philosophy, can in many respects be attributed to one of the intellectual strategies of *das Man*, which means that such leads us astray from understanding the truth of Being.

More detailed critique and even invective against Jaspers were presented by Heidegger in his later works and in his *Black Notebooks*, which were published long after his death and Evola's. Thus, Evola simply could not have known Heidegger's more detailed issues with Jaspers' existentialism. Nevertheless, the substantial divergence between these two Germans' ideas was already widely known throughout closely intertwined intellectual circles in Europe in Evola's time.

Even more erroneous is how Evola attributes to Heidegger, by way of identifying his thought with Sartre's, a perspective that is closed-off to the vertical dimension, and his allegation of Heidegger's "phenomenological agnosticism." The roots of this most crude error lie, once again, in reading Heidegger through Sartre, and in the fact that Evola was fundamentally unfamiliar with Heidegger's detailed and complex theological project as well as Heidegger's views on the role of *mythos* and the sacred in the being of man. In the very same postwar period, however, Heidegger was already publicly professing such perspectives, and he recognized the early experience and exposition of his *Being and Time* to have been unsuccessful and "too phenomenological," even too loaded with "existentiality."

Evola did not grasp the point that is of principal importance to understanding Heidegger's ideas on Being and here-being (*Dasein*), namely, the differentiation between Being (*Sein/Seyn*) and beings (*Seiende*). Evola passes over the most interesting and productive points in the critique of existentialism from theological perspectives. He remarks that "a certain type of existentialism could also lead to another point already established here: that of a positive antitheism, an existential overcoming of the God-figure, the object of faith or doubt."[186] Here, Evola himself figures as an apologist for merging the I, Being, and God (which for him is transcendence) in an apophatic "invisible presence." The difference is that, for Evola, as a radically positioned Traditionalist, what is of principal importance is transcendence, transcending the earthly level and the ordinary through the figure of the Divine and theosis, whereas existentialism and phenomenology are oriented towards the "middle world," to speak in mythological language. An academic phenomenological approach to studying traditions and myths would be developed by Mircea Eliade who, like Evola, considered himself a student of the ideas of René Guénon.

We can find similar affirmations of a merging of the self present in the world with the Divine and Being in Christian mysticism, yet elsewhere Evola rightly notes the obvious Advaitist, Eastern, and Neoplatonic correspondences of some of the necessary preconditions for such an "existential project." Namely, this is the need for a primordial principle that sets destiny and the need to remain true to this principle as one's own I. The "unfavorable soil" of existentialism produces a rift in consciousness and the human being between Sartrean existentialism and this need which permeates the whole vertical. For Evola, such a rift is a sign of decline.

---

186 Evola, *Ride the Tiger*, 81.

Unfortunately, Evola's whole analysis and critique of existentialism has nothing to do with Heidegger and his mature project, which is otherwise rich in all the necessary questions for Traditionalism. It can be argued that Evola was not familiar with this project at all and that he did not understand the key methods of the German master's philosophizing. When Evola writes about Heidegger, he is only expressing illusions, emotions, and issues which, while in some instances being genuinely right from a Traditionalist standpoint, pertain to the "populism" of the thundering, left-wing, unmistakably anti-sacred Sartre and his epigones, whose relation to our German thinker is extremely indirect and far-fetched.

At the same time, there is the fact that both Julius Evola and Martin Heidegger belonged to two very tightly interconnected ideological currents which some scholars and adherents consider to have been a single European intellectual field and cauldron in the early 20th century, namely Traditionalism and the Conservative Revolution. Evola and Heidegger also shared a common circle of friends, including Carl Schmitt, Ernst Jünger, etc.

Furthermore, long after Heidegger's death, a handwritten note was discovered among his remaining estate (*Nachlass*) with a quote from the 1935 German edition of Evola's *Revolt Against the Modern World*.[187] This discovery allows us to claim that Heidegger was indeed familiar with one of the most representative books of the philosophy of Traditionalism. Moreover, not only did Heidegger extract a passage from Evola's programmatic book, but he immediately appropriated it for his own interpretation in a way which substantially illuminates the perspectives of these two philosophies in relation to one another. Heidegger excerpted the following thought[188]:

---

187 See Julius Evola, *Revolt Against the Modern World*, trans. Guido Stucco (Rochester: Inner Traditions, 1995).

188 For the translation and discussion of this fragment, see Collin Cleary, "Heidegger against the Traditionalists" in *Passages: Studies in Traditionalism and Traditions* 1.

| Wenn eine Rasse die Berührung mit dem, was allein Beständigkeit hat und geben kann — mit der Welt des Seyns — verloren hat, dann sinken die von ihr gebildeten kollektiven Organismen, welches immer ihre Größe und Macht sei, schicksalhaft in die Welt der Zufälligkeit herab. | When a race has lost connection with what alone has and can give it constancy – with the world of Beyng, — then the collective organisms formed by it, whatever be their greatness and power, are doomed to sink down into the world of contingency. |

This rendition differs substantially from the original passage in Evola's book[189]:

| Wenn eine Rasse die Berührung mit dem, was allein Beständigkeit hat und geben kann — mit der Welt des "*Seins*" — verloren hat, dann sinken die von ihr gebildeten kollektiven Organismen, welches immer ihre Größe und Macht sei, schicksalhaft in die Welt der Zufälligkeit herab: *werden Beute des Irrationalen, des Veränderlichen, des "Geschichtichen," dessen, was von unten und von außen her bedingt ist.* | When a race has lost connection with what alone has and can give it constancy — with the world of "*Being*" — then the collective organisms formed by it, whatever their greatness and power, are doomed to sink down into the world of contingency: *to become prey to the irrational, the changeable, the 'historical,' of what is conditioned from below and from the outside.* |

What is immediately striking is Heidegger's change of the word *Sein* to *Seyn*. What gives a race[190] its constancy and stability is not simply being-as-beings or a super-being source of the world, but rather, as Heidegger articulates here, the apophatic instance of Beyng-as-Nothing. As a classical Traditionalist, Evola upholds Being as the highest form of all being(s), as the transcendent, as the Platonic world of Ideas. Evola advocates the fundamental doctrine of two natures, higher being and the sublunar world of becoming, which constitutes the classical two-level structure of metaphysics. For Heidegger, however, metaphysics and Plato in particular are a principal milestone in the oblivion of Being

---

189 The italics designate the parts which Heidegger edited or omitted.

190 Here it bears clarifying that Evola did not see race in the biological terms of vulgar racism; his works most often treat race as "race of the spirit," equivalent to the classical estates, castes, varna, or Plato's metallic souls.

and the decline of the whole Western world. Already in this point, we can see that Heidegger fundamentally rejects Evola's metaphysical approach on the one hand, while on the other he immediately adjusts the proportions of this quote in tune with his own train of thought.

Hence also follows the reason why Heidegger omitted the final sentence following the colon: "to become prey to the irrational, the changeable, the 'historical,' of what is conditioned from below and from the outside." For Heidegger, Beyng principally essences historically, especially in the spheres of philosophy and poetry, where the most important words ripen and speak forth, forming the world (*Welt*) in their circles and echoes. Moreover, the being of things is just as fundamentally mutable as culture. The definitions of "thing" and "being" can radically differ from culture to culture. Only in the early 21st century has Traditionalism matured to assimilate and begin to operate with the paradigm of ontological pluralism (the plurality of cultures + the plurality of natures) and the linguistic understanding of Tradition, thereby correcting and overcoming some of the implicit Eurocentric ontological and gnoseological premises of classical Traditionalism itself.[191]

Besides the "horizontal" plurality of the noetic worlds of different peoples and their traditions, the question can be raised as to the temporal mutability of things and beings, their movement and degeneration, decline, dissolution, and oblivion, as well as the shift from authentic thing to utilitarian simulacrum divorced from any sacred source. In such a case, "mutability" is prefigured into the world as the eschatological due. With respect to the "irrational," which Evola imputes as a negative principle, and into which the sublunar world falls in its divorce from Beyng, here it bears only recalling that Heidegger placed irrationalism on an even lower rung than the dry rationality responsible for the oblivion of Beyng and the *Zeitgeist* of modern thinking.

---

[191] See Askr Svarte, *Tradition and Future Shock*; idem., *Polemos: The Dawn of Pagan Traditionalism*, trans. Jafe Arnold (PRAV Publishing, 2020). See also Dugin, "René Guénon: Traditionalism as a Language."

Striving to hold on to the unchanging without fail, to keep oneself at the point of the immovable principle, in the centre within the circle, is, on the whole, quite characteristic of Evola's "personal equation."[192] But Heidegger's structure does not entail a fundamental mutability or mere mutability ("plurality without unity"). In Heidegger's optic, the "immovable" source must be founded in an apophatic instance and be shepherded or guarded by, to use Evola's language, a kind of "elite." One has the impression that, while unmistakably understanding and even directly proclaiming the intention to transcend a personal God towards the apophatic "invisible presence," Evola still regularly slips from the apophatic heights into the cataphatic valley and struggle of values and politics. In this lies one of the qualitative differences between his inner metaphysical orientation, the nature of his soul, and René Guénon's inherent "Brahminical" stake on apophaticism. Of course, neither Guénon nor Evola were integrated into Hinduism or practicing adepts of Vedanta and Tantra. Instead, in this case we are talking about the principles, style, and orientations that were characteristic of their standpoints and thinking.

The American thinker Collin Cleary, an expert on Tantrism and Hegel, points to the naïveté of Traditionalists' notion of the "eternal" or timeless nature of metaphysical tradition. For example, Traditionalists take Plato and Platonism to be the highest, constant form of expressing the ideal order and describing the world of ideas, ignoring the fact that Platonism appeared in an era when the Greek tradition was already in deep decline, and that before Plato there was the thought of the outstanding Presocratics as well as earlier mysteries and cults. Plato is already the Iron Age, but he is voluntaristically exalted as the Sophia Perennis (the Eternal Wisdom). Moreover, across diversely ranging interpretations, especially in Aristotelianism, Plato's philosophy underlies all of the classical and modern socio-political ideologies and doctrines. The glint of the

---

192 See Julius Evola, *The Path of Cinnabar: An Intellectual Autobiography*, trans. Sergio Knipe (United Kingdom: Integral Tradition Publishing, 2009).

primordial light in later doctrines is taken and presented as if it were the light itself.

Besides their obvious contradictions and mutual critiques, Cleary points out how Guénonian Traditionalism and Heideggerian philosophy coincide in many of their assessments of Modernity, as both reject the ideas of the Enlightenment, the "reign of quantity" or calculative thinking, uprooted modern cosmopolitanism, the acceleration of time and history in their dissolution, the destruction of hierarchies and the reduction of beings to singular, universal standards, templates, and mechanisation, Cartesian subject-object dualism and the speculative view of the world from the standpoint of absolute objectivity, etc. We can also directly link the cultural crisis of Western-centric civilisation to Heidegger's bored masses of *das Man* and the culture that the latter produce so as to hide from death (in more Traditionalistic language, from their personal as well as the cosmic eschatology). In the incessant whirl of simulacra and sensations, religions and traditions themselves — even if ultimately credible and authentic in their forms and reconstructions — come to be divorced from Beyng and from the authentic Dasein which might speak their myths, and become merely other projections of simulacra and signs onto screens, completely empty, superficial actions and imitations which do not bind anything and which lead nowhere.

Finally, upon attentively and delicately heeding the nuances of Heidegger's view on the nature of the Divinities, their reasons for abandoning the world, and on the question of the relations between the axes of Heaven-Earth, Divinities-Mortals, and Beyng-Sacred-Myth, we can see that Heidegger in many respects had insight into and thought through similar questions to those concerning Traditionalists, but he arrived at them along a different trajectory and likewise offers a different way out.

Cleary puts forth an even more succinct and rich summation of the comparability of Traditionalism and Martin

Heidegger's philosophy: "while Heidegger is not a Guénonian or Evolian Traditionalist, he is actually *more traditionalist* than the Traditionalists."[193] On the whole, we agree with such an intermediate determination of Heidegger's relation to Traditionalism; furthermore, we seek to bring this "more radical Traditionalism" to its glaring extremes.

In the Russian-speaking space, the largest-scale Traditionalist approach to Martin Heidegger's philosophy has been carried out in the works of Alexander Dugin. Dugin's books on Heidegger are some of the best introductions to the major questions of his philosophy, with all the necessary considerations given for linguistic differences and the problems with translating philosophical terms amidst inevitable semantic shifts.[194] Beyond his completely correct and unbiased presentation of the Black Forest thinker's main ideas and the trajectories of his forest paths of thinking, Heidegger's fundamental-ontology is important to Dugin for constructing a number of philosophical concepts as well as for his own independent attempt at bringing about a convergence between Heidegger and Traditionalism.

Dugin's most important contribution to developing Heidegger's ideas is his substantiation of the thesis of a plurality of Dasein(s). Heidegger himself habitually reduced Dasein to European man and European structures, which he implied by default while periodically emphasizing the special role to be played by the Germans as a people in the "end of one and the beginning of an other Western thinking." Dugin moves to recover what otherwise seems to lie waiting on the surface and draws attention to the fundamental and qualitative differences in the forms of lifeworlds and cultural modes, i.e., the being-in-the-world(s) of different peoples, including those exotic as well as those similar to one another. That is, in different corners of the middle world, in accordance with the

---

193 Cleary, "Heidegger against the Traditionalists."

194 See Dugin, *Martin Heidegger: The Philosophy of Another Beginning*; idem, *Heidegger. Poslednii bog.*

differing grammars and semantics of different languages and differences in the deep structures of thinking, *mythoi* and *logoi*, Dasein exists in different ways which at times are altogether dissimilar. If we take the thesis that "the fate of Europe is the fate of the world" to be true, then the whole diversity of cultures and civilizations should, in the spirit of the modern idea of progress, be reducible to and gravitate towards the Western European path of development and its anthropo-cultural, ontological, and gnoseological paradigm. Rejecting the very idea of a universalism of fate has a long and, without a doubt, truthful and convincing history in European thought itself, one which cannot discount the influence of Heidegger's own critique and relativization of the European *Logos*' claim to absoluteness.[195] In turn, Dugin strives to demonstrate, and at times does so altogether convincingly, that within the world we are dealing not with one Dasein, but with a multiplicity of Dasein's which approximately correspond to or correlate with the nomenclature of extant peoples and civilizations.[196] There exist different Dasein's — regardless of their degree of "primitiveness" or "development," "barbarism" or "civilizedness." This approach overcomes Heidegger's own implicit universalism or Eurocentrism.

When it comes to the eschatology of Beyng, as in the trajectory outlined by Heidegger throughout his works, we can immediately draw the conclusion that such is a specific trait or erroneous result of Western thinking that is Greek at its core. It cannot be ruled out that there are structural errors present in other theologies, predetermined by the very vector of Beyng's concealment, which also lead to collapse; but, being Europeans, we must first and foremost figure out ourselves, our destiny, and

---

195 See Askr Svarte, *Tradition and Future Shock*.

196 See Dugin's *Noomakhia* series, an outline and excerpts of which are available in English at *Eurasianist Internet Archive* [https://eurasianist-archive.com/item/noomakhia/]. See in particular "The Horizons of Cultures: The Geography of Logoi" [https://eurasianist-archive.com/2019/06/20/noomakhia-geosophy-the-horizons-of-cultures-the-geography-of-logoi/]. See also Alexander Dugin, "Plural Anthropology — The Fundamental-Ontological Analysis of Peoples," trans. Michael Millerman, in Jeff Love (ed.), *Heidegger in Russia and Eastern Europe* (London: Rowman & Littlefield, 2017).

our position in the world. In this case, the "planetary" decline affecting other, non-European and even non-Indo-European peoples and tribes would be a product of the imposition of a single fate and eschatology through Abrahamic missionarianism, colonialism, and globalism. Insofar as, in one way or another, all "high" mythologies and theologies bear a universal character, and given that traces of eschatological motifs can be found in all tales and myths, we can speak of an antinomian coincidence and paradox of eschatology. Western civilization spreads its oncological ontology and expands its sphere of influence, with its intrinsic alienation and rapid flight into the structures of the *Gestell* and *das Man*, and thereby denies and liquidates the original, unique trajectories of the eschatologies indicated in the myths of different peoples, replacing them and imposing upon all the West's own being-towards-death. At the same time, however, in denying other cultures their own authentic end to existence can by all means be read as a normative variation of a quite harsh and rapid break of eschatology as such. Moreover, insofar as everything in the middle world is condemned to finitude and death, this means that the global sunset and decline is still, at any rate, a fulfillment of the due — in one way or another, the due decline comes about. Therefore, the fate of the West is the downgoing (*Untergang*) and dragging of the whole world into the abyss with it. Understanding such a fate, Evola maintained the hope that if Europe is condemned to enter the darkness first, then it has the change of being the first to come out on the other side. In the Traditionalist optic, this corresponds to the renewal of the cycle or the metaphor of worldwide initiation — after all, passing through death and rebirth is always at the core of initiation.[197] This intention is complementary to and resonant with Heidegger's ideas on history and Another Beginning.

Similarly, for Dugin, the plurality of Dasein(s) and the possibility of Another Beginning are needed to substantiate

---

[197] For our part, we insist on an extremely literal reading of this structure: the only chance for "salvation" or "another way" for Europe and the world is through completely, literally dismantling and liquidating the modern, science-centric, industrial, digital civilization along with its culture and anthropological types.

the fundamental possibility of an independent, original (or "originary"), unique Russian philosophy, one which will not simply be a continuation of or commentary on Western or Eastern philosophy.[198]

In his endeavor to reconcile Heidegger and Traditionalist metaphysics, Dugin places special import on differentiating between two approaches to the ontology and gnoseology of Neoplatonism.[199] He distinguishes one approach which draws on the *Timaeus* and yields a "closed Platonism," i.e., a world of extant idea-beings and a world of extant copy-beings, between which is situated the extant Demiurge-Creator-being. Such a "closed-off" Platonism deals only with extant beings, albeit very different in their essential qualities, and is therefore "hermetically" sealed off from Nothing and Non-Being. This line is most clearly of all continued in Aristotle's logic, Thomism, ensuing Christian theology (to which the fundamental rift between the Creator and the created world is intrinsic), and post-Christian ontology and gnoseology (where "God is dead").

On the other hand, drawing on Neoplatonism as an original reading of Plato from the standpoint of the *Parmenides*, Dugin points to the Neoplatonists' and especially Plotinus' paradoxical reinterpretation of the key instance of the One. Contrary to Parmenides' thesis that "Being is, Non-Being is not," Plotinus and the Neoplatonists rescue the One from the circle of any categories and from any criteria pertaining to beings, which is to say that they understand the One strictly apophatically: the One is the simplest that is not, i.e., it "is" no-thing. This Platonic topography is therefore open on top, constituting an "open Platonism" which maintains the "primordial instance" of the semantic axis of One-Being-Nothing, access to which is possible ecstatically, but not gnoseologically (since any attempt to know the One-as-Nothing rationally leads only to the opposite of

---

[198] See Alexander Dugin, *Martin Heidegger: Vozmozhnost' russkoi filosofii* [*Martin Heidegger: the Possibility of Russian Philosophy*] (Moscow: Academic Project, 2011).

[199] Dugin, *Heidegger. Poslednii bog.*

knowing the One). The One-Nothing is not divorced from the Intellect and the world of the many (ἕν πολλά), but is immanently co-inherent within.

This Neoplatonism largely inspired the Rhineland mystics, especially Meister Eckhart, whom Heidegger rather reverently references in his works. But Heidegger understood Neoplatonism itself to be a form of ancient mysticism, probably not least because of the late Neoplatonists' emphasis on theurgy, astrology, and magic and their incorporation into a single corpus of emanations. Nevertheless, it is on the basis of such an "open Platonism," to which Heidegger did not pay any attention, that Dugin sees the rightful possibility of a convergence and the possibility of a space for two-directional translation between Heideggerian and Traditionalist philosophy.

For Dugin, Neoplatonism also offers a way for synthesizing Heidegger's philosophy and Orthodox Christian doctrine. Since the Orthodox foundation of the Russian *Logos* is axiomatic for Dugin, he distinguishes therein a Greek Neoplatonic ground that spans all the way to the Christian mysticism and Sophiology of the Russian Silver Age in Vladimir Solovyov and Frs. Sergei Bulgakov and Pavel Florensky. In addition, Dugin argues that it was none other than the Aristotelian-Thomistic, Catholic branch of Christianity, and not Byzantine-Russian Orthodoxy, that was the focus of Heidegger's critique. Accordingly, Russian Heideggerian philosophy — the Russian *Logos* as such — is inevitably reduced to Sophiology, Orthodox theology, and the teachings of the Holy Church Fathers.

The problem with Orthodox Neoplatonism being a bridge and "key" to Heidegger lies at once in three aspects. The first is that Heidegger critiqued not mere individual or strictly Catholic aspects of Christianity, but Christianity's fundamental metaphysical principle of determining God as a being and the principle of the *ens creatum* ("createdness" -> "ready-to-handness") of the world. This dogmatic premise does not depend on any selected branch or on any ensuing development of

Christianity, but lies at the core of Christian (and, more broadly, Abrahamic) metaphysics and ontology (or ontotheology) as such.[200] The second lies in that the mystical branch in Orthodox Christianity was not originally intrinsic to the latter, but was constructed and construed as normative (although remaining disputed to this day[201]) only at a much later time. In addition, it is the position of the Church itself that there is no secret, mystical, initiatic, esoteric doctrine within Christianity, whose very distinctive character is its openness to all people and its universal revelation. This allowed the classical Traditionalists to doubt the initiatic component of Christian doctrine and to prefer apocryphal currents or altogether modern Hermitic-occult esoteric traditions from the Renaissance to our days.[202]

Moreover, such "Christian esotericism" stressed by Dugin largely retains and harbors the intellectual and linguistic structures of pre-Christian mysteries and cults, particularly those pertaining to Platonism and Neoplatonism. The very existence of Christian theology's intimate reliance upon and tight boundedness to Platonism and Neoplatonism exposes and divests Christianity itself — and, once again, it is this intertwined ontotheological construction that Heidegger recognized as being that most erroneous foundation underlying Western thinking.

This situation is manifoldly complicated by the fact that already at the Synod of Constantinople in 543, on the orders of Emperor Justinian, the Fifteen Anathemas denounced Platonism in the guise of Origen and his teachings. Even before then, Justinian had already closed down the Platonic Academy in Athens once and for all in 529. In the 11th century, "Hellenic wisdom" was once again anathematized in the guise

---

200 See Askr Svarte, *Polemos*; idem., *Polemos II: Pagan Perspectives*, trans. Jafe Arnold (PRAV Publishing, 2021).

201 It is worth noting that a number of Orthodox Christian theologians and experts have gone so far as to define Dugin's whole philosophy and theological constructions as "marginal" or altogether "heretical."

202 See Askr Svarte, *Polemos*; idem., *Polemos II*.

of the Neoplatonist John Italus. The anathema against Italus, a student of the Neoplatonist Psellus, came in the same century as the Great Schism of 1054, which divided Christianity into the Catholic and Byzantine branches. Despite this divergence, the key anathemas against Platonism and Neoplatonism remain common to all denominations. Disputes over Neoplatonic influence reemerged in judgements on the orthodoxy of the teachings of Meister Eckhart and the Rhineland mystics, the mystical Hesychastic teachings of Gregory Palamas, and among the Catholics Platonism was once again anathematized in the guise of John Scotus Eriugena.

Dugin himself altogether honestly admits both the "smuggled" and partly heretical character of this (Neo-)Platonic line within Christianity, he acknowledges the negative role of creationism as a gateway and "founding father" of Modernity, which in many respects developed as the secular or inverted continuation of creationism's structures, and he also recognizes the definite proximity between Heidegger's numerical structures and pre-Christian archetypes.[203]

In his fundamental work *Martin Heidegger: The Last God*, Dugin distinguishes four possibilities for the human being to assimilate and take up a relation to the philosophy of the Swabian master. In broad strokes, these options constitute four different "humanities" in the spirit of "race" evoked in the passage that brought together Evola and Heidegger:

1. The possibility of being grounded as *Da-sein*, of becoming *Da-sein*'s "grounding founders." Such a person belongs to the "future ones," the *Zu-Künftigen*. Only the "rare" and "few" — philosophers, thinkers, poets, heroes — can be such.

2. The possibility of being part of a people, i.e., serving as Dasein's surrounding world through directly yet delicately treating beings and the beingful world as natural, near and kin to the people, as that which "sprouts" and "cultivates." Such is the peasant's relation to

---

[203] See Alexander Dugin, *Postfilosofiia: tri paradigmy v istorii mysli* (Moscow: Eurasian Movement, 2009); idem, *V poiskakh temnogo Logosa: filosofsko-bogoslovskie ocherki* (Moscow: Academic Project, 2013). See also the footnotes in Dugin, *Heidegger. Poslednii Bog*.

Da-sein and to the world, which holds the keys to the ancient agrarian metaphors that predetermined the structure of the First Beginning of philosophy among the Presocratics (φύσειν-λέγειν, whence originate "physics" and *Logos*).

3. The possibility of insisting on the old *Logos*, conservatively upholding previous phases of its movement before its collapse in the face of onsetting nihilism. (This position is doomed, because it is based on fear before the *Untergang* and the knowledge that comes with nihilism).

4. The possibility of submitting to the energies of nihilism, optimistically rejoicing in a dayless and nightless world, refusing to pay any attention to any of the catastrophic phenomena around us, and resting content with the last crumbs of the disintegrated *Logos* in the form of improving technologies and primitive corporeal care for oneself (liberalism, globalism, the consumer society, progress).

Until approximately 2013-14, Dugin's philosophical positioning dwelled in the sphere of the first and second anthropological and existential possibilities, but nowadays we are witnessing a conscious retreat or even lapse into apologetics for the third position. In other words, Dugin has moved away from Heideggerian positions and the Traditionalism of Evola's *Ride the Tiger* towards reactionary Modernity, towards mainstream Russian conservatism and political Orthodoxy, and philosophically towards classical metaphysics in its most problematic form, namely, apologetics for Plato and Aristotle against Nietzsche and Heidegger.[204]

We can summate Alexander Dugin's endeavor to work out a convergence between Traditionalism and Heideggerianism thusly: in its premises, it is well-developed, extensive, detailed, and promising, but in its finished, current form, it runs quite contrary to the direct warnings of Heidegger himself as well as to Christian dogma. In the end, this attempt has been thrown and left at an impasse.

---

[204] See Dugin's most recent books: *Internal'nye ontologii. Sakral'naia fizika i oprokinutyi mir* (Moscow: Direktmedia, 2022); idem, *V prostranstve velikikh snov* (Moscow: Academic Project, 2022).

In general, appealing to Martin Heidegger's philosophy is a quite commonplace and normative phenomenon among Traditionalists today. Much productive work and preliminary, albeit often superficial, comparisons have been put forth. It can be said that there is an ongoing aspiration or even "longing" to merge or synthesize these two philosophies. This is not without reason: mastering and appropriating Heidegger's philosophy allows for a deeper and broader grounding of the critique of Modernity, even while Traditionalists leave Modernity's metaphysical core in ancient forms of traditional metaphysics untouched.

In the sphere of socio-political and cultural critique, Heidegger's arguments and original methods are employed and draw interest as instruments for political agitation, such as in the discourse of the European New Right. Many different right-wing conservative forces want to incorporate Heidegger into the ranks of their like-minded thinkers, at times without knowing or even delving into his thoughts on the matter of modern political agitation and other such machinations which lead astray from the foremost guiding question of Being.

In the sphere of postwar theology (predominantly Christian — Catholic and Protestant), Heidegger's ideas have also exerted a rather existential-humanistic influence. Contrary to this philosopher's own direct objections, some of his theses on Dasein, being-in-the-world, and alienation have been incorporated into Christian theological doctrines. But such attempts exhibit a rather extravagant and voluntaristic character in the spirit of "soft" or "minimal" theology.

Yet, as we can see, despite the indisputable congruence between some of their key evaluations, Heidegger and Traditionalism differ so substantially in their reconstructions of the genesis of the crisis of the modern world and their proposed ways out of it, that the situation in many ways resembles a sharp, existential bifurcation of "either-or."

For there to be a convergence between Traditionalism and the philosophy of the Other Beginning along with its theological project, what is needed are non-trivial theological and philosophical moves which would largely transform Traditionalism itself and its strategies through deep reflection on itself in the context of its general preservation of distance and nerve of opposition to the modern world, as well as its inexorable orientation towards sacrocentrism. The so-called "Apollonian" and socio-political dominants of classical Perennialist Traditionalism will be exposed to questioning and revision.

It is necessary to outline some of the principal directions in which a Traditionalist interpretation of Heideggerianism might develop, and conversely, what prospects Traditionalism might have from the standpoint of a fundamental-ontological, existential approach to the modern world and its future.

First, Heidegger's critique and project might simply be dismissed like the temptation of a false concept. Out of intellectual disagreement, many might simply discard the philosophy of the Event and instead fully focus on archaeology and the conservation of knowledge about the previous phases and stages of the decline of metaphysics. This would partially be the case of Evola, who treated Heidegger from a completely erroneous and irrelevant angle. This position often leads to compromises with Modernity.

On this note, it is worth turning to the theological polemic between Advaita-Vedanta and later non-dual Kashmir Shaivism on the one hand and Buddhism on the other, whose polemic bears similarities in spirit to what we are discussing here. The normative view among Hindus was that Buddhism, with its revolt against the varna system, its overriding ethics, and its extravagant teachings, was a test of faith through temptation that the devas put to their faithful people. On the higher level of theology and philosophy, this challenge was taken quite seriously, providing occasion for Advaita masters to sharpen all their arguments and affirm the ultimate superiority of their schools over more secular, and essentially pro-modern, pure Buddhism. The key nerve in this theological dispute boils down to the contrast between theistic and non-theistic monism. Fundamental for Advaitists is tracing back the Being of the whole infinite diversity of beings to the Absolute Consciousness of the Divine, whether Brahma or Shiva. The whole beingful world is the unfolding of the Divine imagination, song, and dialogue with itself. The Divine is the One, and the world and man's difference from it is only an illusion within the cosmic *imaginaire*. The Divine is the source, ground, and essence of all beings — everything is woven out of it and its emanations.

Buddhism is based on a fundamental rejection of any theological foundation of Being. Instead, the ground of everything is posited to be *Śūnyatā*, the void. Thus, Buddhism asserted a peculiarly "empty" monism that relativized even the Divinities, and in some schools and aphorisms it reached the point of an outright anti-theism that rejected the whole structure of classical Vedanta as a lie that clouds the mind and binds one to the chain of rebirths within Samsara.

In their sharp polemic with Buddhism, the advocates of Divine monism and Absolute Consciousness honed the apophaticism and poetics of Advaita-Vedanta, which organically and without contradiction flowed into the more Tantric positions of the Advaita-Shaivism of the Kashmir valley masters, whose perspectives were more metaphysically proper to the unfavorable conditions of the Kali-Yuga. The Nirguna aspect of the apophatic, unmanifest dimension of the Divine nature was freshly accentuated and maximally sharpened in their high theology. This apophatic principle incorporated the doctrine of the creation of the world by speech with the mantra-word. The Advaita masters were thus able to consistently synthesize the doctrine of the Divine ground of the world as the Divine's manifestation in unconcealment-concealment and the (para-) Divine Being of the Nothing. This fully corresponds to the openness of the Divine and the lingual-speech principles of the world, which compensated against the anti-theistic intention of Buddhism and a closed, referential metaphysics in the spirit of Greek Platonism.

Partly due to the special position of the *Śūnyatā* (which later was more adequately articulated in the practices of Zen or receded into the background in Buddhist-Hindu and Buddhist-shamanic dual faith), a philosophical cliché has taken shape which holds that the doctrines of Nothing in Heidegger and Buddhism are either very close or even identical. Well-known is Kitaro Nishida's attempt to bring together the Zen Buddhism of the Kyoto School with the Neoplatonic apophatic theology of Meister Eckhart and Heidegger's philosophy. But in *Contributions to Philosophy (Of the Event)*, in discussing the ways by which man might get out of metaphysics and come to Being, the master issued the reservation: "Not a Buddhism! Just the opposite."[205]

Earlier, we examined the nuance in the structure of Heidegger's thinking that is the primacy of the holy (*das Heilige*) in relation to the Divine, and more precisely to the Divinities as such. But the master traces the roots of the holy, i.e., the abyssal ground of the Divinehood of the Divinities, back to the one apophatic Beyng. The Divinities are needful of Beyng in order to fully flourish and in order to be what they essentially are, even in their totally monistic dimension, as the source of all beings, turned at once to the world as their own manifestation (being-the-world and being-in-the-world) and to the Nothing. This is how the Divine manifests itself at the same time as it facilitates the covering over of the voice of Beyng in silence and concealment.

The alienation and oblivion of the Divinities, seen from within the world, is *avidya*, the veil of ignorance and unknowing, *Maya*. If *avidya* were strictly an individual problem, then it would be fixable and curable — as if by following the instructions of a guru and putting in effort, one might get rid

---

[205] Heidegger, *Contributions to Philosophy (Of the Event)*, 134

of delusion or lay down the trajectory for a more successful rebirth of one's soul in the next cycle. But the force of *avidya* grows on a cosmic scale in proportion to the life cycle of all the worlds descending into the darkness of ignorance, crudeness, inertia, and the sealing off of beings (the dominance of the *guna tamas* at the end of the cycle). Therefore, it is not only the whole of Western mankind that is living in alienation, but all the peoples and cultures poisoned by the modern Western *logos* and the Platonic-Abrahamic metaphysics that developed into and are retained in the paradigm of Modernity. It is obvious that the problem does not lie in personal alienation and falling out of sight of the Divinities; rather, the matter at hand is the great eschatological process. *Avidya* thus becomes innerworldly dominant and the leitmotif of the tale.

This explains the flight of the old Divinities. Mankind finds itself in a situation of dual alienation: people no longer look to the Divinities, and the Divinities themselves have left the world, which means that there is no one left for us to look to.

For Traditionalism, abandoning classical metaphysics (ontotheology) would be equivalent to a gesture of complicity in the decline, an act of nihilism, falling away from the normative Sanatana Dharma of the Vedic era into later illusory Buddhism. But in our case and in our metaphysical situation, this abandonment is not in favor of Modernity, secularism, atheism, the Gestell, and current cultural Postmodernism, but rather in favor of discovering another ground and other possibilities for the holy, theology, and being in the world.

The second line is close to the first and yet is simpler: within the manifest world as *Maya*, everything is possible, but all of this will be annulled and dispelled when the Divine destroys the world. This approach stems from a position that is close to theistic solipsism and insists on literally perceiving the world like a mirage. The world is to be seen as a play of illusions and reflections, which calls for us to not be attached to anything in the world of beings. This position contradicts Heidegger's words on the facticity of Dasein's existing within the world and history. But even these words, like other philosophical and ideological positions, slogans, and maxims, are possible reflections of very convincing dreams and mirages.

The third direction poses the question of the possibility of a bifurcation point in the structure of the world and of *mythos*. There are two key conditions here:

1. In the complete and perfected monistic doctrine, the supreme, absolute Divine (the One Absolute) is the only thing that is genuine and credible, for it is the entirety and fullness of reality. The world is not torn away from the Divine, but is its manifestation, its self-revelation and at the same time its self-concealment. Accordingly, the whole world, and everything within it, cannot in principle bear the character of an illusion or semblance; on the contrary, the world is ultimately, absolutely, unconditionally authentic and real.

2. There is the question of why the world and worlds (the cosmoi and universes of mythologies) are constantly structured as the same type in their foundations upon the renewal of the cosmic cycles of destruction and manifestation. They always appear in the same fundamental and root structures indicated by structuralism, anthropology, comparative mythology, metaphysics, and philosophy — the very same triadicity, cyclicality, binary oppositions, leading metaphors of the tale, the grammar of languages, etc.

From the standpoint of Advaita monism, which is open towards Being-as-Nothing, it could be said that Heidegger's thought exists within and as part of the manifest world, meaning it has the same source as the consciousness of the Absolute as it imagines, thinks, and unfolds itself not within the metaphysical prescription of top to bottom (from the top down, when "somewhere high up" there appears a correlate that is affected by the matter of the phenomenal world, i.e., a thing, appears for thought in the consciousness of the Divine), but as ultimately immanent to the world. Events and thoughts within the world as the manifest Divinity have the same weight of veracity and truth.

Thus, Heidegger's innerworldly thought can be recognized and adopted as a thought of the Divine itself in all its specificity and convincingness.

Heidegger's idea of an other decision on the question of the truth of Beyng implies a full and deep shift in the philosophically structured foundations of Western (and, with certain qualifications, global) thinking, a transition to a different "metaphysics," history, and *modus vivendi* all the way to the details of culture. This intention could be recognized to be the Divine's innerworldly thought on changing the leading structures of its own imagination and how it develops and constitutes its own manifestation. If the cycle ends and we do not come back on the same wheel (understood as literally coinciding in all details with the repetition of one and the same, or as the playing out of the same plot and structural arches in different decorations), then we will find ourselves on grounds which are altogether different from and impossible within the current exposition.

The fourth direction entails a complete departure from the old metaphysics and theology as having logically lost their fire and turned into ashes, to render the famous aphorism of Gustav Mahler. This is foretold in many traditions in a direct and altogether similar way. In Heideggerian philosophy, this would be described as the exhaustion of the metaphysical configuration and Dasein's constitution of traditional, mythopoetic being-in-the-world. The world is as Dasein projects it ahead of itself; thus, when Dasein has committed itself to a number of fatal innerworldly decisions, then it leads the world and itself within it to a state of exhaustion and boredom.

On this note, confronting Heidegger and recognizing the correctness of his posing of questions and analysis is a traumatic experience for Traditionalist thinking, which might have the rug torn out from under it.

Heidegger's proposed path towards Another Beginning — through experiencing the test of God-forsakenness and reaffirming the abyssal ground of the sacred, Divinehood, the word, and thinking through apophatic Beyng-as-Nothing — compels us to set aside the dying and increasingly collapsing traditions of the past that belong to the body of the First Beginning's metaphysics. In such a case, we are dealing with a strong stride forward into a very distant future. Even if now we can still see the pale flickering of the increasingly extinguished light of the Sophia Perennis, we nevertheless understand that these fumes are doomed to apostasy and eschatology, and we, not waiting for their final dissipation in darkness, leave them to set off on our wandering. This is how things seem to stand.

For Traditionalism, one of the key problems is enduring the caesura of the flight of the old Divinities and the still not yet arriving new ones. Within the thrown abandonment of presence in the world, this might seem endlessly long, dragging on until all words and thoughts about the light of the sacred are wiped out and fall silent. In the meanwhile, all miracles, epiphanies, and other "sacred experiences" will be exposed as nothing more than psycho-emotional agitations and phantom pains for the lost ground of the self and the cosmos. We are not talking about a conscious disenchantment of the genuine sacred, as if levelling and denying it, but rather about the fact that today it is surrogate experiences and activities that are mistaken to be the sacred. Our understanding of the sacred must be cleansed of all philistine thirst for the illusions and impressions that are so natural to contemporary believers.

To Georges Bataille, a French scholar of archaic and transgressive forms of the sacred, belong these enigmatic words: "'Night is also a sun', and the absence of myth is also a myth: the coldest, the purest, the only *true* myth."[206] This maxim is structured in the manner of a poetic antiphrasis, which often correlates with a form of irony and lends to various idiomatic expressions carrying the opposite meaning. But in

---

[206] Georges Bataille, *The Absence of Myth: Writings on Surrealism*, trans. Michael Richardson (London: Verso, 1994), 48.

this case, Bataille's words should be taken extremely seriously as a paradoxical and antinomian indication of the untrodden paths of the tale. The absence of myth is akin to when rivers flow into and dissolve amidst oceans. Bataille also points out: "The absence of God is no longer a closure: it is the opening up to the infinite. The absence of God is greater, and more divine, than God..."[207]

The absence of the Divinities and the silence of their tale is a direct removal of all their cataphatic masks without exception, the exposure of the nothing-selfhood of Divinehood. An extreme experience of theophany is offered in the absence of any given form of a Divinity which man might grab onto and fit into a cult, history, or conservatism doomed to ossification. In this radical, apophatic a-theophany, the question of the theism or non-theism of monism is removed.

The task of the single and transitional ones — evidently with some contribution from, and looking back to, the remembering ones — is to prepare in delicacy, in sensitivity, and in attunement to the harmony and voice of a silent telling, the space for the coming-anew of the Divinities and the decision about Being. What is ontologically and existentially important is finding the trail to the forest clearing where a fire can be lit in anticipation of another tale arising out of the silence, one that foretells of the timid steps of the Divinities.

In the meanwhile, looking around us at the surrounding culture, the unbridled rampage of machinations, the gigantism of the petty, and the conservative as well as the futurological projects, trajectories, and aspirations of global man, we conclude that *no Divinities will ever come into such a world, not now and not in the near or distant future.*

---

207 Ibid.

Selected Bibliography

Arnold, Jafe. "The Eternal (Re)Turn: Heidegger and the '*Absolutes Getragensein*' of Myth". *Phainomena: Journal of Phenomenology and Hermeneutics* 31:120-121, 2022: 93-119.

Bataille, Georges. *The Absence of Myth: Writings on Surrealism.* Translated by Michael Richardson. London: Verso, 1994.

_____*The Accursed Shared.* 3 volumes. Translated by Robert Hurley. New York: Zone Books, 1988-1993.

Benoist, Alain de. *Ernst Jünger: Between the Gods and the Titans.* Translated by Greg Johnson and F. Roger Devlin. Budapest: Middle Europe Books, 2022.

Borodai, Sergei. *Iazyk i poznanie. Vvedenie v postreliativizm.* Moscow: Sadra, 2020.

_____"Sovremennoe ponimanie problemy lingvisticheskoi otnositel'nosti: raboty po prostranstvennoi kontseptualizatsii". *Voprosy iazykoznaniia* 4, 2013: 17-54.

Brisson, Luc. *How Philosophers Saved Myths: Allegorical Interpretation and Classical Mythology.* Translated by Catherine Tihanyi. Chicago: University of Chicago Press, 2004.

Castro, Eduardo Viveiros de. "Who is afraid of the ontological wolf?" CUSAS Annual Marilyn Strathern Lecture, 30 May 2014.

Cleary, Collin. "Heidegger Against the Traditionalists." In: Arnold, Jafe, Evgeny Nechkasov, Lucas Griffin, and Luca Siniscalco (eds.). *Passages: Studies in Traditionalism and Traditions* 1. PRAV Publishing, 2023: 285-307.

_____*Summoning the Gods: Essays on Paganism in a God-Forsaken World.* San Francisco: Counter-Currents Publishing, 2011.

_____*What is a Rune? and Other Essays.* San Francisco: Counter-Currents, 2015.

Davydov, I.A. "Transformatsiia chetveritsu Heideggera v digital'nykh proektsiiakh postgumanizma." *Gumanitarnye vedomosti TGPU im. L.N. Tolstogo* 3:43, 2022: 138-147.

Dickins, Bruce. *Runic and Heroic Poems of the Old Teutonic Peoples.* Cambridge: Cambridge University Press, 1915.

Dugin, Alexander. *Filosofiia traditsionalizma.* Moscow: Arktogeia, 2002.

_____*Internal'nye ontologii. Sakral'naia fizika i oprokinutyi mir.* Moscow: Direktmedia, 2022.

_____*Martin Heidegger: The Philosophy of Another Beginning.* Translated by Nina Kouprianova. Arlington: Radix / Washington Summit Publishers, 2014.

_____*Martin Heidegger. Poslednii Bog.* Moscow: Academic Project, 2014.

_____*Martin Heidegger: Vozmozhnost' russkoi filosofii.* Moscow: Academic Project, 2011).

_____"Plural Anthropology — The Fundamental-Ontological Analysis of Peoples." Translated by Michael Millerman. In: Love, Jeff (ed.). *Heidegger in Russia and Eastern Europe.* London: Rowman & Littlefield, 2017.

_____*Postfilosofiia: tri paradigmy v istorii mysli.* Moscow: Eurasian Movement, 2009.

_____"René Guénon: Traditionalism as a Language." In: Arnold, Jafe, Evgeny Nechkasov, Lucas Griffin, and Luca Siniscalco (eds.). *Passages: Studies in Traditionalism and Traditions* 1. PRAV Publishing, 2023: 17-56.

_____*V poiskakh temnogo Logosa: filosofsko-bogoslovskie ocherki.* Moscow: Academic Project, 2013.

_____*V prostranstve velikikh snov.* Moscow: Academic Project, 2022.

Evola, Julius. *Men Among the Ruins: Postwar Reflections of a Radical Traditionalist.* Translated by Guido Stucco. Vermont: Inner Traditions, 2002.

_____*The Path of Cinnabar: An Intellectual Autobiography*. Translated by Sergio Knipe. United Kingdom: Integral Tradition Publishing, 2009.

_____*Revolt Against the Modern World*. Translated by Guido Stucco. Rochester: Inner Traditions, 1995.

_____*Ride the Tiger: A Survival Manual for Aristocrats of the Soul*. Translated by Joscelyn Godwin and Constance Fontana. Rochester: Inner Traditions, 2003.

Falyov, Egor. *Germenevtika Martina Heideggera*. Saint Petersburg: Aleteia, 2008.

Filler, James. *Heidegger, Neoplatonism, and the History of Being: Relation as Ontological Ground*. London: Palgrave MacMillan, 2023.

Findell, Martin. *Runes*. London: Trustees of the British Museum, 2014.

Fink, Eugen. *Osnovnye fenomeny chelovecheskogo bytiia*. Moscow: Kanon+/ Reabilitatsiia, 2017.

Folin, S.L. (ed.). *Friedrich Hölderlin i ideia Evropy*. Saint Petersburg: Platonic Philosophical Society, 2018.

Friedrich, Hugo. *The Structure of Modern Poetry: From the Mid-Nineteenth to the Mid-Twentieth Century*. Translated by Joachim Neugroschel. Evanston: Northwestern University Press, 1974.

Gadamer, Hans-Georg. *Truth and Method*. 2nd rev. ed., translated by Joel Weinsheimer and Donald G. Marshall. London: Bloomsbury, 2020.

Golovin, Evgeny. *Priblizhenie k Snezhnoi Koroleve*. Moscow: Arktogeia, 2003.

Guardini, Romano. *Hölderlin. Kartina mira i bogovdokhnovlennost'*. Moscow: Nauka, 2015.

Hansen, H.T. "Julius Evola's Political Endeavors." In: Evola, Julius. *Men Among the Ruins: Postwar Reflections of a Radical Traditionalist*. Rochester: Inner Traditions, 2002: 1-104.

Harris, Joseph. *"Speak Useful Words or Say Nothing": Old Norse Studies by Joseph Harris*. Edited by Susan E Deskis and Thomas D. Hill. Ithaca: Cornell University Library, 2008.

Heidegger, Martin. *Being and Time*. Translated by Joan Stambaugh. Albany: State University of New York Press, 2010.

―――――――― *Being and Truth*. Translated by Gregory Fried and Richard Polt. Bloomington/Indianapolis: Indiana University Press, 2010.

―――――――― *Contributions to Philosophy (Of the Event)*. Translated by Richard Rojcewicz and Daniela Vallega-Neu. Indianapolis: Indiana University Press, 2012.

―――――――― *Elucidations of Hölderlin's Poetry*. Translated by Keith Hoeller. Amherst: Humanity Books, 2000.

―――――――― "The End of Philosophy and the Task of Thinking." In idem. *Basic Writings: From Being and Time (1927) to The Task of Thinking (1964)*. Edited by David Farrell Krell. London: Harper Perennial, 2008.

―――――――― *The Event*. Translated by Richard Rojcewicz. Bloomington/Indianapolis: Indiana University Press, 2013.

―――――――― *Heraclitus Seminar 1966/67*. Translated by Charles H. Seibert. University of Alabama Press, 1979.

―――――――― *On Inception*. Translated by Peter Hanly. Bloomington: Indiana University Press, 2023.

―――――――― *Kant and the Problem of Metaphysics*. Translated by Richard Taft. Bloomington/Indianapolis: Indiana University Press, 1997.

―――――――― *Mindfulness*. Translated by Parvis Emad and Thomas Kalary. London: Continuum, 2006.

―――――――― "'Only a God Can Save Us': The *Spiegel* Interview (1966)." Translated by William J. Richardson, S.J. In: Sheehan, Thomas (ed.). *Heidegger: The Man and the Thinker*. Chicago: Precedent Publishing, 1981.

_____*Parmenides*. Translated by André Schuwer and Richard Rojcewicz. Bloomington/Indianapolis: Indiana University Press, 1992.

_____*Pathmarks*. Edited by William McNeill. Cambridge: Cambridge University Press, 1998.

_____*Poetry, Language, Thought*. Translated by Albert Hofstadter. London: Harper Perennial, 2001.

_____*Ponderings II-VI: Black Notebooks 1931-1938*. Translated by Richard Rojcewicz. Bloomington/Indianapolis: Indiana University Press, 2016.

_____*On the Way to Language*. Translated by Peter D. Hertz. New York: HarperCollins, 1971.

_____"Why Do I Stay in the Provinces? (1934)". In: Sheehan, Thomas (ed.). *Heidegger: The Man and the Thinker*. Chicago: Precedent Publishing, 1981.

_____*Zametki I-V (Chernyie tetradi 1942-1948)*. Translated into Russian by Aleksei B. Grigor'ev, edited by Mikhail Maiatskii. Moscow: Gaidar Institute, 2022.

Hölderlin, Friedrich. *Selected Poetry*. Translated by David Constantine. Eastburn: Bloodaxe Books, 2018.

Isaeva, N.V. *Isskustvo kak provodnik. Kashmirskii shivaizm: Abhinavagupta i Kshemaraja (v sravnenii s nektoroymi paratearal'nymi opytami soveremennosti)*. Saint Petersburg: Russian Christian Humanitarian Academy, 2014.

_____*Slovo, tvoriashchee mir. Ot rannei vedanty k kashmirskomu shivaizmu: Gaudapada, Bhartrihari, Abhinavagupta*. Moscow: Ladomir, 1996.

Jettmar, Karl. *The Religions of the Hindukush: The Pre-Islamic Heritage of Eastern Afghanistan and Northern Pakistan*. Bangkok: Orchid Press, 2023.

Jünger, Ernst. *The Forest Passage*. Translated by Thomas Friese. Candor: Telos, 2013.

Jünger, Friedrich Georg. *Grecheskie mify*. Moscow: Vladimir Dal', 2006.

───────────────── *Iazyk i myshlenie*. Moscow: Nauka, 2005.

Kaczynski, Theodore John. *Anti-Tech Revolution: Why and How*. Fitch & Madison, 2020.

Kahn, Charles H. *The Verb 'Be' in Ancient Greek*. Indianapolis: Hackett Publishing Company, 2003.

Kazakov, G.A. *Sakral'naia leksika v sisteme iazyka*. Comrat: Comrat State University, 2016.

Kerényi, Carl. *Eleusis: Archetypal Image of Mother and Daughter*. Translated by Ralph Manheim. Princeton: Princeton University Press, 1967.

Kohn, Eduardo. *How Forests Think: Toward an Anthropology Beyond the Human*. Berkeley: University of California Press, 2013.

Kosykhin, V.G. *Ontologiia i nigilism: ot Heideggera k Postmodernu*. Saratov: Saratov State Academy of Law, 2008.

Lakoff, George. *Women, Fire, and Dangerous Things: What Categories Reveal about the Mind*. Chicago: Chicago University Press, 1987.

Lakoff, George and Mark Johnson. *Metaphors We Live By*. Chicago: Chicago University Press, 1980.

Lebedev, A.V. *Logos Geraklita. Rekonstruktsiia mysli i slova*. Moscow: Nauka, 2014.

Lee, Penny. *The Whorf Theory Complex: A Critical Reconstruction*. Amsterdam: John Benjamins, 1996.

Lévi-Strauss, Claude. *Structural Anthropology*. Translated by Claire Jacobson and Brooke Grundfest Schoepf. New York: Basic Books, 1963.

Lukianov, A.V. *Filosofskie idei F. Hölderlina i metafora pustoty*. Ufa: Bashkir State University, 2012.

Maiatskii, Mikhail. *Spor o Platone. Krug Stefana George i nemetskii universitet.* Moscow: HSE University, 2012.

Makar'ev, I.V."*Filosofskie proekty L. Wittgensteina i M. Heideggera v 1920- gody: sravnitel'nyi analiz.*" Values and Meanings 2:78, 2022: 63-78.

Matveichev, O.A. and A.V. Pertsev. "*Vechnost' kak Poslednii Bog, prokhodiashchii mimikhodom (Ob ekzistentsialistskoi mistike M. Heideggera.*" Perevody 6:2, 2017: 57-72.

Mauss, Marcel. *The Gift: Forms and Functions of Exchange in Archaic Societies.* Translated by Ian Cunnison. London: Cohen & West, 1966.

Meillassoux, Quentin. *After Finitude: An Essay on the Necessity of Contingency.* Translated by Ray Brassier. London: Continuum, 2008.

Moiseev, D. *Politicheskaia doktrina Iuliusa Evoly v kontekste 'konservativnoi revoliutsii' v Germanii.* Moscow: Kabinetnyi uchenyi, 2021.

Nietzsche, Friedrich. *The Gay Science.* Translated by Josefine Nacukhoff and Adrian del Caro, ed. Bernard Williams. Cambridge: Cambridge University Press, 2001.

Norton, Robert E. *Secret Germany: Stefan George and his Circle.* Ithaca: Cornell University Press, 2002.

Pandit, B.N. *Specific Principles of Kashmir Śaivism.* New Delhi: Munshiram Manoharlal Publishers, 1997.

Ratgauz, G.I. (ed.). *Zolotoe pero. Nemetskaia, avstriiskaia i shveitsarskaia poeziia v russkikh perevodakh 1812-1970 gg.* Moscow: Progress, 1974.

Reinhardt, Karl. *Mify Platona.* Moscow: Vladimir Dal': 2019.

Romanenko, Y.M. (ed). *M. Heidegger i russkaia filosofskaia mysl'.* Saint Petersburg: Russian Christian Humanitarian Academy, 2020.

Samarina, T.S. "Religioznaia problematika v tvorchestve M. Heideggera i fenomenologiia religii: vziamosviazi i paralelli." *Voprosy filosofii* 9, 2021: 173-183.

Schalow, Frank. *Heidegger and the Quest for the Sacred: From Thought to the Sanctuary of Faith*. Dordrecht: Springer, 2001.

Scott, Cyril. *Baudelaire: The Flowers of Evil*. London: Elkin Mathews, 1909.

Scott, James S. *The Art of Not Being Governed: An Anarchist History of Upland Southeast Asia*. New Haven: Yale University Press, 2009.

Sedgwick, Mark. *Against the Modern World: Traditionalism and the Secret Intellectual History of the Twentieth Century*. Oxford: Oxford University Press, 2004.

_____*Traditionalism: The Radical Project for Restoring Sacred Order*. London: Pelican Books, 2023.

Sessa, Giovanni. "*Heidegger lettore di Evola*." Centro Studi La Runa, 2 February 2016.

Seval'nikov, A.Y. "Kritika estestvennonauchnogo metoda u Heideggera." *Voprosy filosofii* 9, 2022: 98-107.

Shurbelev, A.P. "Chto dobavilos' k filosofii, ili o 'Prosto-naprosto prituplennom slovoupotreblenii' (bloßer dumpfe Wortgebrauch)." Journal of Integrative Cultural Studies 4:1, 2022: 81-91.

Spengler, Oswald. *The Decline of the West. 2 volumes*. Translated by Charles Francis Atkinson. New York: Alfred A. Knopf, 1927/1928.

Steblin-Kamenskii, M.I. *Myth*. Translated by Mary P. Coote and Frederic Amory. Ann Arbor: Karoma, 1982.

Stovba, Aleksei. "*Fenomen Ereignis v filosofii M. Heideggera*." Horizon 11:1, 2022: 276-297.

Svarte, Askr. *Gods in the Abyss: Essays on Heidegger, the Germanic Logos, and the Germanic Myth*. Translated by Iliya Koptilin and Daniil Granovskiy. London: Arktos, 2020.

_____*Identichnost' iazychnika v XXI veke*. Moscow: Veligor, 2020.

_____*Polemos: The Dawn of Pagan Traditionalism*. Translated by Jafe Arnold. PRAV Publishing, 2020.

_____*Polemos II: Pagan Perspectives*. Translated by Jafe Arnold. PRAV Publishing, 2021.

_____*Tradition and Future Shock: Visions of a Future that Isn't Ours*. PRAV Publishing, 2023.

_____*What the Gods have Left: The Askr Svarte Notebooks*. Translated by Jafe Arnold. PRAV Publishing, 2024.

Sweet, Dennis. *Heraclitus: Translation and Analysis*. Lanham: University Press of America, 1995.

Travers, Martin. "Trees, Rivers and Gods: Paganism in the Work of Martin Heidegger." Journal of European Studies 48:2, 2018: 133-143.

Tsendrovskii, O.Y. "Poniatie bytiia (Seyn) v filosofii M. Heideggera i ee metodologicheskie osobennosti." *Filosofskaia mysl'* 9, 2016: 18-36.

_____"Rim protiv Iudei: nitsshevskaia traktovka istorii i genealogii khristianstva." *Filosofiia i kul'tura* 10, 2014: 1478-1487.

Vedder, Ben. *Heidegger's Philosophy of Religion: From God to the Gods*. Pittsburgh: Duquesne University Press, 2006.

West, M.L. *Indo-European Poetry and Myth*. Oxford: Oxford University Press, 2009.

Wittgenstein, Ludwig. *Tractatus Logico-Philosophicus*. Translated by D.F. Pears and B.F. McGuinness. London: Routledge, 1974.

Zenkin, S. *Nebozhestvennoe sakral'noe. Teoriia i khduzhostvennaia praktika*. Moscow: Russian State University for the Humanities, 2014.

Zhigalkin, Sergei. *Metafizika vechnogo vozvrashcheniia*. 2nd ed. Moscow: Kul'turnaia revoliutsiia, 2011.

_____*Ob inykh gorizontakh zdeshnego: apologiia vechnogo vozvrashcheniia*. Moscow: Iazyki slavianskikh kul'tur, 2019.

Edda. Die Götter- und Heldenlieder der Germanen. Anaconda, 2017.

Die Götterlieder der Älteren Edda. Translated by Arnulf Krause. Ditzingen: Reclam, 2015.

An Introduction to Tantric Philosophy: The Paramarthasara of Abhinavagupta with the Commentary of Yogarâja. Translated and edited by Lyne Bansat-Boudon and Kamaleshadatta Tripathi. London: Routledge, 2011.

The Poetic Edda: Stories of the Norse Gods and Heroes. Translated by Jackson Crawford. Indianapolis: Hackett Publishing Company, 2015.

The Satapatha-Brahmana (Part IV). Translated by Julius Eggeling. Sacred Books of the East 43. Oxford: Clarendon Press, 1897.

The Thirteen Principal Upanishads. Translated by Robert Hume. Oxford: Oxford University Press, 1921.

Milton Keynes UK
Ingram Content Group UK Ltd.
UKHW021909101024
449571UK00004B/47